No Gallbladder Diet Cookbook:

The Ultimate Guide with 1900 days of

Nutritious & Tasty Recipes

to aid digestion & reduce inflammation after Surgery

Feya Adler

Table of Content...2

Disclaimer

The information provided in the 'No Gallbladder Diet for Beginners' is for informational purposes only. It is important to note that this guide is not intended as medical or health advice. It should not be used to diagnose, treat, or cure any medical condition or disease. For any such concerns, it is always best to consult with a qualified healthcare professional.

It is important to reiterate that the author and publisher of this guide are not medical professionals. The advice provided here is not intended to replace medical advice. The strategies, tips, and suggestions contained in this guide are not guaranteed to produce specific results and may vary depending on individual circumstances. Therefore, it is strongly advised to consult with a healthcare professional before making any dietary changes or starting any new health regimen.

The author and publisher disclaim any liability directly or indirectly for using the material provided in this guide. By reading this material, you agree that the author and publisher are not responsible for the success or failure of your dietary decisions related to any information presented here.

Preface

This cookbook aims to make the dietary transition after gallbladder removal as seamless and straightforward as possible. It's not just about eliminating foods that might cause discomfort; it's about embracing a diet that supports your body's new way of processing food, ensuring you receive all the necessary nutrients for optimal health, and rediscovering joy in meals. Each recipe and tip within these pages is crafted to ease your body into its new standard, focusing on balance, flavor, and nutrition.

A Personal Note from the Author

As I sat in my doctor's office, the words "gallbladder removal" echoed in my mind. I felt a mix of relief and apprehension. I was relieved that the source of my discomfort would soon be addressed, but I was apprehensive about what life without a gallbladder would mean for my diet and lifestyle. Like many of you, I feared the changes, worried about restrictions, and mourned the loss of my favorite meals. However, this journey has taught me that not only is a fulfilling culinary life possible post-surgery, but it can also be vibrant, delicious, and tailored to promote healing and health. This cookbook is the culmination of my experiences, research, and kitchen experiments. It's designed to guide you gently into the world of the gallbladder-less living, turning apprehension into empowerment.

Chapter 1: Guidance «No gallbladder diet, for beginner»

1.1. Making the Most of Your New Dietary Landscape

Adjusting to life without a gallbladder is a process, one that requires patience, experimentation, and listening to your body. Here are some tips to help you use this cookbook effectively:

Start Slowly: Initially, it's wise to introduce dietary changes gradually. Begin with low-fat, easily digestible foods and slowly increase variety as your body adjusts.

Listen to Your Body: Everyone's experience post-gallbladder removal is unique. Pay close attention to how different foods affect you and adjust your diet accordingly. Keeping a food diary can be incredibly helpful in this regard.

Embrace Small, Frequent Meals: Smaller, more frequent meals can help manage the continuous flow of bile into your intestines, making digestion easier and more comfortable.

Stay Hydrated: Adequate hydration is crucial. Water helps with digestion and can aid in mitigating some of the digestive changes you may experience.

Seek Variety and Nutrition: Feel free of your dietary changes. A vast array of gallbladder-friendly foods is both nutritious and delicious. This cookbook aims to introduce you to them in creative and enjoyable ways.

1.2. Tips for Dining Out

Following a no-gallbladder diet can make eating out difficult, but with a bit of planning, you can still enjoy eating out without compromising your nutritional objectives:

Examine Dining Establishments: Before you leave, do some research on local eateries that accommodate particular dietary requirements or provide healthier options. Look for menu items that feature whole grains, grilled or steamed vegetables, and lean proteins.

Pose inquiries: Be bold and ask your waitress questions about the menu or food preparation. Ask about changes or replacements to make meals more gallbladder-friendly. For example, ask for dressing to be served on the side or substitute steamed veggies for fried sides.

Eat in Moderation: When dining out, watch the portions you eat because large portions can upset your stomach. If smaller servings are not offered, consider splitting an entree or eating less. To prevent overindulging, pay attention to your body's hunger signals.

1.3. Guidance on Portion Size

Managing meal sizes: Managing meal sizes is critical for avoiding discomfort and ensuring proper digestion after cholecystectomy. Here are some suggestions to help you control portion sizes effectively:

Use Portion-Controlled Plates: Invest in portion-controlled dishes or containers to help visualize proper serving sizes for various meal groups. Fill half your plate with veggies, one-fourth with lean protein, and the rest with whole grains or starchy vegetables.

Listen to Your Body: Use your hunger and fullness cues to choose when to stop eating. Eat slowly, savoring each meal, and stop when you're satisfied rather than complete.

Practice Mindful Eating: Focus on the sensory experience of eating and how different foods make you feel. Be mindful of your emotional eating triggers and treat food as nourishment rather than a coping tool.

By implementing these meal planning, dining out, and portion management tactics, you'll be well-prepared to traverse your nutritional path confidently and efficiently.

Chapter 2: Everyday Recipes

2.1 Breakfast

Greek Yogurt Parfait with Granola and Fruit

Time: 5 minutes| Difficulty: Easy| Serving 2

1 cup Greek yogurt
1/2 cup granola (choose a low-fat, low-sugar option)
1/2 cup mixed fruit (such as berries, banana slices)
Honey or maple syrup for drizzling (optional)

1. Layer Greek yoghurt, granola, and mixed fruit in serving glasses or bowls.
2. Repeat the layers until the glasses or bowls are filled.
3. Drizzle honey or maple syrup over the top, if desired.

Per Serving
Calories: 280|Protein: 15g|Carbs: 40g|Fat: 8g|Fiber: 6g

Broccoli and Cheese Breakfast Casserole

Time: 30 minutes| Difficulty: Easy| Serving 2

4 eggs
1 cup chopped broccoli florets
1/2 cup shredded cheese
1/4 cup milk
Salt and pepper to taste
Olive oil for greasing baking dish

1. Preheat the oven to 375°F (190°C) and grease a small baking dish with olive oil.
2. In a mixing bowl, whisk together eggs, milk, salt, and pepper until well beaten.
3. Stir in chopped broccoli florets and shredded cheese.
4. Pour the egg mixture into the prepared baking dish.
5. Bake for 20-25 minutes, or until the eggs are set and the top is golden brown.
6. Allow the casserole to cool slightly before slicing and serving.

Per Serving
Calories: 300|Protein: 20g|Carbs: 8g|Fat: 20g|Fiber: 2g

Apple Cinnamon Overnight Oats

Time: 5 minutes (plus 1 night)| Difficulty: Easy| Serving 2

1 cup rolled oats
1 cup almond milk
1 apple, diced
2 tablespoons maple syrup
1/2 teaspoon cinnamon
1/4 teaspoon vanilla extract
Chopped nuts for topping (optional)

1. In a bowl or jar, mix rolled oats, almond milk, diced apple, maple syrup, cinnamon, and vanilla extract.
2. Stir until well combined.
3. Cover and refrigerate overnight, or for at least 4 hours, to allow the oats to absorb the liquid and soften.
4. Stir well before serving.
5. Top with chopped nuts, if desired.

Per Serving
Calories: 250|Protein: 6g|Carbs: 45g|Fat: 6g|Fiber: 7g

Berry Chia Seed Pudding

Time: 5 minutes (plus chilling time)|Difficulty: Easy| Serving 2

1/4 cup chia seeds
1 cup almond milk
1 tablespoon honey or maple syrup
1/2 teaspoon vanilla extract
Mixed berries for topping

1. In a bowl, whisk together chia seeds, almond milk, honey or maple syrup, and vanilla extract until well combined.
2. Cover the bowl and refrigerate for at least 2 hours or overnight, allowing the chia seeds to absorb the liquid and thicken into a pudding-like consistency.
3. Once chilled and thickened, divide the chia seed pudding into serving bowls.
4. Top with mixed berries just before serving.

Per Serving
Calories: 220|Protein: 5g|Carbs: 25g|Fat: 12g

Peanut Butter Banana Toast

Time: 5 minutes| Difficulty: Easy| Serving 2
2 slices whole-grain bread, toasted
2 tablespoons peanut butter
1 ripe banana, sliced
Honey or maple syrup for drizzling (optional)
1. Spread peanut butter evenly onto each slice of toasted whole-grain bread.
2. Top with sliced banana.
3. Drizzle with honey or maple syrup, if desired.

Per Serving
Calories: 300| Protein: 8g| Carbs: 40g| Fat: 12g| Fiber: 6g

Vegetable Frittata

Time: 20 minutes| Difficulty: Easy| Serving 2
4 eggs
1/2 cup diced bell peppers
1/2 cup diced zucchini
1/4 cup diced onions
1/4 cup grated cheese
Salt and pepper to taste
Olive oil for cooking
1. Preheat the oven to 350°F (175°C).
2. In a mixing bowl, whisk together eggs, salt, and pepper until well beaten.
3. Heat olive oil in an oven-safe skillet over medium heat.
4. Add diced onions and cook until translucent.
5. Add diced bell peppers and zucchini to the skillet and cook until softened.
6. Pour the beaten eggs over the vegetables in the skillet.
7. Cook for a few minutes until the edges start to set.
8. Sprinkle grated cheese evenly over the top.
9. Transfer the skillet to the preheated oven and bake for 10-12 minutes, until the frittata is set and golden brown on top.
10. Remove from the oven and let it cool slightly before slicing and serving.

Per Serving
Calories: 250|Protein: 16g|Carbs: 8g|Fat: 15g|Fiber: 2g

Lemon Blueberry Quinoa Breakfast Bowl

Time: 10 minutes| Difficulty: Easy| Serving 2
1 cup cooked quinoa
1/2 cup almond milk
1 tablespoon honey or maple syrup
Zest of 1 lemon
1/2 cup fresh blueberries
2 tablespoons sliced almonds
Fresh mint leaves for garnish (optional)
1. In a saucepan, heat almond milk over medium heat until warm.
2. Stir in cooked quinoa, honey or maple syrup, and lemon zest.
3. Cook, stirring occasionally, until the quinoa is heated through.
4. Divide the quinoa mixture between two bowls.
5. Top each bowl with fresh blueberries and sliced almonds.
6. Garnish with fresh mint leaves, if desired.

Per Serving
Calories: 250|Protein: 6g|Carbs: 40g|Fat: 7g|Fiber: 5g

Egg and Vegetable Frittata

Time: 20 minutes| Difficulty: Easy| Serving 2
4 eggs
1/2 cup chopped vegetables (such as bell peppers, onions, spinach)
1/4 cup shredded cheese (optional)
Salt and pepper to taste
Olive oil for cooking
1. Preheat the oven to 350°F (175°C).
2. Whisk together eggs, salt, and pepper in a bowl until well beaten.
3. Heat olive oil in an oven-safe skillet over medium heat.
4. Add chopped vegetables to the skillet and cook until softened.
5. Pour the beaten eggs over the vegetables in the skillet, ensuring they are evenly distributed.
6. Cook for 3-4 minutes, until the edges begin to set.
7. Sprinkle shredded cheese over the top (if using).
8. Transfer the skillet to the preheated oven and bake for 10-12 minutes, or until the frittata is set and golden brown on top.
9. Remove from the oven and let it cool slightly before slicing.

Per Serving
Calories: 180|Protein: 12g|Carbs: 8g|Fat: 10g|Fiber: 2g

Avocado Toast with Poached Eggs

Time: 10 minutes| Difficulty: Easy| Serving 2

2 slices whole-grain bread
1 ripe avocado
4 eggs
Fresh herbs for garnish
Red pepper flakes (optional)
Salt and black pepper

1. Toast the slices of whole-grain bread until golden brown.
2. While the bread is toasting, mash the ripe avocado in a small bowl and season with salt, pepper, and red pepper flakes (if using).
3. Poach the eggs in simmering water until the whites are set, but the yolks are still runny.
4. Spread the mashed avocado evenly onto the toasted bread slices.
5. Top each slice with two poached eggs.
6. Garnish with fresh herbs, such as chopped parsley or chives.

Per Serving
Calories: 300|Protein: 12g|Carbs: 20g|Fat: 20g|Fiber: 8g

Mango Coconut Chia Pudding

Time: 5 minutes (plus chilling time)|Difficulty: Easy| Serving 2

1/4 cup chia seeds
1 cup coconut milk
1 ripe mango, diced
2 tablespoons shredded coconut
Honey or maple syrup for sweetening (optional)

1. In a bowl or jar, combine chia seeds and coconut milk.
2. Stir until well combined.
3. Cover and refrigerate for at least 2 hours or overnight, allowing the chia seeds to absorb the liquid and thicken.
4. Once chilled and thickened, divide the chia seed pudding between two serving bowls.
5. Top with diced mango and shredded coconut.
6. Sweeten with honey or maple syrup, if desired

Per serving
Calories: 250|Protein: 5g|Carbs: 30g|Fat: 15g|Fiber: 10g

Protein-Packed Breakfast Bowl

Time: 15 minutes| Difficulty: Easy |Serving 2

2 cups cooked quinoa
4 eggs
1 avocado, sliced
1/2 cup cherry tomatoes, halved
1/4 cup crumbled feta cheese
Salt and pepper to taste
Olive oil for cooking

1. In a skillet, cook eggs to your desired doneness (such as scrambled or sunny-side-up).
2. Divide cooked quinoa between two serving bowls.
3. Top each bowl with cooked eggs, sliced avocado, cherry tomatoes, and crumbled feta cheese.
4. Season with salt and pepper to taste.
5. Drizzle with olive oil, if desired.

Per serving
Calories: 400|Protein: 20g| Carbs: 30g|Fat: 25g|Fiber: 8g

Sweet Potato Hash with Turkey Sausage

Time: 20 minutes| Difficulty: Easy| Serving 2

1 large sweet potato, diced
2 turkey sausage links, sliced
1/2 cup diced bell peppers
1/4 cup diced onions
2 cloves garlic, minced
Salt and pepper to taste
Olive oil for cooking

1. Heat olive oil in a skillet over medium heat.
2. Add diced sweet potatoes to the skillet and cook until tender.
3. Add sliced turkey sausage, diced bell peppers, diced onions, and minced garlic to the skillet.
4. Cook until the sausage is browned and the vegetables are softened.
5. Season with salt and pepper to taste.

Per serving
Calories: 280|Protein: 12g|Carbs: 25g|Fat: 10g|Fiber: 5g

Spinach and Mushroom Omelette

Time: 15 minutes| Difficulty: Easy| Serving 2
4 eggs
1 cup fresh spinach leaves
1/2 cup sliced mushrooms
1/4 cup shredded cheese (optional)
Salt and pepper to taste
Olive oil for cooking
Per serving
Calories: 200|Protein: 14g|Carbs: 5g|Fat: 14g|Fiber: 2g

1. In a bowl, whisk together eggs, salt, and pepper until well beaten.
2. Heat olive oil in a skillet over medium heat.
3. Add sliced mushrooms to the skillet and cook until softened.
4. Add fresh spinach leaves to the skillet and cook until wilted.
5. Pour the beaten eggs over the mushrooms and spinach in the skillet.
6. Cook for 3-4 minutes, until the eggs are set but still moist.
7. Sprinkle shredded cheese over the top (if using).
8. Fold the omelet in half and cook for another minute to melt the cheese.

Quinoa Breakfast Bowl with Sautéed Vegetables

Time: 20 minutes| Difficulty: Easy| Serving 2
1 cup cooked quinoa
1/2 cup diced bell peppers
1/2 cup diced zucchini
1/4 cup diced onions
2 cloves garlic, minced
2 eggs
Salt and pepper to taste
Olive oil for cooking

1. Heat olive oil in a skillet over medium heat.
2. Add diced onions and minced garlic to the skillet and cook until fragrant.
3. Add diced bell peppers and zucchini to the skillet and sauté until softened.
4. Stir in cooked quinoa and continue to cook until heated through.
5. In a separate skillet, cook eggs to your desired doneness (such as sunny-side-up or scrambled).
6. Divide the quinoa and sautéed vegetables between two bowls.
7. Top each bowl with a cooked egg.
8. Season with salt and pepper to taste.

Per serving
Calories: 300|Protein: 12g| Carbs: 30g| Fat: 15g|Fiber: 6g

Smoked Salmon and Cream Cheese Bagel

Time: 10 minutes| Difficulty: Easy| Serving 2

2 whole-grain bagels, halved and toasted
4 tablespoons cream cheese
4 slices smoked salmon
1/4 cup sliced cucumber
1/4 cup sliced red onion
Fresh dill for garnish

1. Spread cream cheese evenly onto each toasted bagel half.
2. Top with smoked salmon, sliced cucumber, and sliced red onion.
3. Garnish with fresh dill.

Per serving
Calories: 350| Protein: 20g|Carbs: 30g|Fat: 15g|Fiber: 6g

Egg Salad Lettuce Wraps

Time: 10 minutes| Difficulty: Easy | Serving 2

4 large eggs

2 tablespoons mayonnaise (look for a low-fat version for a lighter option)

1 teaspoon yellow mustard

Salt and pepper to taste

1/4 cup finely chopped celery

2 tablespoons chopped fresh chives or green onion

8 leaves of butter lettuce or romaine hearts, washed and dried

Paprika (optional, for garnish)

1. Cook Eggs: Place eggs in a saucepan and cover with water. Bring to a boil, then cover, turn off the heat, and let sit for 9-10 minutes. Drain and fill the saucepan with cold water to cool the eggs quickly. Peel them once they're cool.
2. Prepare Egg Salad: Roughly chop the cooled, boiled eggs and place them in a bowl. Add mayonnaise, mustard, salt, and pepper. Gently stir to combine. Fold in the chopped celery and chives or green onion until evenly distributed.
3. Assemble Lettuce Wraps: Lay the lettuce leaves on a flat surface. Spoon the egg salad mixture into the center of each lettuce leaf. If desired, sprinkle a little paprika over each wrap for extra flavor and color.
4. Serve: Fold the sides of the lettuce over the filling and roll up to eat. Serve immediately for the best texture and freshness.

Per serving
Calories: Approx. 300| Carbs: 3g|Fats: 23g|Protein: 19g

Yogurt and Fruit Parfait

Time: 5 minutes| Difficulty: Easy| Serving 2

1 cup Greek yogurt
1 cup mixed fruit (such as berries, banana slices, and diced mango)
1/4 cup granola
Honey or maple syrup for drizzling (optional)

1. In serving glasses or bowls, layer Greek yogurt, mixed fruit, and granola.
2. Repeat the layers until the glasses or bowls are filled.
3. Drizzle with honey or maple syrup, if desired.

Per serving
Calories: 300| Protein: 20g| Carbs: 40g| Fat: 8g| Fiber: 6g

Breakfast Stuffed Sweet Potatoes

Time: 45 minutes| Difficulty: Moderate| Serving 2

2 medium sweet potatoes
4 large eggs, scrambled
1/2 cup black beans, drained and rinsed
1/4 cup diced bell peppers
1/4 cup diced onions
1/4 cup shredded cheese (cheddar or Monterey Jack)
Fresh cilantro for garnish
Salt and pepper to taste
Cooking spray

1. Preheat the oven to 400°F (200°C).
2. Wash and scrub the sweet potatoes, then pierce them several times with a fork.
3. Place the sweet potatoes on a baking sheet lined with parchment paper and bake for 40-45 minutes, or until tender.
4. While the sweet potatoes are baking, prepare the scrambled eggs.
5. Heat a non-stick skillet over medium heat and coat with cooking spray.
6. Sautee the diced onions and bell peppers until softened.
7. Add the scrambled eggs to the skillet and cook until set.
8. Once the sweet potatoes are cooked, slice them open lengthwise and fluff the insides with a fork.
9. Divide the scrambled eggs, black beans, and shredded cheese between the two sweet potatoes.
10. Season with salt and pepper to taste.
11. Garnish with fresh cilantro.
12. Serve immediately.

Per serving
Calories: 320| Protein: 18g| Fat: 12g| Carbs: 35g

Egg and Avocado Breakfast Wrap

Time: 10 minutes| Difficulty: Easy| Serving 2

4 eggs
1 ripe avocado, sliced
2 whole-wheat tortillas
Salt and pepper to taste
Salsa for serving (optional)

1. In a skillet, scramble the eggs until cooked through.
2. Warm the whole-wheat tortillas in the skillet or microwave.
3. Divide scrambled eggs and sliced avocado between the tortillas.
4. Season with salt and pepper to taste.
5. Roll up the tortillas to form wraps.
6. Serve with salsa on the side, if desired

Per serving
Calories: 300| Protein: 14g| Carbs: 20g| Fat: 18g| Fiber: 6g

Vegetable and Quinoa Breakfast Skillet

Time: 25 minutes| Difficulty: Easy| Serving 2

1 tablespoon olive oil
1/2 cup diced bell peppers
1/2 cup diced zucchini
1/4 cup diced onions
1 clove garlic, minced
1 cup cooked quinoa
2 large eggs
Salt and pepper to taste
Fresh parsley for garnish

1. Heat olive oil in a skillet over medium heat.
2. Add the diced onions and garlic to the skillet and cook until softened.
3. Add the diced bell peppers and zucchini to the skillet and sauté until tender.
4. Stir in the cooked quinoa and cook until heated through.
5. Make two wells in the quinoa mixture and crack an egg into each well.
6. Cover the skillet and cook until the eggs are set to your liking (about 3-5 minutes for runny yolks).
7. Season with salt and pepper to taste.
8. Garnish with fresh parsley.
9. Serve immediately.

Per serving
Calories: 290| Protein: 14g| Fat: 12g| Carbs: 30g

Egg and Avocado Breakfast Burrito

Time: 25 minutes| Difficulty: Moderate| Serving 2
4 large eggs
2 whole wheat tortillas
*1 avocado, sliced **and** 1 tablespoon olive oil*
1/2 cup black beans, drained and rinsed
*1/4 cup salsa **and** Salt and pepper to taste*

1. In a bowl, whisk together eggs, salt, and pepper.
2. Heat olive oil in a skillet over medium heat. Pour in the egg mixture and cook, stirring occasionally, until the eggs are scrambled and cooked through.
3. Warm the whole wheat tortillas in the skillet or microwave for a few seconds until they are pliable.
4. Divide the scrambled eggs, sliced avocado, black beans, and salsa between the tortillas.
5. Roll up the tortillas to form burritos, tucking in the sides as you go.
6. Serve immediately, or wrap the burritos in foil for an on-the-go breakfast.

Per serving
Calories: 320| Protein: 15g| Fat: 18g| Carbs: 26g

Vegetarian Breakfast Burrito

Time: 25 minutes| Difficulty: Moderate| Serving 2
2 large whole wheat tortillas
4 large eggs, scrambled
1/2 cup black beans, drained and rinsed
*1/2 cup diced bell peppers **and** 1/4 cup diced onions*
1/2 cup shredded cheese (cheddar or Monterey Jack)
*1/4 cup salsa **and** Salt and pepper to taste*

1. Heat a non-stick skillet over medium heat and coat with cooking spray.
2. Sautee the diced onions and bell peppers until softened.
3. Add the scrambled eggs to the skillet and cook until set.
4. Warm the black beans in the microwave or on the stovetop.
5. Divide the scrambled eggs, black beans, and shredded cheese between the two tortillas.
6. Top each tortilla with salsa and season with salt and pepper to taste.
7. Fold in the sides of the tortillas and roll up tightly to form burritos.
8. Heat a separate skillet over medium heat and lightly toast the burritos on all sides until golden brown.
9. Serve immediately.

Per serving
Calories: 340| Protein: 20g| Fat: 14g| Carbs: 30g

Vegetarian Breakfast Casserole

Time: 45 minutes| Difficulty: Moderate| Serving 2

6 large eggs
1/2 cup milk (or almond milk)
2 cups frozen hash browns, thawed
1 cup chopped mixed vegetables (bell peppers, onions, spinach)
1 cup shredded cheddar cheese
Salt and pepper to taste

1. Preheat the oven to 375°F (190°C). Grease a baking dish with cooking spray.
2. In a mixing bowl, whisk together eggs, milk, salt, and pepper.
3. Spread the thawed hash browns evenly on the bottom of the greased baking dish.
4. Layer the chopped mixed vegetables on top of the hash browns.
5. Pour the egg mixture over the vegetables in the baking dish.
6. Sprinkle shredded cheddar cheese evenly over the top.
7. Bake in the preheated oven for 30-35 minutes, or until the eggs are set and the cheese is melted and golden brown.
8. Remove from the oven and let cool slightly before slicing into squares.
9. Serve warm.

Per serving
Calories: 280| Protein: 15g| Fat: 18g| Carbs: 15g

Healthy Breakfast Burrito Bowl

Time: 20 minutes| Difficulty: Moderate| Serving 2

1 cup cooked quinoa
1/2 cup black beans, drained and rinsed
1/2 avocado, sliced
2 large eggs, scrambled
1/4 cup salsa
1/4 cup shredded cheese (optional)
Salt and pepper to taste

1. In a bowl, layer cooked quinoa, black beans, scrambled eggs, sliced avocado, salsa, and shredded cheese (if using).
2. Season with salt and pepper to taste.
3. Serve immediately.

Per serving
Calories: 380| Protein: 21g| Fat: 17g| Carbs: 36g

Spinach and Mushroom Breakfast Quesadilla

Time: 15 minutes| Difficulty: Moderate| Serving 2
2 large whole wheat tortillas
1 cup fresh spinach leaves
1/2 cup sliced mushrooms
1/2 cup shredded cheese (cheddar or mozzarella)
2 large eggs, scrambled
Salsa and Greek yogurt for serving (optional)
Salt and pepper to taste

1. Heat a non-stick skillet over medium heat and coat with cooking spray.
2. Place one tortilla in the skillet and sprinkle half of the shredded cheese over the entire tortilla.
3. Top one half of the tortilla with fresh spinach leaves, sliced mushrooms, and scrambled eggs.
4. Season with salt and pepper to taste.
5. Fold the other half of the tortilla over the filling to create a half-moon shape.
6. Cook for 2-3 minutes on each side, or until the tortilla is golden brown and crispy, and the cheese is melted.
7. Remove from the skillet and repeat with the remaining tortilla and ingredients.
8. Cut each quesadilla into wedges and serve with salsa and Greek yogurt if desired.
9. Serve immediately.

Per serving
Calories: 320| Protein: 18g| Fat: 15g| Carbs: 28g

Egg and Avocado Breakfast Salad

Time: 15 minutes| Difficulty: Easy| Serving 2
2 large eggs
1 avocado, sliced
2 cups mixed salad greens
1/4 cup cherry tomatoes, halved
2 tablespoons balsamic vinaigrette
Salt and pepper to taste

1. Bring a pot of water to a boil. Carefully add the eggs and boil for 8 minutes.
2. Remove the eggs from the pot and run them under cold water to cool. Peel and slice them.
3. In a large bowl, toss together mixed salad greens, cherry tomatoes, sliced avocado, and balsamic vinaigrette.
4. Divide the salad between two plates.
5. Top each salad with sliced hard-boiled eggs.
6. Season with salt and pepper to taste.
7. Serve immediately.

Per serving
Calories: 320| Protein: 11g| Fat: 24g| Carbs: 14g

Blueberry Banana Pancakes

Time: 20 minutes| Difficulty: Moderate| Serving 2
1 cup whole wheat flour
1 tablespoon baking powder
1 ripe banana, mashed
1 cup almond milk (or any milk of your choice)
1/2 cup fresh blueberries
1 tablespoon maple syrup (optional)

1. In a bowl, whisk together the whole wheat flour and baking powder.
2. Add the mashed banana, almond milk, and maple syrup (if using). Mix until well combined.
3. Gently fold in the fresh blueberries.
4. Heat a non-stick skillet or griddle over medium heat and lightly grease with cooking spray or butter.
5. Pour 1/4 cup of the pancake batter onto the skillet for each pancake.
6. Cook until bubbles form on the surface, then flip and cook for another 1-2 minutes until golden brown.
7. Repeat with the remaining batter.
8. Serve warm with additional fresh blueberries and maple syrup if desired.

Per serving
Calories: 220| Protein: 6g| Fat: 2g| Carbs: 45g

Healthy Breakfast Pizza

Time: 20 minutes| Difficulty: Moderate| Serving 2
2 whole wheat English muffins, split and toasted
1/2 cup marinara sauce
1/2 cup shredded mozzarella cheese
2 large eggs
1/4 cup sliced bell peppers and 1/4 cup sliced mushrooms
*Salt and pepper to taste **and** Fresh basil for garnish*

1. Preheat the oven to 375°F (190°C).
2. Place toasted English muffins on a baking sheet lined with parchment paper.
3. Spread marinara sauce evenly over each English muffin half.
4. Sprinkle shredded mozzarella cheese over the marinara sauce.
5. Crack an egg onto each English muffin half.
6. Arrange sliced bell peppers and mushrooms around the eggs.
7. Season with salt and pepper to taste.
8. Bake in the preheated oven for 12-15 minutes, or until the eggs are set and the cheese is melted.
9. Garnish with fresh basil.
10. Serve immediately.

Per serving
Calories: 340| Protein: 19g| Fat: 14g| Carbs: 35g

Mediterranean Breakfast Plate

Time: 15 minutes| Difficulty: Easy| Serving 2

2 large eggs, boiled and sliced
1/2 cup cherry tomatoes, halved
1/4 cucumber, sliced
1/4 cup hummus
2 whole wheat pita bread, toasted
Kalamata olives for garnish
Fresh parsley for garnish

1. Arrange boiled egg slices, cherry tomatoes, cucumber slices, and whole wheat pita bread on a plate.
2. Serve with a dollop of hummus.
3. Garnish with Kalamata olives and fresh parsley.
4. Serve immediately.

Per serving
Calories: 340| Protein: 18g| Fat: 14g| Carbs: 38g

Indian Spiced Oats

Time: 20 minutes| Difficulty: Easy| Serving 2

1 cup rolled oats
2 cups water
1 tsp. turmeric
1/2 tsp. cumin
1 small carrot, grated
1/4 cup peas
Salt to taste
1 tbsp. chopped cilantro for garnish

1. Cook oats in water with turmeric and cumin until soft.
2. Stir in carrots and peas, cooking until tender.
3. Garnish with cilantro before serving.

Per serving
Calories: 200| Protein: 6g| Fat: 3g| Carbs: 36g

Brazilian Tapioca Crepes

Time: 20 minutes| Difficulty: Moderate| Serving 2

1 cup tapioca flour
1/2 cup water
Pinch of salt
1/2 cup shredded low-fat cheese
1 tomato, sliced
1/2 avocado, sliced

1. Mix tapioca flour, salt, and water to form a batter.
2. Pour into a hot non-stick pan, forming thin crepes.
3. Sprinkle cheese on top, allowing it to melt.
4. Add tomato and avocado before folding and serving.

Per serving
Calories: 280| Protein: 6g| Fat: 12g| Carbs: 36g

Moroccan Shakshuka

Time: 30 minutes| Difficulty: Moderate| Serving 2

4 large eggs
1 can (14 oz.) diced tomatoes
1 small onion, diced
1 red bell pepper, diced
2 cloves garlic, minced
1 tsp. cumin
1 tsp. paprika
1/2 tsp. chili powder (optional)
Salt and pepper to taste
2 tbsp. fresh parsley, chopped
1 tbsp. olive oil

1. Heat olive oil in a large skillet over medium heat.
2. Sauté onion, bell pepper, and garlic until soft.
3. Add tomatoes and spices, simmering until the mixture thickens.
4. Crack eggs into the pan over the tomatoes. Cover and cook until eggs are done to your liking.
5. Garnish with fresh parsley before serving.

Per serving
Calories: 220| Protein: 14g| Fat: 12g| Carbs: 15g

Japanese Miso Soup with Tofu

Time: 15 minutes| Difficulty: Easy| Serving 2

3 cups water
2 tbsp. miso paste
1/2 block silken tofu, diced
2 green onions, sliced
*1 tbsp. dried seaweed, rehydrated **and** 1 tsp. sesame oil*

1. Bring water to a simmer and dissolve the miso paste in it.
2. Add tofu and seaweed, and cook gently for 3 minutes.
3. Stir in sesame oil and green onions just before serving.

Per serving
Calories: 150| Protein: 10g| Fat: 7g| Carbs: 10g

Thai Mango Sticky Rice

Time: 40 minutes| Difficulty: Moderate| Serving 2

1 cup sticky rice, soaked overnight
1/2 cup light coconut milk
2 tbsp. sugar and 1/4 tsp. salt
1 ripe mango, sliced
1 tbsp. toasted sesame seeds

1. Cook sticky rice until tender.
2. Heat coconut milk with sugar and salt until dissolved, mix into the rice.
3. Serve with fresh mango and sprinkle with sesame seeds.

Per serving
Calories: 320| Protein: 5g| Fat: 8g| Carbs: 58g

Turkish Menemen (Scrambled Eggs with Vegetables)

Time: 25 minutes| Difficulty: Easy| Serving 2

4 eggs
1 onion, chopped
1 green bell pepper, chopped
2 tomatoes, diced
1/2 tsp. paprika
Salt and pepper to taste
2 tbsp. parsley, chopped
1 tbsp. olive oil

1. Heat olive oil in a skillet and sauté onions and bell pepper until soft.
2. Add tomatoes and paprika, cooking until the mixture is saucy.
3. Scramble eggs into the mixture until cooked.
4. Garnish with parsley before serving.

Per serving
Calories: 240| Protein: 14g| Fat: 17g| Carbs: 10g

Mexican Chia Pudding

Time: Overnight (plus 15 minutes active prep)| Difficulty: Easy| Serving 2

1/4 cup chia seeds
1 cup almond milk
1 tbsp. honey
1/2 tsp. vanilla extract
1/2 tsp. cinnamon
Fresh berries for topping

1. Mix chia seeds, almond milk, honey, vanilla, and cinnamon in a bowl.
2. Refrigerate overnight until set.
3. Top with fresh berries before serving.

Per serving
Calories: 250| Protein: 5g| Fat: 15g| Carbs: 25g

Caribbean Coconut Water Smoothie

Time: 10 minutes| Difficulty: Easy| Serving 2

1 cup coconut water
1 banana
1/2 cup pineapple chunks
1/2 cup mango chunks
Ice as needed

1. Blend all ingredients until smooth.

Per serving
Calories: 180| Protein: 2g| Fat: 0.5g| Carbs: 44g

Ethiopian Injera with Veggie Toppings

Time: Overnight (for batter to ferment) + 20 minutes cooking| Difficulty: Challenging| Serving 2

1 cup teff flour
2 cups water
Salt to taste
1/2 tsp. baking powder
Mixed vegetables (carrots, cabbage, and spinach), lightly sautéed

1. Mix teff flour with water and let sit overnight to ferment.
2. Stir in salt and baking powder, then cook in a non-stick pan like pancakes.
3. Top with sautéed vegetables and serve.

Per serving
Calories: 210| Protein: 8g| Fat: 1g| Carbs: 46g

Hawaiian Acai Bowl

Time: 15 minutes| Difficulty: Easy| Serving 2

1 acai berry packet (frozen)
1/2 banana
1/2 cup mixed berries
1/4 cup granola
1 tbsp. shredded coconut
1/4 cup almond milk

1. Blend the acai packet with banana and almond milk until smooth.
2. Pour into a bowl and top with berries, granola, and shredded coconut.

Per serving
Calories: 315| Protein: 4g| Fat: 10g| Carbs: 53g

Lebanese Foul Mudammas

Time: 20 minutes| Difficulty: Easy| Serving 2

1 can (15 oz.) fava beans, drained and rinsed
2 cloves garlic, minced
1 lemon, juiced
2 tablespoons olive oil
1 teaspoon cumin
Salt and pepper to taste
Fresh parsley, chopped for garnish

1. In a pan, heat the olive oil over medium heat and sauté garlic until golden.
2. Add fava beans, lemon juice, cumin, salt, and pepper.
3. Cook until beans are warm. Mash slightly if desired.
4. Garnish with fresh parsley before serving.

Per serving
Calories: 250| Protein: 12g| Fat: 9g| Carbohydrates: 33g

Indonesian Coconut Rice (Nasi Uduk)

Time: 30 minutes| Difficulty: Moderate| Serving 2

1 cup jasmine rice
1 cup coconut milk
1 pandan leaf (optional)
1 lemongrass stalk, bruised
1/2 teaspoon salt

1. Rinse rice until water runs clear.
2. In a pot, combine rice, coconut milk, pandan leaf, lemongrass, and salt.
3. Bring to a boil, then cover and reduce to a simmer for 20 minutes, or until rice is fluffy.
4. Remove pandan leaf and lemongrass before serving.

Per serving
Calories: 320| Protein: 5g| Fat: 14g| Carbs: 44g

Egyptian Ful Medames

Time: Overnight soaking + 30 minutes cooking| Difficulty: Moderate| Serving 2

1 cup dried fava beans, soaked overnight
1 teaspoon baking soda (for soaking)
2 cloves garlic, minced
1 lemon, juiced
2 tablespoons olive oil
Salt to taste
*Chopped parsley **and** tomato for garnish*

1. Rinse soaked beans and cook with fresh water and baking soda until tender.
2. Drain beans and mix with garlic, lemon juice, olive oil, and salt.
3. Mash lightly and garnish with parsley and tomato.

Per serving
Calories: 260| Protein: 13g| Fat: 10g| Carbs: 34g

Spanish Pan con Tomate

Time: 15 minutes| Difficulty: Easy| Serving 2

2 large ripe tomatoes, grated
1 clove garlic, cut in half
2 slices of whole grain bread
1 tablespoon olive oil
Salt to taste

1. Toast the bread until crisp.
2. Rub the garlic over the toasted bread.
3. Spread the grated tomato over the bread, drizzle with olive oil, and sprinkle with salt.

Per serving
Calories: 180| Protein: 4g| Fat: 7g| Carbs: 26g

Turkish Poached Eggs with Yogurt (Çilbir)

Time: 20 minutes| Difficulty: Moderate| Serving 2

4 eggs
1 cup plain low-fat yogurt
2 cloves garlic, minced
1 tablespoon olive oil
1 teaspoon paprika
Fresh dill for garnish

1. Whisk yogurt with minced garlic and set aside at room temperature.
2. Poach eggs in simmering water until the whites are set but yolks are still runny.
3. Place yogurt on a plate, top with poached eggs, drizzle with olive oil, sprinkle paprika, and garnish with dill.

Per serving
Calories: 230| Protein: 16g| Fat: 15g| Carbs: 7g

Brazilian Tapioca Crepes

Time: 20 minutes| Difficulty: Easy| Serving

1 cup tapioca flour
1/4 cup water
Pinch of salt
*Filling: 1/2 banana **and** 1 tablespoon honey*

1. Mix tapioca flour with water and salt to form a batter.
2. Pour batter into a hot non-stick skillet, forming a thin crepe.
3. Cook until edges lift, then fill with banana and honey, fold, and serve.

Per serving
Calories: 200| Protein: 0g| Fat: 0g| Carbs: 50g

Moroccan Semolina Porridge (Sellou)

Time: 25 minutes| Difficulty: Moderate| Serving 2

1/2 cup fine semolina
2 cups water
1 tablespoon honey
1/2 teaspoon cinnamon
Almonds and sesame seeds for topping

1. In a saucepan, bring water to a boil and slowly whisk in the semolina.
2. Reduce heat and continue to stir until thickened.
3. Stir in honey and cinnamon.
4. Serve topped with almonds and sesame seeds.

Per serving
Calories: 210| Protein: 5g| Fat: 3g| Carbs: 40g

Vietnamese Rice Congee

Time: 35 minutes| Difficulty: Easy| Serving 2
*1/2 cup jasmine rice, rinsed **and** 4 cups water*
1 chicken breast (optional, poached and shredded)
1 inch ginger, finely chopped
*Salt to taste **and** Green onions **and** cilantro for garnish*
1. Combine rice, water, and ginger in a pot; bring to a boil.
2. Reduce heat to a simmer; cook until rice is very soft and the mixture is thick.
3. Add shredded chicken, season with salt.
4. Serve garnished with green onions and cilantro.

Per serving (without chicken):
Calories: 120| Protein: 2g| Fat: 0g| Carbs: 27g

Egyptian Foul Mudammas

Time: 15 minutes| Difficulty: Easy| Serving 2
1 can (15 oz.) fava beans, drained and rinsed
*1 small onion, chopped **and** 2 cloves garlic, minced*
*1 lemon, juiced **and** 2 tbsp. olive oil **and** 1 tsp. cumin*
Salt and pepper to taste and Parsley for garnish
1. Heat olive oil in a pan, sauté onion and garlic until translucent.
2. Add fava beans, cumin, and a bit of water; cook until heated through.
3. Mash lightly, stir in lemon juice, season with salt and pepper.

Per serving
Calories: 200| Protein: 8g| Fat: 10g| Carbs: 20g

Peruvian Quinoa Porridge

Time: 25 minutes| Difficulty: Easy| Serving 2
1/2 cup quinoa, rinsed
*1 cup almond milk **and** 1 banana, sliced*
*2 tbsp. honey **and** 1/2 tsp. cinnamon*
1. Combine quinoa and almond milk in a pot; bring to a boil.
2. Reduce heat to low; simmer covered until quinoa is tender and creamy.
3. Stir in banana, honey, and cinnamon before serving.

Per serving
Calories: 270| Protein: 6g| Fat: 4g| Carbs: 52g

Filipino Tapsilog (Tapa, Sinangag, at Itlog)

Time: 30 minutes (if using pre-cooked tapa)|
Difficulty: Moderate| Serving 2

1/2 cup beef tapa (pre-cooked Filipino cured beef)
*1 cup cooked rice **and** 1 clove garlic, minced*
2 eggs and 1 tablespoon vegetable oil
1. Fry the garlic in oil until golden, then add rice and cook until crisp.
2. In another pan, fry the tapa until cooked through.
3. Fry eggs to your liking.
4. Serve tapa, fried rice, and eggs together.

Per serving
Calories: 320| Protein: 25g| Fat: 15g| Carbs: 20g

2.2 Salad Recipes

Tuna Salad Lettuce

Time: 10 minutes| Difficulty: Easy| Serving 2
1 can tuna, drained
2 tablespoons Greek yogurt
1 tablespoon lemon juice
Salt and pepper, to taste
Lettuce leaves, for wrapping
Tomato slices, for topping
1. In a bowl, mix together tuna, Greek yogurt, lemon juice, salt, and pepper.
2. Spoon tuna salad onto lettuce leaves.
3. Top with tomato slices.
4. Roll up lettuce leaves to form wraps.
5. Serve immediately for a protein-rich and satisfying snack.

Per serving
Calories: 150| Protein: 15g| Carbs: 5g| Fat: 7g| Fiber: 2g

Vegetable and Quinoa Breakfast Skillet

Time: 20 minutes| Difficulty: Easy| Serving 2
*1 cup cooked quinoa **and** 1/2 cup diced bell peppers*
*1/2 cup diced zucchini **and** 1/4 cup diced onions*
*2 cloves garlic, minced **and** 2 eggs **and** Salt and pepper*
1. In a skillet, heat olive oil over medium heat.
2. Add diced onions and minced garlic to the skillet and cook until fragrant.
3. Add diced bell peppers and zucchini to the skillet and sauté until softened.
4. Stir in cooked quinoa and continue to cook until heated through.
5. Make two wells in the quinoa and vegetable mixture.
6. Crack an egg into each well and cook until the eggs are set to your desired doneness.

Per serving
Calories: 300|Protein: 12g|Carbs: 30g|Fat: 15g|Fiber: 6g

Mediterranean Chickpea Salad

Time: 20 minutes| Difficulty: Easy| Serving 2

1 can (15 oz.) chickpeas, rinsed and drained
1 cucumber, diced
1 cup cherry tomatoes, halved
1/2 red onion, finely chopped
1/4 cup parsley, chopped
1/4 cup feta cheese, crumbled (optional)
2 tablespoons lemon juice
1 tablespoon olive oil
Salt and pepper to taste

Per serving
Calories: 250 | Carbs: 30g| Fats: 10g| Protein: 9g

1. In a large bowl, mix chickpeas, cucumber, cherry tomatoes, red onion, and parsley.
2. Add feta cheese if using.
3. In a small bowl, whisk together lemon juice, olive oil, salt, and pepper.
4. Drizzle the dressing over the salad and toss gently to combine.
5. Serve chilled or at room temperature.

Beet and Goat Cheese Salad

Time: 15 minutes (plus time to roast beets if using fresh)| Difficulty: Easy| Serving 2

2 medium beets, roasted, peeled, and diced
2 cups mixed salad greens
1/4 cup goat cheese, crumbled
2 tablespoons walnuts, chopped
2 tablespoons balsamic reduction
Salt and pepper to taste

1. Place the mixed greens in a salad bowl.
2. Top with diced beets, goat cheese, and walnuts.
3. Drizzle with balsamic reduction and season with salt and pepper.
4. Toss gently to combine and serve immediately.

Per serving
Calories: 235 per serving| Carbs: 15g| Fats: 15g| Protein: 8g

Grilled Chicken Salad with Mixed Greens

Time: 35 minutes| Difficulty: Easy| Serving 2

2 boneless, skinless chicken breasts (about 6 oz. each)
1 tablespoon olive oil, plus extra for grilling
4 cups mixed greens (such as lettuce, arugula, and spinach)
1 medium cucumber, thinly sliced
1/2 cup cherry tomatoes, halved
1/4 red onion, thinly sliced
1/4 cup crumbled feta cheese
2 tablespoons balsamic vinegar
1 teaspoon honey
1 teaspoon Dijon mustard
1 tablespoon water
Salt and pepper to taste

1. Preheat Grill: Preheat your grill medium-high heat and brush it with a bit of olive oil.
2. Season Chicken: Season the chicken breasts with salt and pepper, then drizzle with 1 tablespoon of olive oil to coat evenly.
3. Grill Chicken: Place the chicken on the grill and cook for about 5-7 minutes on each side, or until fully cooked through and the internal temperature reaches 165°F (74°C). Once cooked, remove from the grill and let it rest for a few minutes. Then, slice thinly.
4. Prepare Salad Dressing: In a small bowl, whisk together balsamic vinegar, honey, Dijon mustard, and water until well combined. Season with a pinch of salt and pepper to taste.
5. Assemble the Salad: In a large bowl, combine mixed greens, cucumber slices, cherry tomatoes, and red onion slices. Drizzle with the prepared dressing and toss gently to coat.
6. Serve: Divide the salad onto plates, top with sliced grilled chicken and crumbled feta cheese. Serve immediately.

Per serving
Calories: 350| Carbohydrates: 12g| Fats: 16g| Protein: 36g

Black Bean and Corn Salad with Avocado

Time: 15 minutes| Difficulty: Easy| Serving 2

1 can (15 ounces) black beans, rinsed and drained
1 cup corn kernels (fresh, canned, or frozen)
1 avocado, diced
1/2 red bell pepper, diced
1/4 cup red onion, finely chopped
1/4 cup fresh cilantro, chopped
Juice of 1 lime
2 tablespoons extra virgin olive oil
1 teaspoon ground cumin
Salt and pepper to taste

1. Prepare the Salad Ingredients: In a large mixing bowl, combine the black beans, corn kernels, diced avocado, diced red bell pepper, chopped red onion, and chopped cilantro.
2. Make the Dressing: In a small bowl, whisk together the lime juice, extra virgin olive oil, ground cumin, salt, and pepper until well combined.
3. Combine Salad and Dressing: Pour the dressing over the salad ingredients in the mixing bowl. Gently toss until everything is evenly coated with the dressing.
4. Adjust Seasoning: Taste the salad and adjust the seasoning with additional salt and pepper if needed.
5. Serve: Transfer the black bean and corn salad to serving bowls or plates. Enjoy immediately as a light and refreshing meal or side dish.

Per serving
Calories: 250| Carbs: 27g| Fats: 13g| Protein: 6g

Shrimp and Quinoa Salad

Time: 35 minutes| Difficulty: Moderate| Serving 2

1/2 cup quinoa, rinsed
1 cup water
200g (about 7 oz.) shrimp, peeled and deveined
1 tablespoon olive oil
1/2 teaspoon paprika
Salt and pepper to taste
1 cup cherry tomatoes, halved
1/2 cucumber, diced
1/4 red onion, finely sliced
1 avocado, diced
1/4 cup chopped fresh cilantro (or parsley, if preferred)
Juice of 1 lime
2 tablespoons extra-virgin olive oil
Mixed greens (optional, for serving)

1. Cook Quinoa: In a medium saucepan, bring 1 cup of water to a boil. Add quinoa and a pinch of salt, reduce heat to low, cover, and simmer for 15 minutes or until all the water is absorbed. Remove from heat and let it sit, covered, for 5 minutes. Fluff with a fork and let cool.
2. Prepare Shrimp: While the quinoa is cooking, season shrimp with 1 tablespoon of olive oil, paprika, salt, and pepper. Heat a pan over medium-high heat and cook the shrimp for 2-3 minutes on each side, or until they turn pink and opaque. Remove from heat and set aside to cool.
3. Assemble Salad: In a large bowl, combine the cooked quinoa, cooled shrimp, cherry tomatoes, cucumber, red onion, and avocado. Add the chopped cilantro (or parsley) and gently mix to combine.
4. Dressing: In a small bowl, whisk together lime juice and 2 tablespoons of extra-virgin olive oil. Season with salt and pepper to taste. Pour the dressing over the salad and toss to evenly coat.
5. Serve: Serve the salad on a bed of mixed greens, if using, for an additional nutrient boost.

Per serving Calories: Approx. 400|Carbohydrates: 33g| Fats: 22g| Protein: 24g

Cucumber Avocado Salad

Time: 10 minutes| Difficulty: Very Easy| Serving 2

2 medium cucumbers, thinly sliced
1 ripe avocado, diced
2 tablespoons lime juice
1 tablespoon olive oil
Salt and pepper to taste
1/4 cup fresh cilantro, chopped

1. In a large bowl, combine the cucumbers and avocado.
2. In a small bowl, whisk together lime juice, olive oil, salt, and pepper.
3. Pour the dressing over the cucumber and avocado, add cilantro, and toss gently

Per serving
Calories: 180| Carbs: 12g| Fats: 14g| Protein: 2g

Tuna Salad Lettuce Wraps

Time: 15 minutes| Difficulty: Easy| Serving 2

1 can (5 ounces) tuna in water, drained
1/4 cup plain Greek yogurt
1 tablespoon Dijon mustard
1/4 cup red onion, finely chopped
1/4 cup celery, finely chopped
1/4 cup cucumber, finely diced
1 tablespoon capers, rinsed and drained
Salt and pepper to taste
8 large lettuce leaves (such as Bibb or butter lettuce)
Optional garnish: *chopped fresh herbs (parsley, dill, or chives)*

1. Prepare the Tuna Mixture: In a mixing bowl, combine the drained tuna, Greek yogurt, Dijon mustard, chopped red onion, celery, cucumber, and capers. Stir until all ingredients are well incorporated. Season with salt and pepper to taste.
2. Prepare the Lettuce Wraps: Rinse the lettuce leaves and pat them dry with paper towels. Choose the most substantial leaves to hold the tuna mixture.
3. Assemble the Wraps: Spoon an equal portion of the tuna salad onto the center of each lettuce leaf. If desired, garnish with chopped fresh herbs for added flavor and color.
4. Serve: Fold the lettuce leaves over the tuna mixture to form wraps. Serve immediately for the best texture and freshness.

Per serving
Calories: 200| Carbs: 6g| Fats: 2g|Protein: 34g

Quinoa and Black Bean Salad

Time: 30 minutes| Difficulty: Easy| Serving 2

1 cup cooked quinoa (cooled)
1 can (15 oz) black beans, rinsed and drained
1 red bell pepper, diced
1/4 cup fresh cilantro, chopped
2 green onions, sliced
Juice of 1 lime
2 tablespoons olive oil
Salt and pepper to taste

1. In a large bowl, combine the quinoa, black beans, red bell pepper, cilantro, and green onions.
2. In a small bowl, whisk together lime juice, olive oil, salt, and pepper.
3. Pour the dressing over the quinoa mixture and toss to combine.
4. Serve immediately or refrigerate until ready to serve.

Per serving
Calories: 320 | Carbs: 45g| Fats: 9g| Protein: 12g

Strawberry Spinach Salad with Poppy Seed Dressing

Time: 15 minutes| Difficulty: Easy| Serving 2

4 cups fresh spinach leaves
1 cup sliced strawberries
1/4 cup sliced almonds
1/4 cup crumbled feta cheese
Juice of 1 lemon
2 tablespoons extra virgin olive oil
1 tablespoon honey
1 teaspoon poppy seeds
Salt and pepper to taste

1. In a large bowl, combine the fresh spinach leaves, sliced strawberries, sliced almonds, and crumbled feta cheese.
2. In a small bowl, whisk together the lemon juice, extra virgin olive oil, honey, poppy seeds, salt, and pepper to make the dressing.
3. Pour the dressing over the salad ingredients and toss until well combined.

Per serving
Calories: 250| Carbohydrates: 20g| Fats: 15g| Protein: 6g

Greek Salad with Grilled Chicken

Time: 35 minutes| Difficulty: Easy| Serving 2

2 boneless, skinless chicken breasts (about 6 ounces each)
1 tablespoon olive oil
1 teaspoon dried oregano
Salt and pepper to taste
4 cups mixed salad greens (like romaine, arugula, and spinach)
1 large tomato, chopped
1 cucumber, sliced
1/2 red onion, thinly sliced
1/2 cup olives, pitted
1/2 cup crumbled feta cheese

Ingredients for the Dressing:
3 tablespoons extra virgin olive oil
1 tablespoon red wine vinegar
1 teaspoon Dijon mustard
1 garlic clove, minced
Salt and pepper to taste

1. Prep the Chicken: Preheat your grill or grill pan over medium heat. Season the chicken breasts with olive oil, dried oregano, salt, and pepper.
2. Grill the Chicken: Place the chicken on the grill and cook for about 5 minutes per side, or until fully cooked through and the internal temperature reaches 165°F (74°C). Once cooked, let it rest for a few minutes before slicing thinly.
3. Mix the Dressing: In a small bowl, whisk together the extra virgin olive oil, red wine vinegar, Dijon mustard, minced garlic, salt, and pepper. Set aside.
4. Assemble the Salad: In a large salad bowl, combine the mixed greens, chopped tomato, sliced cucumber, red onion, olives, and crumbled feta cheese. Toss to mix.
5. Add Chicken and Dressing: Add the sliced grilled chicken to the salad and drizzle with the prepared dressing. Toss lightly to ensure everything is well coated.
6. Serve: Divide the salad between two plates and serve immediately.

Per serving
Calories: 550| Carbohydrates: 12g| Fats: 36g| Protein: 44g

Caprese Salad with Basil and Balsamic Glaze

Time: 10 minutes| Difficulty: Easy| Serving 2

2 large ripe tomatoes, sliced
125g (about 4.4 oz.) fresh mozzarella cheese, sliced
Fresh basil leaves, to taste
2 tablespoons balsamic glaze
1 tablespoon extra-virgin olive oil
Salt and pepper to taste

1. Arrange the Salad: On a large plate or platter, alternate slices of tomato and mozzarella cheese. Tuck fresh basil leaves between each slice.
2. Season: Drizzle the balsamic glaze and extra virgin olive oil over the arranged tomatoes, mozzarella, and basil. Season with salt and pepper to your liking.
3. Serve: Allow the salad to sit for a few minutes for the flavors to meld together before serving. Enjoy as a refreshing appetizer or light meal.

Per serving
Calories: 250| Carbohydrates: 10g| Fats: 18g| Protein: 12g

Apple Walnut Spinach Salad

Time: 15 minutes| Difficulty: Easy| Serving 2

3 cups baby spinach, washed
1 apple, cored and thinly sliced
1/4 cup walnuts, chopped (lightly toasted, optional)
2 tablespoons dried cranberries
2 tablespoons balsamic vinegar
1 tablespoon olive oil
Salt and pepper to taste

1. Place spinach in a large salad bowl.
2. Top with apple slices, walnuts, and dried cranberries.
3. In a small bowl, whisk together balsamic vinegar, olive oil, salt, and pepper.
4. Drizzle the dressing over the salad just before serving and toss gently to coat.

Per serving
Calories: 220| Carbs: 24g| Fats: 12g| Protein: 3g

Quinoa and Spinach Salad with Cranberries and Almonds

Time: 20 minutes| Difficulty: Easy| Serving 2

1 cup cooked quinoa, cooled
2 cups fresh spinach leaves
1/4 cup dried cranberries
1/4 cup sliced almonds
1/4 cup crumbled feta cheese
Juice of 1 lemon
2 tablespoons extra virgin olive oil
Salt and pepper to taste

1. In a large bowl, combine the cooked quinoa, spinach leaves, dried cranberries, sliced almonds, and crumbled feta cheese.
2. In a small bowl, whisk together the lemon juice, extra virgin olive oil, salt, and pepper to make the dressing.
3. Pour the dressing over the salad ingredients and toss until well combined.

Per serving
Calories: 300| Carbohydrates: 30g| Fats: 15g| Protein: 10g

Mediterranean Chickpea Salad

Time: 15 minutes| Difficulty: Easy| Serving 2

1 can (15 ounces) chickpeas, rinsed and drained
1 cup cherry tomatoes, halved
1 cucumber, diced
1/4 cup red onion, thinly sliced
1/4 cup of olives, pitted and halved
2 tablespoons chopped fresh parsley
Juice of 1 lemon
2 tablespoons extra virgin olive oil
Salt and pepper to taste

1. In a large bowl, combine the chickpeas, cherry tomatoes, cucumber, red onion, olives, and chopped parsley.
2. In a small bowl, whisk together the lemon juice, extra virgin olive oil, salt, and pepper to make the dressing.
3. Pour the dressing over the salad ingredients and toss until well combined.

Per serving
Calories: 250| Carbohydrates: 30g| Fats: 10g| Protein: 10g

Chicken Caesar Salad

Time: 20 minutes| Difficulty: Easy| serving 2
2 boneless, skinless chicken breasts
4 cups chopped romaine lettuce
1/4 cup grated Parmesan cheese
1/4 cup croutons (optional)
Caesar dressing (store-bought or homemade)
Salt and pepper to taste

1. Season the chicken breasts with salt and pepper, then grill until cooked through. Let them rest for a few minutes before slicing thinly.
2. In a large bowl, combine the chopped romaine lettuce, grated Parmesan cheese, and croutons.
3. Add the sliced grilled chicken to the salad.
4. Drizzle Caesar dressing over the salad and toss until well combined.
5. Serve immediately as a satisfying main dish salad.

Per serving
Calories: 300| Carbohydrates: 10g| Fats: 15g| Protein: 30g

Asian Cabbage Salad with Grilled Chicken

Time: 25 minutes| Difficulty: Moderate| Serving 2
2 boneless, skinless chicken breasts
4 cups shredded cabbage (green or Napa)
1 cup shredded carrots
1/4 cup sliced green onions
1/4 cup chopped cilantro
1/4 cup chopped peanuts
2 tablespoons sesame seeds
2 tablespoons rice vinegar
1 tablespoon soy sauce
1 tablespoon honey
1 teaspoon grated ginger
1 garlic clove, minced **and** *Salt and pepper to taste*

1. Season the chicken breasts with salt and pepper, then grill until cooked through. Let them rest for a few minutes before slicing thinly.
2. In a large bowl, combine the shredded cabbage, shredded carrots, sliced green onions, chopped cilantro, chopped peanuts, and sesame seeds.
3. In a small bowl, whisk together the rice vinegar, soy sauce, honey, grated ginger, minced garlic, salt, and pepper to make the dressing.
4. Pour the dressing over the salad ingredients and toss until well combined.
5. Serve the salad topped with sliced grilled chicken.

Per Serving
Calories: 350| Carbohydrates: 20g| Fats: 15g| Protein: 30g

Warm Quinoa and Vegetable Salad

Time: 20 minutes| Difficulty: Easy| Serving 2
1 cup cooked quinoa
1/2 cup diced carrots
1/2 cup diced zucchini
1/2 cup cherry tomatoes, halved
1 tbsp. olive oil
2 tbsp. lemon juice and Salt and pepper to taste
Fresh parsley, chopped
1. Heat olive oil in a pan and sauté carrots and zucchini until tender.
2. Mix in the cooked quinoa and cherry tomatoes until heated through.
3. Remove from heat, add lemon juice, parsley, salt, and pepper.
4. Serve warm.

Per serving
Calories: 200| Protein: 6g| Fat: 7g| Carbs: 29g

Warm Beetroot and Goat Cheese Salad

Time: 25 minutes| Difficulty: Easy| Serving 2
2 medium beetroots, peeled and diced
50g goat cheese, crumbled
2 cups arugula
1 tbsp olive oil
2 tbsp balsamic glaze and Salt and pepper to taste
1. Roast beetroot in a preheated oven at 400°F for 20 minutes.
2. Toss warm beetroot with arugula and goat cheese.
3. Drizzle with olive oil and balsamic glaze, season with salt and pepper, and serve.

Per serving
Calories: 180| Protein: 6g| Fat: 10g| Carbs: 18g

Warm Lentil and Turkey Salad

Time: 30 minutes| Difficulty: Medium| Serving 2
1 cup cooked lentils
1/2 lb. cooked turkey breast, shredded
1 red bell pepper, diced
1/2 red onion, thinly sliced
1 tbsp. olive oil
2 tbsp. cider vinegar
1 tsp. Dijon mustard
Salt and pepper to taste
1. In a skillet, heat olive oil over medium heat.
2. Add bell pepper and onion, sauté until soft.
3. Stir in lentils and turkey, cook until warm.
4. Whisk together cider vinegar, mustard, salt, and pepper.
5. Toss the warm salad with the dressing and serve.

Per serving
Calories: 260| Protein: 28g| Fat: 8g| Carbs: 20g

Warm Broccoli and Chicken Salad

Time: 20 minutes| Difficulty: Easy| Serving 2
2 cups broccoli florets
1 cooked chicken breast, sliced
- 1/4 cup sliced almonds
- 2 tbsp. dried cranberries
- 1 tbsp. olive oil
- 1 tbsp. lemon juice
- Salt and pepper to taste
1. Steam broccoli until tender-crisp, about 5 minutes.
2. In a skillet, toast almonds until lightly golden.
3. Toss warm broccoli, chicken, almonds, and cranberries together.
4. Drizzle with olive oil and lemon juice, season with salt and pepper, and serve warm.

Per serving
Calories: 280| Protein: 25g| Fat: 14g| Carbs: 16g

Warm Spinach and Mushroom Salad

Time: 15 minutes| Difficulty: Easy| Serving 2
2 cups fresh spinach
1 cup sliced mushrooms
1 small red onion, thinly sliced
1 garlic clove, minced
1 tbsp olive oil
2 tbsp balsamic vinegar
Salt and pepper to taste
1. Heat olive oil in a pan over medium heat.
2. Sauté garlic, onion, and mushrooms until soft.
3. Add spinach and cook until just wilted.
4. Drizzle with balsamic vinegar, season with salt and pepper, and serve warm.

Per serving
Calories: 120| Protein: 3g| Fat: 7g| Carbs: 11g

Warm Chicken and Avocado Salad

Time: 20 minutes| Difficulty: Easy| Serving 2
2 cooked chicken breasts, sliced
1 ripe avocado, sliced
2 cups mixed salad greens
1/2 cucumber, sliced
1 tbsp. olive oil
2 tbsp. lime juice and Salt and pepper to taste
1. In a bowl, combine chicken, avocado, and cucumber.
2. Over medium heat, briefly warm the mixture in a skillet just to take the chill off.
3. Remove from heat and toss with salad greens.
4. Dress with olive oil, lime juice, salt, and pepper, and serve immediately.

Per serving
Calories: 290| Protein: 25g| Fat: 17g| Carbs: 8g

Warm Quinoa and Roasted Vegetable Salad

Time: 30 minutes| Difficulty: Easy| Serving 2
1 cup cooked quinoa
2 cups mixed roasted vegetables (e.g., bell peppers, eggplant, squash)
1/4 cup crumbled feta cheese
2 tbsp. chopped fresh parsley
1 tbsp. balsamic vinegar
1 tbsp. olive oil
Salt and pepper to taste

1. In a bowl, combine cooked quinoa and roasted vegetables.
2. Drizzle with olive oil and balsamic vinegar, season with salt and pepper, and toss to combine.
3. Sprinkle with crumbled feta cheese and chopped parsley, and serve warm.

Per serving
Calories: 260| Protein: 8g| Fat: 10g| Carbs: 35g

Warm Farro and Beet Salad

Time: 40 minutes| Difficulty: Easy| Serving 2
1 cup cooked farro
1 cup roasted beets, diced
1/4 cup crumbled goat cheese
2 tbsp. chopped fresh dill
1 tbsp. lemon juice
1 tbsp. olive oil
Salt and pepper to taste

1. In a bowl, combine cooked farro and roasted beets.
2. Drizzle with olive oil and lemon juice, season with salt and pepper, and toss to combine.
3. Sprinkle with crumbled goat cheese and chopped dill, and serve warm.

Per serving
Calories: 280| Protein: 10g| Fat: 10g| Carbs: 35g

Warm Shrimp and Avocado Salad

Time: 20 minutes| Difficulty: Easy| Serving 2
1 lb cooked shrimp, peeled and deveined
1 avocado, diced
2 cups mixed salad greens
1/4 cup sliced cherry tomatoes
2 tbsp chopped fresh cilantro
1 tbsp lime juice
1 tbsp olive oil and Salt and pepper to taste

1. In a large bowl, combine cooked shrimp, avocado, salad greens, and cherry tomatoes.
2. Drizzle with olive oil and lime juice, season with salt and pepper, and toss to combine.
3. Sprinkle with chopped cilantro, and serve warm.

Per serving:
Calories: 240| Protein: 20g| Fat: 14g| Carbs: 10g

Warm Tofu and Edamame Salad

Time: 25 minutes| Difficulty: Easy| Serving 2
1 block firm tofu, cubed
1 cup cooked edamame
2 cups baby spinach
1/4 cup sliced green onions
2 tbsp. soy sauce
1 tbsp. rice vinegar
1 tbsp. sesame oil
1 tsp. grated ginger and Salt and pepper to taste

1. In a skillet, heat sesame oil over medium heat. Add tofu cubes and cook until lightly browned.
2. In a large bowl, combine cooked tofu, edamame, spinach, and green onions.
3. In a small bowl, whisk together soy sauce, rice vinegar, grated ginger, salt, and pepper.
4. Drizzle the dressing over the salad, toss to combine, and serve warm.

Per serving
Calories: 210| Protein: 17g| Fat: 10g| Carbs: 16g

Warm Chicken and Couscous Salad

Time: 30 minutes| Difficulty: Easy| Serving 2
2 boneless, skinless chicken breasts
1 cup cooked couscous
1/4 cup sliced almonds and 1/4 cup dried cranberries
2 tbsp. chopped fresh parsley
1 tbsp. lemon juice
1 tbsp. olive oil and Salt and pepper to taste

1. Season chicken breasts with salt and pepper.
2. Grill or pan-fry chicken until cooked through. Slice into strips.
3. In a large bowl, combine cooked couscous, sliced chicken, almonds, cranberries, and parsley.
4. Drizzle with olive oil and lemon juice, toss to combine, and serve warm.

Per serving
Calories: 300| Protein: 25g| Fat: 12g| Carbs: 23g

Warm Potato and Green Bean Salad

Time: 25 minutes| Difficulty: Easy| Serving 2
2 cups small potatoes, halved
1 cup green beans, trimmed
2 tbsp olive oil
2 tbsp red wine vinegar
1 tsp Dijon mustardand Salt and pepper to taste

1. Boil potatoes until tender, add green beans in the last 4 minutes of cooking.
2. Drain and while still warm, toss with olive oil, vinegar, mustard, salt, and pepper.
3. Serve warm.

Per serving:
Calories: 220| Protein: 4g| Fat: 10g| Carbs: 30g

Warm Black Bean and Corn Salad

Time: 20 minutes| Difficulty: Easy| Serving 2

1 can (15 oz.) black beans, rinsed and drained
1 cup frozen corn, thawed
1/2 red bell pepper, diced
1/4 cup chopped red onion
2 tbsp. chopped fresh cilantro
1 tbsp. lime juice
1 tbsp. olive oil
1/2 tsp. ground cumin and Salt and pepper to taste

1. In a skillet, heat olive oil over medium heat. Add corn and cook until lightly browned.
2. In a large bowl, combine black beans, corn, bell pepper, onion, and cilantro.
3. In a small bowl, whisk together lime juice, olive oil, cumin, salt, and pepper.
4. Drizzle the dressing over the salad, toss to combine, and serve warm.

Per serving
Calories: 180| Protein: 7g| Fat: 5g| Carbs: 28g

Warm Brussels Sprouts and Bacon Salad

Time: 25 minutes| Difficulty: Easy| Serving 2
2 cups Brussels sprouts, halved
2 slices turkey bacon, chopped
1/4 cup chopped pecans
1 tbsp olive oil
1 tbsp balsamic vinegar and Salt and pepper to taste

1. In a skillet, cook bacon until crisp. Remove and set aside.
2. In the same skillet, add olive oil and Brussels sprouts. Sauté until tender.
3. Toss in pecans and cooked bacon.
4. Drizzle with balsamic vinegar, season with salt and pepper, and serve warm.

Per serving
Calories: 220|Protein: 8g| Fat: 16g| Carbs: 14g

Warm Lentil and Roasted Vegetable Salad

Time: 35 minutes| Difficulty: Easy| Serving 2
1 cup cooked lentils
1 cup mixed roasted vegetables (e.g., carrots, bell peppers, zucchini)
2 tbsp. chopped fresh parsley
1 tbsp. lemon juice
1 tbsp. olive oil and Salt and pepper to taste

1. Toss cooked lentils and roasted vegetables in a bowl.
2. Drizzle with olive oil and lemon juice, season with salt and pepper, and toss to combine.
3. Sprinkle with chopped parsley and serve warm.

Per serving
Calories: 230| Protein: 10g| Fat: 7g| Carbs: 32g

Warm Chicken Caesar Salad

Time: 25 minutes| Difficulty: Easy| Serving 2

2 boneless, skinless chicken breasts
4 cups chopped Romaine lettuce
1/4 cup grated Parmesan cheese
1/4 cup Caesar dressing
1 tbsp. olive oil
Salt and pepper to taste

1. Season chicken breasts with salt and pepper.
2. Heat olive oil in a skillet over medium-high heat. Cook chicken for 6-8 minutes per side until cooked through.
3. Slice cooked chicken into strips.
4. In a large bowl, combine Romaine lettuce, sliced chicken, Parmesan cheese, and Caesar dressing. Toss to coat.
5. Serve warm.

Per serving
Calories: 280| Protein: 28g| Fat: 14g| Carbs: 10g

Warm Eggplant and Tomato Salad

Time: 30 minutes| Difficulty: Easy| Serving 2

1 large eggplant, diced
2 cups cherry tomatoes, halved
2 cloves garlic, minced
2 tbsp chopped fresh basil
1 tbsp balsamic vinegar
1 tbsp olive oil
Salt and pepper to taste

1. Preheat oven to 400°F. Spread diced eggplant on a baking sheet and roast for 20-25 minutes until tender.
2. In a skillet, heat olive oil over medium heat. Add garlic and cook until fragrant.
3. Add cherry tomatoes to the skillet and cook until softened.
4. In a large bowl, combine roasted eggplant, cooked tomatoes, basil, balsamic vinegar, salt, and pepper. Toss to combine and serve warm.

Per serving
Calories: 160| Protein: 3g| Fat: 7g| Carbs: 23g

Warm Cauliflower and Chickpea Salad

Time: 30 minutes| Difficulty: Easy| Serving 2

2 cups cauliflower florets
1 cup canned chickpeas, rinsed and drained
1/4 cup sliced black olives
2 tbsp. chopped fresh parsley
1 tbsp. lemon juice
1 tbsp. olive oil
Salt and pepper to taste

1. Roast cauliflower florets in the oven at 400°F for 20 minutes.
2. In a skillet, heat olive oil over medium heat. Add chickpeas and cook until lightly browned.
3. Combine roasted cauliflower, chickpeas, olives, and parsley in a bowl.
4. Drizzle with lemon juice, season with salt and pepper, and toss to coat. Serve warm.

Per serving
Calories: 180| Protein: 7g| Fat: 7g| Carbs: 23g

Warm Potato and Bacon Salad

Time: 40 minutes| Difficulty: Moderate| Serving 2
2 cups baby potatoes, halved
4 slices bacon, cooked and crumbled
1/4 cup diced red onion
2 tablespoons chopped parsley
2 tablespoons olive oil
1 tablespoon white wine vinegar
1 teaspoon Dijon mustard
Salt and pepper to taste

1. Boil baby potatoes in salted water until fork-tender. Drain and set aside.
2. In a skillet, heat olive oil over medium heat. Add diced red onion and sauté until softened.
3. In a small bowl, whisk together white wine vinegar, Dijon mustard, salt, and pepper to make the dressing.
4. In a large bowl, combine cooked baby potatoes, crumbled bacon, sautéed red onion, chopped parsley, and dressing. Toss gently to combine.

Per serving
Calories: 300 Protein: 8g Fat: 18g Carbs: 25g

Warm Quinoa and Roasted Vegetable Salad

Time: 35 minutes| Difficulty: Moderate| Serving 2

1 cup quinoa
2 cups mixed vegetables (zucchini, bell peppers, onions)
2 tablespoons olive oil
1 teaspoon Italian seasoning
Salt and pepper to taste
2 cups baby spinach
1/4 cup crumbled feta cheese
2 tablespoons balsamic vinegar

1. Cook quinoa according to package instructions.
2. Toss mixed vegetables with olive oil, Italian seasoning, salt, and pepper. Roast in the oven at 400°F (200°C) for 20-25 minutes until tender.
3. In a large bowl, combine cooked quinoa, roasted vegetables, baby spinach, and crumbled feta cheese.
4. Drizzle balsamic vinegar over the salad and toss gently to combine.

Per serving
Calories: 320| Protein: 10g| Fat: 12g| Carbs: 45g

Warm Spinach and Bacon Salad

Time: 25 minutes| Difficulty: Easy| Serving 2

4 cups baby spinach
4 slices bacon, cooked and crumbled
1/4 cup sliced red onion
1/4 cup sliced mushrooms
2 tablespoons olive oil
2 tablespoons apple cider vinegar
1 teaspoon Dijon mustard
Salt and pepper to taste

1. In a skillet, cook bacon until crispy. Remove from skillet and crumble.
2. In the same skillet, add sliced mushrooms and red onion. Sauté until softened.
3. In a small bowl, whisk together olive oil, apple cider vinegar, Dijon mustard, salt, and pepper to make the dressing.
4. In a large bowl, combine baby spinach, crumbled bacon, sautéed mushrooms, and red onion.
5. Drizzle dressing over the salad and toss gently to combine.

Per serving
Calories: 280 Protein: 8g Fat: 22g Carbs: 8g

Warm Lentil and Roasted Vegetable Salad

Time: 40 minutes| Difficulty: Moderate| Serving 2

1 cup dried green lentils
2 cups mixed vegetables (carrots, red onion, bell peppers)
2 tablespoons olive oil
1 teaspoon cumin
Salt and pepper to taste
2 cups arugula
1/4 cup crumbled goat cheese
2 tablespoons lemon juice

1. Cook lentils according to package instructions.
2. Toss mixed vegetables with olive oil, cumin, salt, and pepper. Roast in the oven at 400°F (200°C) for 25 minutes.
3. In a large bowl, combine cooked lentils, roasted vegetables, arugula, and crumbled goat cheese.
4. Drizzle lemon juice over the salad and toss gently to combine.

Per serving
Calories: 320 Protein: 18g Fat: 10g Carbs: 40g

Warm Chickpea and Spinach Salad

Time: 25 minutes| Difficulty: Easy| Serving 2

1 can chickpeas, drained and rinsed
2 cups baby spinach
1 red bell pepper, sliced
1/4 cup sliced red onion
2 tablespoons olive oil
1 tablespoon balsamic vinegar
Salt and pepper to taste

1. In a skillet, heat olive oil over medium heat. Add chickpeas and sauté until golden brown, about 5-7 minutes.
2. Add sliced bell pepper and red onion to the skillet and sauté for another 3-4 minutes until softened.
3. Transfer the chickpea mixture to a large bowl. Add baby spinach and toss until spinach is slightly wilted.
4. Drizzle balsamic vinegar over the salad, season with salt and pepper, and toss gently to combine.

Per serving
Calories: 240 Protein: 9g Fat: 10g Carbs: 28g

Warm Lentil and Bacon Salad

Time: 40 minutes| Difficulty: Moderate| Serving 2

1 cup green lentils
4 slices bacon, cooked and crumbled
1/4 cup diced red onion
1/4 cup diced bell pepper
2 tablespoons olive oil
2 tablespoons red wine vinegar
1 teaspoon honey
Salt and pepper to taste

1. Cook lentils according to package instructions.
2. In a skillet, heat olive oil over medium heat. Add diced red onion and bell pepper. Sauté until softened.
3. In a small bowl, whisk together red wine vinegar, honey, salt, and pepper to make the dressing.
4. In a large bowl, combine cooked lentils, crumbled bacon, sautéed red onion, and bell pepper. Drizzle dressing over the salad and toss gently to combine.

Per serving
Calories: 320 Protein: 18g Fat: 12g Carbs: 35g

Warm Brussels Sprouts and Bacon Salad

Time: 30 minutes| Difficulty: Easy| Serving 2

2 cups Brussels sprouts, halved
4 slices bacon, cooked and crumbled
1/4 cup sliced almonds
2 tablespoons olive oil
1 tablespoon balsamic vinegar
1 teaspoon honey
Salt and pepper to taste

1. Preheat the oven to 400°F (200°C).
2. Toss Brussels sprouts with olive oil, salt, and pepper. Roast in the oven for 20-25 minutes until crispy and golden brown.
3. In a small bowl, whisk together balsamic vinegar, honey, salt, and pepper to make the dressing.
4. In a large bowl, combine roasted Brussels sprouts, crumbled bacon, sliced almonds, and dressing. Toss gently to combine.

Per serving
Calories: 280 Protein: 10g Fat: 20g Carbs: 15g

2.3 Soup Recipes

Vegetable Soup

Time: 30 minutes| Difficulty: Easy| Serving 2
4 cups vegetable broth
1 onion, chopped
2 carrots, sliced
2 celery stalks, sliced
1 zucchini, diced
1 cup chopped tomatoes
1 cup chopped spinach
1 tablespoon olive oil
Salt and pepper to taste

1. Heat olive oil in a large pot over medium heat. Add chopped onion and cook until translucent.
2. Add carrots, celery, and zucchini to the pot and cook for a few minutes until slightly softened.
3. Pour in vegetable broth and bring to a boil. Reduce heat and simmer for 15-20 minutes.
4. Add chopped tomatoes and spinach to the pot and cook for an additional 5 minutes.
5. Season with salt and pepper to taste. Serve hot.

Per serving
Calories: 100| Carbohydrates: 15g| Fats: 4g| Protein: 3g

Tomato Basil Soup

Time: 35 minutes| Difficulty: Easy| Serving 2
4 cups canned crushed tomatoes
2 cups vegetable broth
1 onion, chopped
2 garlic cloves, minced
1/4 cup chopped fresh basil
2 tablespoons olive oil
Salt and pepper to taste

1. Heat olive oil in a large pot over medium heat. Add chopped onion and minced garlic, cook until softened.
2. Add canned crushed tomatoes and vegetable broth to the pot. Bring to a simmer.
3. Cook for 20-25 minutes, stirring occasionally.
4. Stir in chopped fresh basil and cook for another 5 minutes.
5. Season with salt and pepper to taste.
6. Serve hot.

Per serving
Calories: 150| Carbohydrates: 20g| Fats: 6g| Protein: 3g

Chicken and Rice Soup

Time: 40 minutes| Difficulty: Moderate| Serving 2
4 cups chicken broth
2 boneless, skinless chicken breasts
1/2 cup uncooked rice
1 onion, chopped
2 carrots, sliced
2 celery stalks, sliced
1 garlic clove, minced
*1 tablespoon olive oil **and** Salt and pepper to taste*

1. In a large pot, heat olive oil over medium heat. Add chopped onion and minced garlic, cook until fragrant.
2. Add sliced carrots and celery to the pot and cook for a few minutes.
3. Pour in chicken broth and bring to a boil. Add chicken breasts and rice to the pot.
4. Reduce heat and simmer for 20-25 minutes, or until chicken is cooked through and rice is tender.
5. Remove chicken breasts from the pot, shred with forks, and return to the pot.
6. Season with salt and pepper to taste.

Per Serving
Calories 250|Carbohydrates: 20g| Fats: 6g| Protein: 25g

Lentil Soup

Time: 45 minutes| Difficulty: Easy| Serving 2
1 cup dried lentils, rinsed and drained
4 cups vegetable broth
1 onion, chopped
2 carrots, sliced
2 celery stalks, sliced
2 garlic cloves, minced
1 teaspoon ground cumin
1 teaspoon ground coriander
*1 tablespoon olive oil **and** Salt and pepper to taste*

1. Heat olive oil in a large pot over medium heat. Add chopped onion and minced garlic, cook until softened.
2. Add sliced carrots and celery to the pot and cook for a few minutes.
3. Stir in dried lentils, ground cumin, and ground coriander. Cook for another minute.
4. Pour in vegetable broth and bring to a boil. Reduce heat and simmer for 30-35 minutes, or until lentils are tender.
5. Season with salt and pepper to taste.

Per Serving
Calories: 200|Carbohydrates: 30g| Fats: 3g| Protein: 12g

Butternut Squash Soup

Time: 50 minutes| Difficulty: Moderate| Serving 2

4 cups diced butternut squash
2 cups vegetable broth
1 onion, chopped
2 garlic cloves, minced
1/2 teaspoon ground cinnamon
1/4 teaspoon ground nutmeg
2 tablespoons olive oil
Salt and pepper to taste

1. Preheat oven to 400°F (200°C). Place diced butternut squash on a baking sheet, drizzle with olive oil, and season with salt and pepper. Roast for 25-30 minutes, or until tender.
2. Heat olive oil in a large pot over medium heat. Add chopped onion and minced garlic, cook until softened.
3. Add roasted butternut squash to the pot. Stir in ground cinnamon and ground nutmeg.
4. Pour in vegetable broth and bring to a simmer. Cook for 15-20 minutes.
5. Use an immersion blender to puree the soup until smooth.
6. Season with salt and pepper to taste.

Per serving
Calories: 180| Carbs: 25g| Fats: 8g| Protein: 2g

Egg Drop Soup

Time: 20 minutes| Difficulty: Easy | Serving 2

4 cups chicken broth
2 eggs, beaten
2 green onions, thinly sliced
1 teaspoon grated ginger
1 tablespoon soy sauce
Salt and pepper to taste

1. Bring chicken broth to a simmer in a large pot.
2. Stir in grated ginger and soy sauce.
3. Slowly pour beaten eggs into the simmering broth while stirring gently with a fork. Cook for 1-2 minutes until eggs are cooked through.
4. Stir in sliced green onions.
5. Season with salt and pepper to taste

Per serving
Calories: 100| Carbs: 5g| Fats: 6g| Protein: 8g

Minestrone Soup

Time: 40 minutes| Difficulty: Moderate| Serving 2

4 cups vegetable broth
1 can (15 ounces) diced tomatoes
1 onion, chopped
2 carrots, sliced
2 celery stalks, sliced
1 zucchini, diced
1 cup cooked pasta (such as small shells or elbow macaroni)
1/2 cup cooked kidney beans
1/4 cup chopped fresh parsley
1 tablespoon olive oil
Salt and pepper to taste

1. Heat olive oil in a large pot over medium heat. Add chopped onion and cook until translucent.
2. Add sliced carrots, sliced celery, and diced zucchini to the pot. Cook for a few minutes until slightly softened.
3. Pour in vegetable broth and diced tomatoes with their juices. Bring to a boil, then reduce heat and simmer for 20-25 minutes.
4. Stir in cooked pasta, cooked kidney beans, and chopped fresh parsley. Cook for an additional 5 minutes.

Per serving
Calories: 220| Carbs: 35g| Fats: 5g| Protein: 8g

Corn Chowder

Time: 45 minutes| Difficulty: Moderate| Serving 2

4 cups vegetable broth
2 cups corn kernels
2 potatoes, peeled and diced
1 onion, chopped
2 garlic cloves, minced
1/4 cup chopped fresh parsley
2 tablespoons olive oil
Salt and pepper to taste

1. Heat olive oil in a large pot over medium heat. Add chopped onion and minced garlic, cook until softened.
2. Add diced potatoes to the pot. Pour in vegetable broth and bring to a boil.
3. Reduce heat and simmer for 20-25 minutes, or until potatoes are tender.
4. Stir in corn kernels and chopped fresh parsley. Cook for another 5 minutes.
5. Season with salt and pepper to taste.

Per serving
Calories: 220| Carbs: 30g| Fats: 7g| Protein: 5g

Potato Leek Soup

Time: 45 minutes| Difficulty: Moderate| Serving 2

4 cups vegetable broth
4 potatoes, peeled and diced
2 leeks, white and light green parts only, sliced
1 onion, chopped
2 garlic cloves, minced
1/4 cup chopped fresh parsley
2 tablespoons olive oil
Salt and pepper to taste

1. Heat olive oil in a large pot over medium heat. Add chopped onion and sliced leeks, cook until softened.
2. Add minced garlic to the pot and cook for another minute.
3. Add diced potatoes to the pot. Pour in vegetable broth and bring to a boil. Reduce heat and simmer for 20-25 minutes, or until potatoes are tender.
4. Use an immersion blender to puree the soup until smooth.
5. Stir in chopped fresh parsley.
6. Season with salt and pepper to taste.

Per serving
Calories: 200| Carbs: 30g| Fats: 5g| Protein: 4g

Mushroom Barley Soup

Time: 50 minutes| Difficulty: Moderate| Serving 2

4 cups vegetable broth
1 cup pearl barley
8 ounces mushrooms, sliced
1 onion, chopped
2 garlic cloves, minced
1/4 cup chopped fresh dill
2 tablespoons olive oil
Salt and pepper to taste

1. Heat olive oil in a large pot over medium heat. Add chopped onion and minced garlic, cook until softened.
2. Add sliced mushrooms to the pot and cook until tender.
3. Stir in pearl barley and vegetable broth. Bring to a boil, then reduce heat and simmer for 30-35 minutes, or until barley is tender.
4. Stir in chopped fresh dill.
5. Season with salt and pepper to taste.
6. Serve hot.

Per serving
Calories: 200| Carbs: 30g| Fats: 5g| Protein: 7g

Broccoli Cheddar Soup

Time: 35 minutes| Difficulty: Moderate| Serving 2

4 cups vegetable broth
2 cups chopped broccoli florets
1 onion, chopped
2 garlic cloves, minced
1 cup shredded cheddar cheese
1/2 cup milk (or dairy-free alternative)
2 tablespoons olive oil
Salt and pepper to taste

1. Heat olive oil in a large pot over medium heat. Add chopped onion and minced garlic, cook until softened.
2. Add chopped broccoli florets to the pot. Pour in vegetable broth and bring to a boil. Reduce heat and simmer for 15-20 minutes, or until broccoli is tender.
3. Use an immersion blender to puree the soup until smooth.
4. Stir in shredded cheddar cheese and milk, continue to cook until cheese is melted and soup is heated through.
5. Season with salt and pepper to taste.

Per serving
Calories: 250| Carbs: 15g| Fats: 15g| Protein: 10g

Cauliflower Soup

Time: 40 minutes| Difficulty: Moderate| Serving 2

4 cups vegetable broth
1 head cauliflower, chopped
1 onion, chopped
2 garlic cloves, minced
1/4 cup chopped fresh parsley
2 tablespoons olive oil
Salt and pepper to taste

1. Heat olive oil in a large pot over medium heat. Add chopped onion and minced garlic, cook until softened.
2. Add chopped cauliflower to the pot. Pour in vegetable broth and bring to a boil.
3. Reduce heat and simmer for 20-25 minutes, or until cauliflower is tender.
4. Use an immersion blender to puree the soup until smooth.
5. Stir in chopped fresh parsley.
6. Season with salt and pepper to taste.

Per serving
Calories: 150| Carbs: 20g| Fats: 6g| Protein: 5g

Chicken Noodle Soup

Time: 40 minutes| Difficulty: Easy| Serving 2

4 cups chicken broth
2 boneless, skinless chicken breasts
1 cup uncooked egg noodles
1 carrot, sliced
1 celery stalk, sliced
1/2 onion, chopped
2 garlic cloves, minced
1 tablespoon olive oil
Salt and pepper to taste

1. Heat olive oil in a large pot over medium heat. Add chopped onion and minced garlic, cook until softened.
2. Add sliced carrot and celery to the pot. Pour in chicken broth and bring to a boil.
3. Add boneless, skinless chicken breasts to the pot. Reduce heat and simmer for 20-25 minutes, or until chicken is cooked through.
4. Remove chicken breasts from the pot, shred with forks, and return to the pot.
5. Stir in uncooked egg noodles and cook for 8-10 minutes, or until noodles are tender.
6. Season with salt and pepper to taste.

Per serving
Calories: 300| Carbs: 20g| Fats: 8g| Protein: 30g

Spinach and White Bean Soup

Time: 40 minutes| Difficulty: Easy| Serving 2

4 cups vegetable broth
1 can (15 ounces) white beans, rinsed and drained
2 cups fresh spinach leaves
1 onion, chopped
2 garlic cloves, minced
1 teaspoon dried thyme
1 tablespoon olive oil
Salt and pepper to taste

1. Heat olive oil in a large pot over medium heat. Add chopped onion and minced garlic, cook until softened.
2. Stir in dried thyme.
3. Pour in vegetable broth and add white beans to the pot. Bring to a boil, then reduce heat and simmer for 15-20 minutes.
4. Add fresh spinach leaves to the pot and cook until wilted.
5. Season with salt and pepper to taste.

Per serving
Calories: 180| Carbs: 25g| Fats: 3g| Protein: 10g

Black Bean Soup

Time: 45 minutes| Difficulty: Easy| Serving 2

4 cups vegetable broth
2 cans (15 ounces each) black beans, rinsed and drained
1 onion, chopped
2 garlic cloves, minced
1 bell pepper, chopped
1 jalapeno pepper, seeded and chopped (optional)
1 teaspoon ground cumin
1 teaspoon chili powder
2 tablespoons olive oil
Salt and pepper to taste

1. Heat olive oil in a large pot over medium heat. Add chopped onion and minced garlic, cook until softened.
2. Add chopped bell pepper and jalapeno pepper to the pot. Cook for a few minutes until softened.
3. Stir in ground cumin and chili powder.
4. Pour in vegetable broth and add black beans to the pot. Bring to a boil, then reduce heat and simmer for 20-25 minutes.
5. Use an immersion blender to puree some of the soup, leaving some beans whole for texture.

Per serving
Calories: 220| Carbs: 30g| Fats: 5g| Protein: 10g

Roasted Red Pepper Soup

Time: 40 minutes| Difficulty: Moderate| Serving 2

4 cups vegetable broth
3 large red bell peppers
1 onion, chopped
2 garlic cloves, minced
1 can (14 ounces) diced tomatoes
2 tablespoons olive oil
Salt and pepper to taste

1. Preheat oven to 450°F (230°C). Place whole red bell peppers on a baking sheet and roast for 20-25 minutes, or until skins are charred. Remove from oven and let cool. Peel off skins, remove seeds, and chop peppers.
2. Heat olive oil in a large pot over medium heat. Add chopped onion and minced garlic, cook until softened.
3. Add chopped roasted red peppers and diced tomatoes to the pot. Pour in vegetable broth and bring to a simmer.
4. Cook for 15-20 minutes, then remove from heat.
5. Use an immersion blender to puree the soup until smooth.

Per serving
Calories: 200| Carbs: 25g| Fats: 8g| Protein: 5g

Thai Coconut Soup

Time: 35 minutes| Difficulty: Moderate| Serving 2

4 cups vegetable broth
1 can (14 ounces) coconut milk
8 ounces tofu, cubed
1 red bell pepper, sliced
1 onion, chopped
2 garlic cloves, minced
1 tablespoon grated ginger
1 tablespoon soy sauce
1 tablespoon lime juice
*2 tablespoons olive oil **and** Salt and pepper to taste*

1. Heat olive oil in a large pot over medium heat. Add chopped onion and minced garlic, cook until softened.
2. Stir in grated ginger and sliced red bell pepper. Cook for a few minutes until softened.
3. Pour in vegetable broth and coconut milk. Bring to a simmer.
4. Add cubed tofu to the pot. Cook for 10-15 minutes.
5. Stir in soy sauce and lime juice.
6. Season with salt and pepper to taste.

Per serving
Calories: 250| Carbs: 15g| Fats: 18g| Protein: 10g

Beef and Vegetable Soup

Time: 50 minutes| Difficulty: Moderate| Serving 2

4 cups beef broth
8 ounces beef stew meat, cubed
2 carrots, sliced
2 celery stalks, sliced
1 onion, chopped
2 garlic cloves, minced
*1/4 cup chopped fresh parsley **and** 2 tablespoons olive oil*

1. Heat olive oil in a large pot over medium heat. Add chopped onion and minced garlic, cook until softened.
2. Add cubed beef stew meat to the pot. Cook until browned on all sides.
3. Pour in beef broth and bring to a boil. Reduce heat and simmer for 30-35 minutes, or until beef is tender.
4. Add sliced carrots and celery to the pot. Cook for an additional 10-15 minutes, or until vegetables are tender.
5. Season with salt and pepper to taste.
6. Stir in chopped fresh parsley.

Per Serving
Calories: 300| Carbs: 15g| Fats: 15g| Protein: 25g

Sweet Potato Soup

Time: 45 minutes| Difficulty: Moderate| Serving 2

4 cups vegetable broth
2 large sweet potatoes, peeled and diced
1 onion, chopped
2 garlic cloves, minced
1/4 cup coconut milk
2 tablespoons olive oil
1 teaspoon ground cumin
1/2 teaspoon ground cinnamon
Salt and pepper to taste

1. Heat olive oil in a large pot over medium heat. Add chopped onion and minced garlic, cook until softened.
2. Add diced sweet potatoes to the pot. Stir in ground cumin and ground cinnamon.
3. Pour in vegetable broth and bring to a boil. Reduce heat and simmer for 20-25 minutes, or until sweet potatoes are tender.
4. Use an immersion blender to puree the soup until smooth.
5. Stir in coconut milk.
6. Season with salt and pepper to taste.
7. Serve hot.

Per serving
Calories: 200| Carbs: 30g| Fats: 8g| Protein: 3g

Italian Wedding Soup

Time: 50 minutes| Difficulty: Moderate| Serving 2

4 cups chicken broth
8 ounces ground turkey
1/4 cup uncooked orzo pasta
1 carrot, sliced
1 celery stalk, sliced
1/2 onion, chopped
2 garlic cloves, minced
1/4 cup chopped fresh parsley
1 tablespoon olive oil
Salt and pepper to taste

1. Heat olive oil in a large pot over medium heat. Add chopped onion and minced garlic, cook until softened.
2. Add ground turkey to the pot. Cook until browned, breaking it apart with a spoon.
3. Pour in chicken broth and bring to a boil. Add sliced carrot and celery to the pot.
4. Stir in uncooked orzo pasta. Reduce heat and simmer for 10-12 minutes, or until pasta is cooked through.
5. Stir in chopped fresh parsley.

Per serving
Calories: 250| Carbs: 20g| Fats: 10g| Protein: 20g

Mexican Chicken Tortilla Soup

Time: 50 minutes| Difficulty: Easy| Serving 2

2 chicken breasts, cooked and shredded
1 onion, chopped
3 cups chicken broth
1 can diced tomatoes
1 cup black beans, drained and rinsed
1 cup corn kernels
2 cloves garlic, minced
2 tbsp. olive oil
1 tbsp. chili powder
Salt and pepper to taste
Tortilla strips for garnish

1. Sauté onion and garlic until softened.
2. Add diced tomatoes, chicken broth, black beans, and corn kernels. Simmer for 30 minutes.
3. Stir in shredded chicken and chili powder. Cook for another 10 minutes.
4. Season with salt and pepper before serving. Garnish with tortilla strips.

Per serving
Calories: 280| Protein: 20g| Fat: 7g| Carbs: 30g

Savory Beef Stew

Time:1 hour| Difficulty: Medium| Serving 2

1 lb. beef stew meat, cubed
1 onion, chopped
3 cups beef broth
2 carrots, chopped
2 potatoes, diced
1 cup green peas
2 cloves garlic, minced
2 tbsp. olive oil
Salt and pepper to taste

1. Sauté onion and garlic until softened. Add beef and cook until browned.
2. Pour in beef broth and bring to a boil. Reduce heat and simmer for 30 minutes.
3. Add carrots, potatoes, and green peas. Simmer for another 20 minutes until vegetables are tender.
4. Season with salt and pepper before serving.

Per serving
Calories: 280| Protein: 22g| Fat: 10g| Carbs: 25g

Creamy Pumpkin Soup

Time: 40 minutes| Difficulty: Easy| Serving 2
2 cups pumpkin puree
1 onion, chopped
2 cloves garlic, minced
3 cups vegetable broth
1/2 cup coconut milk
1 tsp. ground cinnamon **and** Salt and pepper to taste
1. Sauté onion and garlic until soft.
2. Add pumpkin puree, vegetable broth, and cinnamon. Simmer for 20 minutes.
3. Blend until smooth, then stir in coconut milk.
4. Season with salt and pepper.

Per serving
Calories: 120| Protein: 2g| Fat: 5g| Carbs: 18g

Christmas Corn Chowder

Time: 40 minutes| Difficulty: Easy| Serving 2
2 cups corn kernels
1 onion, diced
2 potatoes, peeled and diced
3 cups vegetable broth
1 cup almond milk
2 tbsp. olive oil
2 cloves garlic, minced **and** Salt and pepper to taste
1. Sauté onion and garlic until soft, then add potatoes and corn. Cook for 5 minutes.
2. Add vegetable broth and simmer until potatoes are tender.
3. Blend half of the soup until smooth, then return to the pot.
4. Stir in almond milk, and season with salt and pepper.

Per serving
Calories: 160| Protein: 3g| Fat: 6g| Carbs: 25g

Holiday Beetroot Soup

Time: 50 minutes| Difficulty: Easy| Serving 2
2 beetroots, peeled and diced
1 potato, peeled and diced
1 onion, chopped
3 cups vegetable broth
1/4 cup Greek yogurt (optional)
2 cloves garlic, minced
2 tbsp. olive oil **and** Salt and pepper to taste
1. Sauté onion and garlic until softened.
2. Add beetroots, potato, and vegetable broth. Simmer until vegetables are tender.
3. Blend until smooth, then return to the pot.
4. Stir in Greek yogurt if desired, and season with salt and pepper.

Per serving
Calories: 130| Protein: 3g| Fat: 6g| Carbs: 17g

Winter Root Vegetable Soup

Time: 50 minutes| Difficulty: Easy| Serving 2

2 parsnips, peeled and diced
2 carrots, peeled and diced
2 potatoes, peeled and diced
1 onion, chopped
3 cups vegetable broth
2 cloves garlic, minced
2 tbsp. olive oil
1/4 tsp. dried thyme
Salt and pepper to taste

1. Sauté onion and garlic until softened.
2. Add parsnips, carrots, and potatoes. Cook for 5 minutes.
3. Pour in vegetable broth and add thyme. Simmer for 30 minutes.
4. Blend half of the soup until smooth, then return to the pot.
5. Season with salt and pepper.

Per serving
Calories: 170| Protein: 3g| Fat: 6g| Carbs: 27g

Holiday Spinach and Potato Soup

Time: 45 minutes| Difficulty: Easy| Serving 2

2 potatoes, peeled and diced
2 cups spinach, chopped
1 onion, diced
3 cups vegetable broth
1/2 cup coconut milk
2 cloves garlic, minced
2 tbsp. olive oil
Salt and pepper to taste

1. Sauté onion and garlic until softened.
2. Add potatoes and vegetable broth. Simmer until potatoes are cooked.
3. Stir in spinach and coconut milk. Cook until spinach wilts.
4. Blend half of the soup until smooth, then return to the pot.
5. Season with salt and pepper.

Per serving
Calories: 150| Protein: 3g| Fat: 6g| Carbs: 22g

Creamy Carrot Ginger Soup

Time: 40 minutes| Difficulty: Easy| Serving 2

5 large carrots, peeled and chopped
1 onion, chopped
3 cups vegetable broth
1 tbsp. ginger, grated
1 clove garlic, minced
1 cup light coconut milk
Salt and pepper to taste
Fresh parsley for garnish

1. In a large pot, sauté onions, garlic, and ginger until onion is translucent.
2. Add carrots and vegetable broth. Bring to a boil, then simmer until carrots are soft.
3. Puree the mixture in a blender until smooth. Return to pot.
4. Stir in coconut milk, heat through. Season with salt and pepper.
5. Serve garnished with parsley.

Per serving
Calories: 160| Protein: 3g| Fat: 7g| Carbs: 23g

Minty Pea Soup

Time: 25 minutes| Difficulty: Easy| Serving 2

2 cups frozen peas
1 onion, diced
2 cups vegetable stock
1/4 cup fresh mint leaves
1 tbsp. olive oil
Salt and pepper to taste
Yogurt for garnish (optional)

1. In a pot, heat olive oil and sauté onion until translucent.
2. Add peas and vegetable stock, bring to a boil, then simmer for 10 minutes.
3. Add mint leaves, blend until smooth with an immersion blender.
4. Season with salt and pepper.
5. Serve with a dollop of yogurt if desired.

Per serving
Calories: 120| Protein: 5g| Fat: 4g| Carbs: 17g

2.4 Meat-based Recipes

Turkey and Avocado Wrap with Whole Wheat Tortilla

Time: 10 minutes| Difficulty: Easy| Serving 2

2 whole wheat tortillas
6 slices of turkey breast
1 avocado, sliced
1/2 cup shredded lettuce
1/4 cup sliced cucumber
2 tablespoons Greek yogurt
1 tablespoon Dijon mustard
Salt and pepper to taste

1. Lay out the whole wheat tortillas on a clean surface.
2. Spread Greek yogurt and Dijon mustard evenly over each tortilla.
3. Place three slices of turkey breast on each tortilla.
4. Arrange avocado slices, shredded lettuce, and sliced cucumber over the turkey.
5. Season with salt and pepper to taste.
6. Roll up the tortillas tightly, folding in the sides as you go.
7. Slice each wrap in half diagonally.
8. Serve immediately or wrap in parchment paper for later.

Per serving
Calories: 300| Carbs: 25g| Fats: 15g| Protein: 20g

Chicken and Vegetable Kabobs with Quinoa

Time: 40 minutes| Difficulty: Moderate| Serving 2

2 boneless, skinless chicken breasts, cut into cubes
1 zucchini, sliced
1 bell pepper, cut into chunks
1 red onion, cut into chunks
8 cherry tomatoes
1 cup quinoa
2 cups vegetable broth
2 tablespoons olive oil
2 tablespoons balsamic vinegar
2 cloves garlic, minced
1 teaspoon dried oregano
Salt and pepper to taste
Wooden skewers, soaked in water for 30 minutes

1. In a small bowl, whisk together olive oil, balsamic vinegar, minced garlic, dried oregano, salt, and pepper to make the marinade.
2. Place the chicken cubes in a shallow dish and pour half of the marinade over them. Toss to coat evenly, then cover and refrigerate for at least 15 minutes.
3. In the meantime, cook quinoa according to package instructions, using vegetable broth instead of water for added flavor.
4. Preheat grill or grill pan to medium-high heat.
5. Thread marinated chicken cubes, sliced zucchini, bell pepper chunks, red onion chunks, and cherry tomatoes onto the soaked wooden skewers, alternating between the ingredients.
6. Brush the assembled skewers with the remaining marinade.
7. Grill the kabobs for 8-10 minutes, turning occasionally, until the chicken is cooked through and the vegetables are charred and tender.
8. Serve the chicken and vegetable kabobs hot over a bed of cooked quinoa.

Per serving
Calories: 400| Carbs: 40g| Fats: 10g| Protein: 35g

Turkey and Vegetable Skewers with Quinoa

Time: 30 minutes| Difficulty: Moderate| Serving 2

2 turkey breasts, cut into cubes
1 zucchini, sliced
1 bell pepper, cut into chunks
1 onion, cut into chunks
8 cherry tomatoes
1 cup quinoa
2 cups vegetable broth
2 tablespoons olive oil
2 tablespoons balsamic vinegar
2 cloves garlic, minced
1 teaspoon dried oregano
Salt and pepper to taste
Wooden skewers, soaked in water for 30 minutes

1. In a small bowl, whisk together olive oil, balsamic vinegar, minced garlic, dried oregano, salt, and pepper to make the marinade.
2. Place the turkey cubes in a shallow dish and pour half of the marinade over them. Toss to coat evenly, then cover and refrigerate for at least 15 minutes.
3. In the meantime, cook quinoa according to package instructions, using vegetable broth instead of water for added flavor.
4. Preheat grill or grill pan to medium-high heat.
5. Thread marinated turkey cubes, sliced zucchini, bell pepper chunks, onion chunks, and cherry tomatoes onto the soaked wooden skewers, alternating between the ingredients.
6. Brush the assembled skewers with the remaining marinade.
7. Grill the skewers for 8-10 minutes, turning occasionally, until the turkey is cooked through and the vegetables are charred and tender.
8. Serve the turkey and vegetable skewers hot over a bed of cooked quinoa.

Per 1/2 of the recipe
Calories: 400| Carbs: 40g| Fats: 10g| Protein: 35g

Pork Tenderloin with Apple Compote

Time: 40 minutes| Difficulty: Moderate| Serving 2
1 pork tenderloin (about 1 pound)
2 tablespoons olive oil
2 apples, peeled, cored, and diced
*1/4 cup apple cider vinegar **and** 2 tablespoons honey*
1/2 teaspoon ground cinnamon

1. Preheat oven to 375°F (190°C).
2. Season pork tenderloin with salt and pepper.
3. Heat olive oil in an oven-safe skillet over medium-high heat.
4. Sear pork tenderloin on all sides until browned, about 2-3 minutes per side.
5. Transfer skillet to the preheated oven and roast pork tenderloin for 20-25 minutes, or until cooked through and internal temperature reaches 145°F (63°C).

In the meantime, prepare the apple compote: In a saucepan, combine diced apples, apple cider vinegar, honey, and ground cinnamon. Cook over medium heat until apples are soft and mixture has thickened.
Serve sliced pork tenderloin with apple compote on the side.
Per Serving
Calories: 300| Carbs: 20g| Fats: 10g| Protein: 25g

Chicken Fajitas

Time: 30 minutes| Difficulty: Easy| Serving 2
2 boneless, skinless chicken breasts, sliced
1 bell pepper, sliced
1 onion, sliced
1 tablespoon olive oil
2 tablespoons fajita seasoning
8 small whole wheat tortillas
Optional toppings: *shredded lettuce, diced tomatoes, shredded cheese, Greek yogurt*

1. Heat olive oil in a skillet over medium-high heat.
2. Add sliced chicken breasts to the skillet and sprinkle with fajita seasoning. Cook until chicken is browned and cooked through, about 5-7 minutes.
3. Add sliced bell pepper and onion to the skillet and cook until vegetables are tender, about 3-4 minutes.
4. Warm whole wheat tortillas in the microwave or on a skillet.
5. Serve chicken and vegetable mixture in warmed tortillas, topped with optional toppings as desired.

Per serving 2 fajitas with toppings
Calories: 350| Carbs: 30g| Fats: 10g|Protein: 30g

Baked Lemon Herb Chicken

Time: 30 minutes| Difficulty: Easy| Serving 2

2 boneless, skinless chicken breasts
1 lemon, thinly sliced
2 cloves garlic, minced
1 tablespoon fresh rosemary, chopped
1 tablespoon fresh thyme, chopped
Salt and pepper to taste
1 tablespoon olive oil

1. Preheat your oven to 375°F (190°C).
2. In a small bowl, mix together the minced garlic, chopped rosemary, chopped thyme, salt, pepper, and olive oil.
3. Place the chicken breasts in a baking dish. Rub the herb mixture over both sides of the chicken breasts.
4. Arrange the lemon slices on top of the chicken breasts.
5. Cover the baking dish with foil and bake in the preheated oven for 25-30 minutes, or until the chicken is cooked through and no longer pink in the center.
6. Remove the foil during the last 5 minutes of baking to allow the chicken to brown slightly.
7. Serve the baked lemon herb chicken hot, garnished with additional fresh herbs if desired.

Per serving
Calories: 250| Protein: 30g| Carbs: 4g| Fat: 12g| Fiber: 1g

Turkey and Cranberry Wrap

Time: 10 minutes| Difficulty: Easy| Serving 2
2 whole wheat tortillas
6 slices of turkey breast
2 tablespoons cranberry sauce
1/4 cup shredded lettuce
1/4 cup sliced cucumber
2 tablespoons Greek yogurt (optional)

1. Lay out the whole wheat tortillas on a clean surface.
2. Spread a tablespoon of cranberry sauce evenly over each tortilla.
3. Place three slices of turkey breast on each tortilla.
4. Arrange shredded lettuce and sliced cucumber over the turkey.
5. If desired, spread a tablespoon of Greek yogurt over the ingredients.
6. Season with salt and pepper to taste.
7. Roll up the tortillas tightly, folding in the sides as you go.
8. Slice each wrap in half diagonally.
9. Serve immediately or wrap in parchment paper for later

Per serving 1 wrap
Calories: 250| Carbs: 25g| Fats: 5g|Protein: 20g

Lamb Chops with Mint Yogurt Sauce

Time: 35 minutes| Difficulty: Moderate| Serving 2
4 lamb chops
2 tablespoons olive oil
2 cloves garlic, minced
1 tablespoon chopped fresh rosemary
Salt and pepper to taste
1/2 cup Greek yogurt
1 tablespoon chopped fresh mint
1 tablespoon lemon juice

1. Preheat grill to medium-high heat.
2. Rub lamb chops with olive oil, minced garlic, chopped rosemary, salt, and pepper.
3. Grill lamb chops for 4-5 minutes on each side, or until cooked to desired doneness.
4. In a small bowl, mix together Greek yogurt, chopped mint, and lemon juice to make the mint yogurt sauce.
5. Serve hot lamb chops with mint yogurt sauce on the side.

Per 1 lamb chop with sauce
Calories: 300| Carbs: 2g| Fats: 20g| Protein: 25g

Beef Stir-Fry with Vegetables

Time: 30 minutes| Difficulty: Easy| Serving 2

8 ounces beef sirloin, thinly sliced
1 tablespoon soy sauce
1 tablespoon oyster sauce
1 tablespoon olive oil
2 cloves garlic, minced
1 bell pepper, sliced
1 onion, sliced
1 cup broccoli florets
Cooked rice or quinoa for serving

1. In a bowl, marinate beef slices with soy sauce and oyster sauce for 10-15 minutes.
2. Heat olive oil in a skillet or wok over medium-high heat.
3. Add minced garlic and stir-fry for 30 seconds.
4. Add marinated beef slices and stir-fry until browned, about 2-3 minutes.
5. Add sliced bell pepper, onion, and broccoli florets to the skillet. Stir-fry for an additional 3-4 minutes, or until vegetables are tender-crisp.
6. Serve hot over cooked rice or quinoa.

Per 1/2 of the recipe without rice/quinoa
Calories: 300| Carbs: 10g| Fats: 15g| Protein: 25g

Pork Tenderloin with Honey Mustard Glaze

Time: 35 minutes| Difficulty: Easy| Serving 2

1 pork tenderloin (about 1 pound)
2 tablespoons Dijon mustard
1 tablespoon honey
1 tablespoon olive oil
2 cloves garlic, minced
Salt and pepper to taste

1. Preheat oven to 375°F (190°C).
2. In a small bowl, whisk together Dijon mustard, honey, olive oil, minced garlic, salt, and pepper to make the glaze.
3. Place pork tenderloin on a baking sheet lined with parchment paper.
4. Brush the glaze over the pork tenderloin, coating it evenly.
5. Bake in the preheated oven for 25-30 minutes, or until pork is cooked through and internal temperature reaches 145°F (63°C).
6. Let the pork rest for 5 minutes before slicing.
7. Serve hot with roasted vegetables or a side salad.

Per 4 oz. pork tenderloin
Calories: 200| Carbs: 5g| Fats: 10g| Protein: 25g

Turkey Meatballs in Tomato Sauce

Time: 40 minutes| Difficulty: Easy| Serving 2

1 pound ground turkey
1/4 cup breadcrumbs
1 egg
2 cloves garlic, minced
1/4 cup grated Parmesan cheese
1 tablespoon chopped fresh parsley
Salt and pepper to taste
2 cups tomato sauce

1. Preheat oven to 375°F (190°C). Line a baking sheet with parchment paper.
2. In a bowl, combine ground turkey, breadcrumbs, egg, minced garlic, Parmesan cheese, chopped parsley, salt, and pepper. Mix until well combined.
3. Shape the mixture into small meatballs and place them on the prepared baking sheet.
4. Bake in the preheated oven for 20-25 minutes, or until meatballs are cooked through and golden brown.
5. Meanwhile, heat tomato sauce in a saucepan over medium heat.
6. Once meatballs are cooked, add them to the tomato sauce and simmer for 5-10 minutes.
7. Serve hot with your choice of side dishes.

Per 4 meatballs with sauce
Calories: 300| Carbs: 10g| Fats: 15g| Protein: 25g

Beef and Mushroom Skewers

Time: 30 minutes| Difficulty: Moderate| Serving 2

1 pound beef sirloin, cut into cubes
1 cup mushrooms, sliced
1 red bell pepper, cut into chunks
1 onion, cut into chunks
2 tablespoons olive oil
2 cloves garlic, minced
1 tablespoon Worcestershire sauce
Salt and pepper to taste

1. In a bowl, combine beef cubes, sliced mushrooms, red bell pepper chunks, onion chunks, olive oil, minced garlic, Worcestershire sauce, salt, and pepper. Mix well to coat.
2. Thread the beef, mushrooms, bell pepper, and onion onto skewers.
3. Preheat grill to medium-high heat.
4. Grill skewers for 8-10 minutes, turning occasionally, until beef is cooked to desired doneness and vegetables are tender.
5. Serve hot with your favorite side dish.

Per 1/4 of the recipe
Calories: 300| Carbs: 5g| Fats: 15g| Protein: 30g

Lamb Kebabs with Yogurt Sauce

Time: 30 minutes| Difficulty: Moderate| Serving 2

1 pound lamb cubes
1/4 cup olive oil
2 cloves garlic, minced
1 tablespoon lemon juice
1 teaspoon ground cumin
1 teaspoon paprika
Wooden skewers, soaked in water for 30 minutes
1/2 cup Greek yogurt
1 tablespoon chopped fresh mint
1 tablespoon chopped fresh parsley

1. In a bowl, mix together olive oil, minced garlic, lemon juice, ground cumin, paprika, salt, and pepper to make the marinade.
2. Thread lamb cubes onto the soaked wooden skewers.
3. Brush the marinade over the lamb kebabs.
4. Grill kebabs for 8-10 minutes, turning occasionally, until lamb is cooked through.
5. In a small bowl, mix together Greek yogurt, chopped mint, and chopped parsley to make the yogurt sauce.
6. Serve hot lamb kebabs with yogurt sauce on the side.

Per 1/2 of the recipe without sauce
Calories: 350| Carbs: 2g| Fats: 25g\ Protein: 30g

Pork and Vegetable Stir-Fry

Time: 30 minutes| Difficulty: Easy| Serving 2

1 pound pork loin, thinly sliced
2 tablespoons soy sauce
1 tablespoon oyster sauce
1 tablespoon olive oil
2 cloves garlic, minced
1 bell pepper, sliced
1 cup broccoli florets
1 carrot, julienned

1. In a bowl, marinate pork slices with soy sauce and oyster sauce for 10-15 minutes.
2. Heat olive oil in a skillet or wok over medium-high heat.
3. Add minced garlic and stir-fry for 30 seconds.
4. Add marinated pork slices to the skillet and stir-fry until browned, about 2-3 minutes.
5. Add sliced bell pepper, broccoli florets, and julienned carrot to the skillet. Stir-fry for an additional 3-4 minutes, or until vegetables are tender-crisp.

Per 1/2 of the recipe without rice/quinoa
Calories: 300| Carbs: 10g| Fats: 15g| Protein: 25g

Turkey Chili

Time: 45 minutes| Difficulty: Easy| Serving 2

tablespoon olive oil
1 onion, chopped
2 cloves garlic, minced
1 pound ground turkey
1 bell pepper, diced
1 can (14 ounces) diced tomatoes
1 can (14 ounces) kidney beans, drained and rinsed
1 cup vegetable broth
*2 tablespoons chili powder **and** 1 teaspoon ground cumin*
***Optional toppings:** shredded cheese, diced avocado, Greek yogurt*

1. Heat olive oil in a large pot over medium heat.
2. Add chopped onion and minced garlic, and sauté until softened.
3. Add ground turkey to the pot and cook until browned.
4. Stir in diced bell pepper, diced tomatoes, kidney beans, vegetable broth, chili powder, ground cumin, salt, and pepper.
5. Bring chili to a simmer and let cook for 30 minutes, stirring occasionally.
6. Serve hot, topped with shredded cheese, diced avocado, and Greek yogurt if desired.

Per Serving
Calories: 250| Carbs: 15g| Fats: 10g| Protein: 20g

Grilled Steak with Chimichurri Sauce

Time: 40 minutes| Difficulty: Moderate| Serving 2

2 beef
2 tablespoons olive oil
2 cloves garlic, minced
1/4 cup chopped fresh parsley
2 tablespoons chopped fresh cilantro
2 tablespoons red wine vinegar
1/2 teaspoon dried oregano

1. Preheat grill to medium-high heat.
2. Season steaks with salt and pepper.
3. In a small bowl, mix together olive oil, minced garlic, chopped parsley, chopped cilantro, red wine vinegar, dried oregano, salt, and pepper to make the chimichurri.
4. Grill steaks for 4-6 minutes on each side, or until desired doneness.
5. Let steaks rest for 5 minutes before slicing.
6. Serve hot with chimichurri sauce drizzled over the top.

Per 1 steak with sauce
Calories: 400| Carbs: 2g| Fats: 25g| Protein: 40g

Turkey and Spinach Stuffed Bell Peppers

Time: 45 minutes| Difficulty: Moderate| Serving 2
4 bell peppers, halved and seeded
1 pound ground turkey
1 cup cooked quinoa
1 cup spinach, chopped
1/2 cup shredded mozzarella cheese
1/4 cup chopped fresh parsley
1 teaspoon dried Italian seasoning
1 cup tomato sauce

1. Preheat oven to 375°F (190°C). Arrange bell pepper halves in a baking dish.
2. In a skillet, cook ground turkey until browned. Drain excess fat.
3. In a large bowl, combine cooked ground turkey, cooked quinoa, chopped spinach, shredded mozzarella cheese, chopped parsley, dried Italian seasoning, salt, and pepper. Mix well.
4. Spoon the turkey and spinach mixture into the bell pepper halves.
5. Pour tomato sauce over the stuffed bell peppers.
6. Cover the baking dish with foil and bake in the preheated oven for 30-35 minutes, or until peppers are tenders.
7. Serve hot, garnished with additional parsley if desired.

Per 1 stuffed bell pepper half
Calories: 250| Carbs: 15g| Fats: 10g| Protein: 25g

Beef and Bean Chili

Time: 1 hour| Difficulty: Moderate| Serving 2
1 tablespoon olive oil
1 onion, chopped
2 cloves garlic, minced
1 pound ground beef
1 can (14 ounces) diced tomatoes
1 can (14 ounces) kidney beans, drained and rinsed
1 cup beef broth
2 tablespoons chili powder and 1 teaspoon ground cumin
Optional toppings: *shredded cheese, diced avocado, Greek yogurt*

1. Heat olive oil in a large pot over medium heat.
2. Add chopped onion and minced garlic, and sauté until softened.
3. Add ground beef to the pot and cook until browned.
4. Stir in diced tomatoes, kidney beans, beef broth, chili powder, ground cumin, salt, and pepper.
5. Bring chili to a simmer and let cook for 30-40 minutes, stirring occasionally.
6. Serve hot, topped with optional toppings as desired.

Per 1/6 of the recipe without toppings
Calories: 300| Carbs: 15g| Fats: 15g| Protein: 25g

Chicken and Broccoli Casserole

Time: 50 minutes| Difficulty: Moderate| Serving 2
2 boneless, skinless chicken breasts, cooked and shredded
2 cups broccoli florets, steamed
1 cup cooked quinoa
1 cup shredded cheddar cheese
1/2 cup Greek yogurt
1/4 cup milk
2 cloves garlic, minced
Salt and pepper to taste
1/4 cup breadcrumbs (optional)

1. Preheat oven to 375°F (190°C). Grease a casserole dish.
2. In a large bowl, combine cooked and shredded chicken, steamed broccoli florets, cooked quinoa, shredded cheddar cheese, Greek yogurt, milk, minced garlic, salt, and pepper. Mix well.
3. Transfer the mixture to the prepared casserole dish and spread evenly.
4. If desired, sprinkle breadcrumbs over the top of the casserole.
5. Bake in the preheated oven for 25-30 minutes, or until bubbly and golden brown on top.
6. Serve hot, garnished with chopped parsley if desired.

Per serving
Calories: 300| Carbs: 20g| Fats: 15g| Protein: 25g

Balsamic Glazed Pork Tenderloin

Time: 40 minutes| Difficulty: Moderate| Serving 2
1 pork tenderloin (about 1 pound)
2 tablespoons olive oil
2 cloves garlic, minced
1/4 cup balsamic vinegar
2 tablespoons honey
1 teaspoon dried thyme

1. Preheat oven to 375°F (190°C).
2. Season pork tenderloin with salt and pepper.
3. In an oven-safe skillet, heat olive oil over medium-high heat.
4. Sear pork tenderloin on all sides until browned, about 2-3 minutes per side.
5. Add minced garlic to the skillet and cook for 1 minute.
6. In a small bowl, whisk together balsamic vinegar, honey, dried thyme, salt, and pepper.
7. Pour the balsamic glaze over the pork tenderloin in the skillet.
8. Transfer the skillet to the preheated oven and roast for 20-25 minutes, or until pork is cooked through.
9. Let the pork rest for 5 minutes before slicing.
10. Serve hot, garnished with fresh parsley.

Per 4 oz. pork tenderloin
Calories: 250| Carbs: 10g| Fats: 10g|Protein: 25g

2.5 Fish-based Recipes

Lemon Herb Baked Salmon

Time: 25 minutes| Difficulty: Easy| Serving 2

2 salmon fillets (6 ounces each)
2 tablespoons olive oil
1 tablespoon lemon juice
1 teaspoon lemon zest
2 cloves garlic, minced
1 teaspoon dried thyme
Salt and pepper to taste
Fresh parsley for garnish

1. Preheat oven to 375°F (190°C).
2. In a small bowl, mix together olive oil, lemon juice, lemon zest, minced garlic, dried thyme, salt, and pepper.
3. Place salmon fillets on a baking sheet lined with parchment paper.
4. Brush the salmon fillets with the lemon herb mixture.
5. Bake in the preheated oven for 12-15 minutes, or until the salmon is cooked through and flakes easily with a fork.
6. Garnish with fresh parsley before serving.

Per 1 salmon fillet
Calories: 350| Carbs: 0g| Fats: 20g| Protein: 35g

Lemon Garlic Tilapia

Time: 20 minutes| Difficulty: Easy| Serving 2

2 tilapia fillets (6 ounces each)
2 tablespoons olive oil
2 cloves garlic, minced
1 tablespoon lemon juice
1 teaspoon lemon zest
1 teaspoon dried oregano
Salt and pepper to taste
Fresh parsley for garnish

1. Preheat oven to 375°F (190°C).
2. Place tilapia fillets on a baking sheet lined with parchment paper.
3. In a small bowl, mix together olive oil, minced garlic, lemon juice, lemon zest, dried oregano, salt, and pepper.
4. Brush the tilapia fillets with the lemon garlic mixture.
5. Bake in the preheated oven for 12-15 minutes, or until the tilapia is cooked through and flakes easily with a fork.
6. Garnish with fresh parsley before serving.

Per 1 tilapia fillet
Calories: 250| Carbs: 0g| Fats: 15g| Protein: 30g

Garlic Butter Grilled Shrimp

Time: 20 minutes| Difficulty: Easy| Serving 2

1 pound large shrimp, peeled and deveined
3 tablespoons melted butter
3 cloves garlic, minced
1 tablespoon chopped fresh parsley
1 tablespoon lemon juice
Salt and pepper to taste
Wooden skewers, soaked in water for 30 minutes

1. Preheat grill to medium-high heat.
2. In a bowl, combine melted butter, minced garlic, chopped parsley, lemon juice, salt, and pepper.
3. Thread the shrimp onto the soaked wooden skewers.
4. Brush the shrimp skewers with the garlic butter mixture.
5. Grill the shrimp skewers for 2-3 minutes on each side, or until shrimp are pink and opaque.
6. Serve hot with additional lemon wedges for squeezing.

Per 1/4 of the recipe
Calories: 200| Carbs: 0g| Fats: 10g| Protein: 25g

Pan-Seared Mahi-Mahi with Mango Salsa

Time: 25 minutes| Difficulty: Easy| Serving 2

2 mahi-mahi fillets (6 ounces each)
2 tablespoons olive oil
1 teaspoon paprika
Salt and pepper to taste
1 ripe mango, peeled and diced
1/2 red bell pepper, diced
1/4 red onion, finely chopped
1 tablespoon chopped fresh cilantro
1 tablespoon lime juice

1. Season mahi-mahi fillets with paprika, salt, and pepper.
2. Heat olive oil in a skillet over medium-high heat.
3. Add mahi-mahi fillets to the skillet and cook for 3-4 minutes on each side, or until fish is cooked through and golden brown.
4. In a bowl, combine diced mango, diced red bell pepper, chopped red onion, chopped cilantro, and lime juice to make the salsa.
5. Serve pan-seared mahi-mahi with mango salsa on top.

Per 1 mahi-mahi fillet with salsa
Calories: 300| Carbs: 20g| Fats: 10g| Protein: 30g

Grilled Swordfish with Mango Salsa

Time: 25 minutes| Difficulty: Easy| Serving 2

2 swordfish steaks (6 ounces each)
2 tablespoons olive oil
1 teaspoon paprika
1/2 teaspoon ground cumin
Salt and pepper to taste
1 ripe mango, peeled and diced
1/2 red onion, finely chopped
1 jalapeño, seeded and minced
2 tablespoons chopped fresh cilantro
1 tablespoon lime juice

1. Preheat grill to medium-high heat.
2. Brush swordfish steaks with olive oil and season with paprika, ground cumin, salt, and pepper.
3. Grill swordfish steaks for 4-5 minutes on each side, or until fish is cooked through and has grill marks.
4. In a bowl, combine diced mango, chopped red onion, minced jalapeño, chopped cilantro, and lime juice to make the salsa.
5. Serve grilled swordfish steaks with mango salsa on top.

Per 1 swordfish steak with salsa
Calories: 300| Carbs: 15g| Fats: 15g| Protein: 30g

Grilled Halibut with Asparagus

Time: 25 minutes| Difficulty: Easy| Serving 2

2 halibut fillets (6 ounces each)
2 tablespoons olive oil
2 cloves garlic, minced
1 tablespoon lemon juice
1 bunch asparagus, trimmed
Lemon wedges for serving

1. Preheat grill to medium-high heat.
2. In a small bowl, mix together olive oil, minced garlic, lemon juice, salt, and pepper.
3. Brush halibut fillets with the olive oil mixture.
4. Place halibut fillets and asparagus on the grill.
5. Grill halibut for 4-5 minutes on each side, or until fish is cooked through and flakes easily with a fork.
6. Grill asparagus for 3-4 minutes, or until tender-crisp.
7. Serve grilled halibut and asparagus hot with lemon wedges on the side.

Per 1 halibut fillet with asparagus
Calories: 300| Carbs: 5g| Fats: 15g| Protein: 35g

Baked Cod with Tomato and Olive Relish

Time: 30 minutes| Difficulty: Easy| Serving 2

2 cod fillets (6 ounces each)
1 tablespoon olive oil
2 cloves garlic, minced
1 cup cherry tomatoes, halved
1/4 cup pitted olives, chopped
1 tablespoon capers
1 tablespoon chopped fresh parsley
Salt and pepper to taste
Lemon wedges for serving

1. Preheat oven to 375°F (190°C).
2. Place cod fillets on a baking sheet lined with parchment paper.
3. In a small bowl, mix together olive oil, minced garlic, cherry tomatoes, chopped olives, capers, chopped parsley, salt, and pepper.
4. Spoon the tomato and olive relish over the cod fillets.
5. Bake in the preheated oven for 15-18 minutes, or until the cod is cooked through and flakes easily with a fork.
6. Serve hot with lemon wedges on the side.

Per 1 cod fillet with relish
Calories: 250| Carbs: 5g| Fats: 10g| Protein: 35g

Lemon Pepper Tuna Steaks

Time: 20 minutes| Difficulty: Easy| Serving 2

2 tuna steaks (6 ounces each)
2 tablespoons olive oil
Zest and juice of 1 lemon
1 teaspoon cracked black pepper
Salt to taste
Fresh parsley for garnish

1. Preheat grill or grill pan to medium-high heat.
2. In a small bowl, mix together olive oil, lemon zest, lemon juice, cracked black pepper, and salt.
3. Brush both sides of the tuna steaks with the lemon pepper mixture.
4. Grill tuna steaks for 3-4 minutes on each side, or until desired doneness.
5. Serve hot, garnished with fresh parsley.

Per 1 tuna steak
Calories: 250| Carbs: 0g| Fats: 15g| Protein 30g

Coconut Curry Shrimp

Time: 30 minutes| Difficulty: Moderate| Serving 2
1 pound large shrimp, peeled and deveined
1 tablespoon olive oil
2 cloves garlic, minced
1 tablespoon curry powder
1 can (14 ounces) coconut milk
1 red bell pepper, sliced
1 cup snap peas
Salt and pepper to taste
Cooked rice for serving
Chopped fresh cilantro for garnish
1. Heat olive oil in a skillet over medium heat.
2. Add minced garlic and curry powder to the skillet, and cook for 1 minute.
3. Stir in coconut milk, sliced red bell pepper, and snap peas. Simmer for 5 minutes.
4. Add shrimp to the skillet and cook for 3-4 minutes, or until shrimp are pink and cooked through.
5. Season with salt and pepper to taste.
6. Serve coconut curry shrimp over cooked rice, garnished with chopped fresh cilantro.

Per 1/4 of the recipe without rice)
Calories: 250| Carbs: 10g| Fats: 15g| Protein: 25g

Teriyaki Glazed Salmon

Time: 30 minutes| Difficulty: Easy| Serving 2

2 salmon fillets (6 ounces each)
1/4 cup soy sauce (or tamari for gluten-free)
2 tablespoons honey
1 tablespoon rice vinegar
1 clove garlic, minced
1 teaspoon minced ginger
1 teaspoon sesame oil
Sesame seeds and sliced green onions for garnish
1. In a small saucepan, combine soy sauce, honey, rice vinegar, minced garlic, minced ginger, and sesame oil. Heat over medium heat and simmer until the sauce thickens slightly, about 5-7 minutes.
2. Preheat the grill or grill pan to medium-high heat.
3. Brush the salmon fillets with the teriyaki sauce and grill for 4-5 minutes on each side, or until the salmon is cooked through and flakes easily with a fork.
4. Serve hot, garnished with sesame seeds and sliced green onions.

Per 1 salmon fillet
Calories: 350| Carbs: 15g| Fats: 20g Protein: 30g

Lemon Garlic Baked Cod

Time: 20 minutes| Difficulty: Easy| Serving 2
2 cod fillets (6 ounces each)
2 tablespoons olive oil
2 cloves garlic, minced
1 tablespoon lemon juice
1 teaspoon lemon zest
Chopped fresh parsley for garnish
1. Preheat oven to 375°F (190°C).
2. Place cod fillets on a baking sheet lined with parchment paper.
3. In a small bowl, mix together olive oil, minced garlic, lemon juice, lemon zest, salt, and pepper.
4. Brush the cod fillets with the lemon garlic mixture.
5. Bake in the preheated oven for 12-15 minutes, or until the cod is cooked through and flakes easily with a fork.
6. Garnish with chopped fresh parsley before serving.

Per 1 cod fillet
Calories: 200| Carbs: 0g| Fats: 10g| Protein: 30g

Mediterranean Baked Cod

Time: 25 minutes| Difficulty: Easy| Serving 2
2 cod fillets (6 ounces each)
2 tablespoons olive oil
2 cloves garlic, minced
1 teaspoon dried oregano
1 teaspoon dried thyme
1/2 cup cherry tomatoes, halved
1/4 cup pitted olives, chopped
1/4 cup crumbled feta cheese
1. Preheat oven to 375°F (190°C).
2. Place cod fillets on a baking sheet lined with parchment paper.
3. In a small bowl, mix together olive oil, minced garlic, dried oregano, dried thyme, salt, and pepper.
4. Brush the cod fillets with the olive oil mixture.
5. Arrange cherry tomatoes and chopped olives around the cod fillets on the baking sheet.
6. Bake in the preheated oven for 15-18 minutes, or until the cod is cooked through and flakes easily with a fork.
7. Sprinkle crumbled feta cheese over the baked cod and garnish with fresh parsley before serving.

Per 1 cod fillet
Calories: 300| Carbs: 5g| Fats: 15g| Protein: 30g

Coconut Lime Shrimp Skewers

Time: 20 minutes| Difficulty: Easy| Serving 2

1 pound large shrimp, peeled and deveined
1/4 cup coconut milk
Zest and juice of 1 lime
2 tablespoons chopped fresh cilantro
1 tablespoon olive oil
Salt and pepper to taste
Wooden skewers, soaked in water for 30 minutes

1. In a bowl, combine coconut milk, lime zest, lime juice, chopped cilantro, olive oil, salt, and pepper to make the marinade.
2. Thread shrimp onto the soaked wooden skewers.
3. Brush shrimp skewers with the coconut lime marinade.
4. Preheat the grill or grill pan to medium-high heat.
5. Grill shrimp skewers for 2-3 minutes on each side, or until shrimp are pink and cooked through.

Per 1/4 of the recipe
Calories: 150| Carbs: 1g| Fats: 5g| Protein: 25g

Pan-Seared Sea Bass with Citrus Salsa

Time: 25 minutes| Difficulty: Easy| Serving 2

2 sea bass fillets (6 ounces each)
2 tablespoons olive oil
Salt and pepper to taste
1 orange, segmented
1 grapefruit, segmented
1/4 red onion, finely chopped
1 tablespoon chopped fresh cilantro
1 tablespoon lime juice
1 tablespoon honey

1. Heat olive oil in a skillet over medium-high heat.
2. Season sea bass fillets with salt and pepper.
3. Sear sea bass fillets for 3-4 minutes on each side, or until fish is golden brown and cooked through.
4. In a bowl, combine orange segments, grapefruit segments, chopped red onion, chopped cilantro, lime juice, and honey to make the salsa.
5. Serve pan-seared sea bass with citrus salsa on top.

Per 1 sea bass fillet with salsa
Calories: 300| Carbs: 20g| Fats: 10g| Protein: 30g

Cajun Spiced Catfish

Time: 25 minutes| Difficulty: Easy| Serving 2
2 catfish fillets (6 ounces each)
2 tablespoons olive oil
1 tablespoon Cajun seasoning
1 teaspoon paprika
1/2 teaspoon garlic powder
1/2 teaspoon onion powder
Salt and pepper to taste
Lemon wedges for serving

1. Preheat oven to 375°F (190°C).
2. Rub catfish fillets with olive oil and season with Cajun seasoning, paprika, garlic powder, onion powder, salt, and pepper.
3. Heat olive oil in a skillet over medium-high heat.
4. Sear catfish fillets for 2-3 minutes on each side until browned.
5. Transfer catfish fillets to a baking dish and bake in the preheated oven for 10-12 minutes, or until fish is cooked through and flakes easily with a fork.
6. Serve hot with lemon wedges on the side.

Per 1 catfish fillet
Calories: 300| Carbs: 5g| Fats: 15g| Protein: 35g

Honey Garlic Glazed Salmon

Time: 30 minutes| Difficulty: Easy| Serving 2
2 salmon fillets (6 ounces each)
2 tablespoons honey
2 tablespoons soy sauce
1 tablespoon olive oil
2 cloves garlic, minced
1 teaspoon grated ginger
Sesame seeds for garnish
Sliced green onions for garnish

1. In a small bowl, whisk together honey, soy sauce, minced garlic, and grated ginger to make the glaze.
2. Heat olive oil in a skillet over medium-high heat.
3. Season salmon fillets with salt and pepper, then place them skin-side down in the skillet.
4. Cook salmon for 3-4 minutes on each side, or until browned and cooked through.
5. Brush salmon fillets with the honey garlic glaze during the last minute of cooking.
6. Sprinkle sesame seeds and sliced green onions over the glazed salmon before serving.

Per 1 salmon fillet
Calories: 350| Carbs: 15g| Fats: 20g| Protein: 30g

Baked Salmon with Garlic and Herbs

Time: 25 minutes| Difficulty: Easy| Serving 2

2 salmon fillets
2 tablespoons olive oil
2 cloves garlic, minced
1 tablespoon chopped fresh parsley
1 teaspoon dried thyme

1. Preheat oven to 375°F (190°C).
2. Place salmon fillets on a baking sheet lined with parchment paper.
3. In a small bowl, mix together olive oil, minced garlic, chopped parsley, dried thyme, salt, and pepper.
4. Spread the garlic and herb mixture evenly over the salmon fillets.
5. Bake in the preheated oven for 12-15 minutes, or until salmon is cooked through and flakes easily with a fork.
6. Serve hot with steamed vegetables or a side salad.

Per 1 salmon fillet
Calories: 250| Carbs: 0g| Fats: 15g| Protein: 25g

Pesto Baked Cod

Time: 20 minutes| Difficulty: Easy| Serving 2

2 cod fillets (6 ounces each)
2 tablespoons prepared pesto
1 tablespoon olive oil
Fresh basil leaves for garnish

1. Preheat oven to 375°F (190°C).
2. Place cod fillets on a baking sheet lined with parchment paper.
3. Spread a tablespoon of prepared pesto over each cod fillet.
4. Drizzle olive oil over the pesto-coated cod fillets.
5. Season cod fillets with salt and pepper to taste.
6. Bake in the preheated oven for 12-15 minutes, or until the cod is cooked through and flakes easily with a fork.
7. Garnish with fresh basil leaves before serving.

Per 1 cod fillet
Calories: 250| Carbs: 2g| Fats: 15g| Protein: 30g

Blackened Red Snapper

Time: 20 minutes| Difficulty: Easy| Serving 2

2 red snapper fillets (6 ounces each)
2 tablespoons olive oil
1 tablespoon Cajun seasoning
1 tablespoon paprika
1 teaspoon garlic powder
1 teaspoon onion powder
Fresh lemon wedges for serving

1. Preheat grill or grill pan to medium-high heat.
2. Rub red snapper fillets with olive oil and season with Cajun seasoning, paprika, garlic powder, onion powder, and salt.
3. Grill red snapper fillets for 3-4 minutes on each side, or until fish is cooked through and flakes easily with a fork.
4. Serve hot with fresh lemon wedges on the side.

Per 1 red snapper fillet
Calories: 250| Carbs: 2g| Fats: 15g| Protein: 30g

Asian-Inspired Salmon Salad

Time: 30 minutes| Difficulty: Easy| Serving 2

2 salmon fillets (6 ounces each)
2 tablespoons soy sauce
1 tablespoon sesame oil
1 tablespoon rice vinegar
1 teaspoon grated ginger
1 teaspoon honey
Mixed salad greens
Sliced cucumber
Sliced bell peppers
Sliced radishes

1. Preheat oven to 375°F (190°C).
2. In a small bowl, whisk together soy sauce, sesame oil, rice vinegar, grated ginger, and honey.
3. Place salmon fillets on a baking sheet lined with parchment paper.
4. Brush salmon fillets with the soy sauce mixture.
5. Bake in the preheated oven for 12-15 minutes, or until salmon is cooked through and flakes easily with a fork.
6. Arrange mixed salad greens, sliced cucumber, sliced bell peppers, and sliced radishes on plates.
7. Place baked salmon fillets on top of the salad.

Per 1 salmon fillet with salad
Calories: 350| Carbs: 15g| Fats: 20g| Protein: 30g

2.6 Vegan and Vegetarian Recipes

Healthy Vegetarian Burrito

Time: 15 minutes| Difficulty: Easy| Serving 2
4 large eggs
1/2 cup black beans, drained and rinsed
1/2 cup diced bell peppers
1/4 cup diced onion
1/2 cup diced tomatoes
1/2 cup shredded cheese (optional)
2 whole-wheat tortillas
Salt and pepper to taste
Olive oil for cooking

1. In a skillet, heat olive oil over medium heat.
2. Add diced onions and bell peppers to the skillet and cook until softened.
3. In a separate bowl, whisk together eggs, salt, and pepper.
4. Pour the beaten eggs into the skillet with the cooked vegetables.
5. Cook, stirring occasionally, until the eggs are scrambled and cooked through.
6. Warm the black beans and tortillas in the microwave or on the stovetop.
7. Divide the scrambled eggs, black beans, diced tomatoes, and shredded cheese (if using) evenly between the tortillas.
8. Roll up the tortillas to form burritos.
9. Serve warm and enjoy this protein-packed breakfast!

Per serving
Calories: 350| Protein: 20g| Carbs: 30g| Fat: 15g| Fiber: 8g

Veggie Sushi Rolls

Time: 15 minutes| Difficulty: Moderate| Serving 2
2 nori sheets
1/2 cup cooked quinoa
1/2 cup cucumber, julienned
1/2 cup carrot, julienned
1/2 avocado, sliced
Soy sauce, for dipping

1. Place a nori sheet on a bamboo sushi mat.
2. Spread cooked quinoa evenly over the nori sheet, leaving a 1-inch border at the top.
3. Arrange cucumber, carrot, and avocado slices in a line across the quinoa.
4. Roll up the nori sheet tightly, using the bamboo mat to help shape the roll.
5. Slice the sushi roll into bite-sized pieces.
6. Serve with soy sauce for dipping.

Per serving
Calories: 200| Protein: 5g| Carbs: 25g| Fat: 8g|Fiber: 5g

Ratatouille with Quinoa

Time: 45 minutes| Difficulty: Moderate| Serving 2
1 cup quinoa
2 cups water or vegetable broth
2 tablespoons olive oil
2 cloves garlic, minced
1 onion, diced
1 eggplant, diced
2 zucchini, diced
1 bell pepper, diced
2 cups diced tomatoes
1 tablespoon tomato paste
1 teaspoon dried thyme
1 teaspoon dried oregano
Salt and pepper to taste
Fresh basil leaves for garnish

1. Rinse quinoa under cold water, then combine with water or vegetable broth in a saucepan. Bring to a boil, then reduce heat to low, cover, and simmer for 15-20 minutes, or until quinoa is cooked and liquid is absorbed.
2. Heat olive oil in a large skillet or Dutch oven over medium heat. Add minced garlic and diced onion, and cook until softened and fragrant.
3. Add diced eggplant, diced zucchini, diced bell pepper, diced tomatoes, tomato paste, dried thyme, dried oregano, salt, and pepper to the skillet. Stir to combine.
4. Cover and simmer for 20-25 minutes, or until vegetables are tender and flavors are blended.
5. Serve ratatouille over cooked quinoa.
6. Garnish with fresh basil leaves before serving.

Per 1/2 of the recipe
Calories: 300| Carbs: 40g| Fats: 10g| Protein: 10g

Baked Sweet Potato with Black Beans and Salsa

Time: 45 minutes| Difficulty: Easy| Serving 2

2 medium sweet potatoes
1 can (15 ounces) black beans, drained and rinsed
1 cup salsa
1 avocado, sliced
Fresh cilantro for garnish
Salt and pepper to taste

1. Preheat oven to 400°F (200°C).
2. Scrub sweet potatoes and pierce them several times with a fork. Place them on a baking sheet lined with parchment paper.
3. Bake sweet potatoes in the preheated oven for 40-45 minutes, or until tender.
4. Once sweet potatoes are cooked, remove them from the oven and let them cool slightly.
5. Slice each sweet potato open lengthwise, and then fluff the flesh with a fork.
6. Top each sweet potato with black beans, salsa, and sliced avocado.
7. Season with salt and pepper to taste.
8. Garnish with fresh cilantro before serving.

Per serving
Calories: 400| Carbs: 60g| Fats: 10g| Protein: 10g

Grilled Veggie Sandwich with Hummus

Time: 30 minutes| Difficulty: Easy| Serving 2
4 slices whole grain bread
1/2 cup hummus
1 zucchini, sliced lengthwise
1 yellow squash, sliced lengthwise
1 red bell pepper, sliced into strips
1 onion, sliced into rounds
1 tablespoon olive oil
Fresh basil leaves for garnish

1. Preheat grill or grill pan to medium-high heat.
2. Brush sliced zucchini, yellow squash, red bell pepper, and onion with olive oil. Season with salt and pepper.
3. Grill vegetables for 3-4 minutes on each side, or until tender and grill marks appear.
4. Toast whole grain bread slices on the grill for 1-2 minutes, or until lightly browned.
5. Spread hummus evenly on each slice of toasted bread.
6. Arrange grilled vegetables on top of the hummus.

Per 1 sandwich
Calories: 300| Carbs: 35g| Fats: 10g|Protein: 10g

Zucchini Noodles with Pesto and Cherry Tomatoes

Time: 20 minutes| Difficulty: Easy| Serving 2
4 medium zucchini
1 cup cherry tomatoes, halved
1/4 cup prepared pesto
2 tablespoons olive oil
Salt and pepper to taste
Optional: *grated Parmesan cheese and fresh basil leaves for garnish*

1. Use a spiralizer to turn zucchini into noodles.
2. Heat olive oil in a large skillet over medium heat. Add zucchini noodles and cherry tomatoes to the skillet.
3. Sauté for 3-4 minutes or until zucchini noodles are tender.
4. Add prepared pesto to the skillet and toss everything together until well combined.
5. Season with salt and pepper to taste.
6. Serve hot, garnished with grated Parmesan cheese and fresh basil leaves if desired.

Per 1/2 of the recipe
Calories: 200| Carbs: 10g| Fats: 15g| Protein: 5g

Veggie Omelette with Whole Wheat Toast

Time: 20 minutes| Difficulty: Easy| Serving 2

4 large eggs
2 tablespoons milk or water
1/2 cup diced bell peppers
1/2 cup diced tomatoes
1/4 cup diced onion
1/4 cup sliced mushrooms
1/4 cup chopped spinach
2 slices whole wheat bread, toasted

1. In a bowl, whisk together eggs and milk or water until well combined.
2. Heat a non-stick skillet over medium heat. Add diced bell peppers, diced tomatoes, diced onion, sliced mushrooms, and chopped spinach to the skillet. Sauté until vegetables are softened.
3. Pour egg mixture over the sautéed vegetables in the skillet. Cook until edges are set.
4. Using a spatula, gently lift the edges of the omelet and tilt the skillet to allow uncooked eggs to flow to the bottom.
5. Once the omelet is set, fold it in half and cook for an additional minute.
6. Slide the omelet onto a plate and serve hot with toasted whole wheat bread on the side.

Per 1 omelet with 1 slice of toast
Calories: 300| Carbs: 25g| Fats: 15g|Protein: 20g

Chickpea and Vegetable Curry

Time: 45 minutes| Difficulty: Moderate| Serving 2

1 cup cooked chickpeas
1 tablespoon olive oil
1 onion, diced
2 cloves garlic, minced
1 tablespoon grated ginger
1 bell pepper, diced
1 zucchini, diced
1 cup diced tomatoes
1 can (13.5 ounces) coconut milk
2 tablespoons curry powder
1 teaspoon ground turmeric
Fresh cilantro for garnish

1. Heat olive oil in a large skillet or Dutch oven over medium heat. Add diced onion, minced garlic, and grated ginger, and sauté until softened and fragrant.
2. Add diced bell pepper and diced zucchini to the skillet. Cook for 5-7 minutes, or until vegetables are tender.
3. Stir in diced tomatoes, cooked chickpeas, coconut milk, curry powder, ground turmeric, salt, and pepper. Bring to a simmer.
4. Cover and simmer for 20-25 minutes, stirring occasionally, until curry is thickened and flavors are blended.
5. Serve hot, garnished with fresh cilantro.
6. Serve over cooked brown rice or quinoa if desired.

Per 1/2 of the recipe
Calories: 350| Carbs: 25g| Fats: 20g| Protein: 10g

Roasted Vegetable Quinoa Bowl

Time: 40 minutes| Difficulty: Easy| Serving 2
1 cup quinoa
2 cups water or vegetable broth
2 tablespoons olive oil
1 sweet potato, peeled and diced
1 red onion, sliced
1 bell pepper, sliced
1 zucchini, sliced
1 cup cherry tomatoes
2 cloves garlic, minced
1 teaspoon dried thyme
1 teaspoon dried rosemary
Fresh parsley for garnish

1. Rinse quinoa under cold water, then combine with water or vegetable broth in a saucepan. Bring to a boil, then reduce heat to low, cover, and simmer for 15-20 minutes, or until quinoa is cooked and liquid is absorbed.
2. Preheat oven to 400°F (200°C). Arrange diced sweet potato, sliced red onion, sliced bell pepper, sliced zucchini, and cherry tomatoes on a baking sheet lined with parchment paper.
3. Drizzle olive oil over the vegetables and sprinkle minced garlic, dried thyme, dried rosemary, salt, and pepper.
4. Toss everything together until vegetables are evenly coated with oil and seasonings.
5. Roast vegetables in the preheated oven for 25-30 minutes, or until tender and caramelized.
6. Serve roasted vegetables over cooked quinoa.
7. Garnish with fresh parsley before serving.

Per 1/2 of the recipe
Calories: 350| Carbs: 50g| Fats: 10g| Protein: 10g

Spinach and Mushroom Quesadillas

Time: 25 minutes| Difficulty: Easy| Serving 2

4 whole wheat tortillas
2 cups baby spinach
1 cup sliced mushrooms
1/2 cup shredded mozzarella cheese
1/2 cup shredded cheddar cheese
1 tablespoon olive oil
Salt and pepper to taste
Optional: *salsa, guacamole, and Greek yogurt for serving*

1. Heat olive oil in a skillet over medium heat. Add sliced mushrooms and sauté until tender.
2. Add baby spinach to the skillet and cook until wilted. Season with salt and pepper to taste.
3. Place one whole wheat tortilla in a non-stick skillet over medium heat. Sprinkle half of the tortilla with shredded mozzarella cheese and shredded cheddar cheese.
4. Spoon sautéed spinach and mushrooms over the cheese.
5. Fold the empty half of the tortilla over the filling to create a half-moon shape.
6. Cook quesadilla for 2-3 minutes on each side, or until cheese is melted and tortilla is golden brown.
7. Repeat the process with remaining tortillas and filling.
8. Slice quesadillas into wedges and serve hot with salsa, guacamole, and Greek yogurt on the side.

Per 1/2 of a quesadilla
Calories: 300| Carbs: 25g| Fats: 15g| Protein: 15g

Tofu and Vegetable Stir-Fry with Brown Rice

Time: 30 minutes| Difficulty: Easy| Serving 2

1 cup brown rice
2 cups water or vegetable broth
1 block (14 ounces) extra-firm tofu, drained and pressed
2 tablespoons soy sauce or tamari
1 tablespoon rice vinegar
1 tablespoon sesame oil
2 tablespoons olive oil
2 cloves garlic, minced
1 onion, sliced
2 carrots, julienned
1 bell pepper, sliced
1 cup broccoli florets
1 cup snap peas
Salt and pepper to taste

Optional: *sliced green onions and sesame seeds for garnish*

1. Rinse brown rice under cold water, and then combine with water or vegetable broth in a saucepan. Bring to a boil, then reduce heat to low, cover, and simmer for 35-40 minutes, or until rice is cooked and liquid is absorbed.
2. Cut pressed tofu into cubes and place them in a bowl. In a separate bowl, whisk together soy sauce or tamari, rice vinegar, and sesame oil. Pour the sauce over the tofu cubes and let them marinate for 10-15 minutes.
3. Heat olive oil in a large skillet or wok over medium-high heat. Add minced garlic and sliced onion, and cook until softened and fragrant.
4. Add julienned carrots, sliced bell pepper, broccoli florets, and snap peas to the skillet. Stir-fry for 5-7 minutes, or until vegetables are tender-crisp.
5. Push vegetables to the side of the skillet and add marinated tofu cubes to the center. Cook tofu for 3-4 minutes on each side, or until golden brown.
6. Once tofu is cooked, toss everything together in the skillet until well combined.
7. Season with salt and pepper to taste.
8. Serve tofu and vegetable stir-fry over cooked brown rice.
9. Garnish with sliced green onions and sesame seeds if desired.

Per 1/2 of the recipe
Calories: 400| Carbs: 45g| Fats: 15g| Protein: 20g

Asian-inspired Tofu Stir-Fry with Brown Rice

Time: 30 minutes| Difficulty: Easy| Serving 2

1 cup brown rice
2 cups water or vegetable broth
1 block (14 ounces) extra-firm tofu, drained and pressed
2 tablespoons soy sauce or tamari
1 tablespoon rice vinegar
1 tablespoon sesame oil
2 tablespoons olive oil
2 cloves garlic, minced
1 onion, sliced
2 carrots, julienned
1 bell pepper, sliced
1 cup broccoli florets
1 cup snap peas
Salt and pepper to taste

Optional: *sliced green onions and sesame seeds for garnish*

1. Rinse brown rice under cold water, then combine with water or vegetable broth in a saucepan. Bring to a boil, then reduce heat to low, cover, and simmer for 35-40 minutes, or until rice is cooked and liquid is absorbed.
2. Cut pressed tofu into cubes and place them in a bowl. In a separate bowl, whisk together soy sauce or tamari, rice vinegar, and sesame oil. Pour the sauce over the tofu cubes and let them marinate for 10-15 minutes.
3. Heat olive oil in a large skillet or wok over medium-high heat. Add minced garlic and sliced onion, and cook until softened and fragrant.
4. Add julienned carrots, sliced bell pepper, broccoli florets, and snap peas to the skillet. Stir-fry for 5-7 minutes, or until vegetables are tender-crisp.
5. Push vegetables to the side of the skillet and add marinated tofu cubes to the center. Cook tofu for 3-4 minutes on each side, or until golden brown.
6. Once tofu is cooked, toss everything together in the skillet until well combined.
7. Season with salt and pepper to taste.
8. Serve tofu and vegetable stir-fry over cooked brown rice.
9. Garnish with sliced green onions and sesame seeds if desired.

Per 1/2 of the recipe
Calories: 400| Carbs: 45g| Fats: 15g| Protein: 20g

Vegan Chickpea and Vegetable Stir-Fry

Time: 30 minutes| Difficulty: Easy| Serving 2

1 tablespoon olive oil
1 onion, diced
2 cloves garlic, minced
1 bell pepper, sliced
1 zucchini, sliced
1 carrot, julienned
1 cup broccoli florets
1 cup snap peas
1 can (14 ounces) chickpeas, drained and rinsed
2 tablespoons soy sauce or tamari
1 tablespoon rice vinegar
1 teaspoon sesame oil
1 teaspoon cornstarch (optional, for thickening)
Salt and pepper to taste
Cooked brown rice for serving

1. Heat olive oil in a large skillet or wok over medium heat. Add diced onion and minced garlic, and sauté until softened and fragrant.
2. Add sliced bell pepper, sliced zucchini, julienned carrot, broccoli florets, and snap peas to the skillet. Stir-fry for 5-7 minutes, or until vegetables are tender-crisp.
3. Add drained and rinsed chickpeas to the skillet, and cook for an additional 2-3 minutes.
4. In a small bowl, whisk together soy sauce or tamari, rice vinegar, sesame oil, and cornstarch (if using).
5. Pour the sauce over the vegetable and chickpea mixture in the skillet. Stir well to coat evenly.
6. Cook for 2-3 minutes, or until the sauce has thickened slightly.
7. Season with salt and pepper to taste.
8. Serve hot, over cooked brown rice.

Per 1/2 of the recipe without rice
Calories: 300| Carbs: 40g| Fats: 10g| Protein: 15g

Quinoa and Vegetable Stir-Fry

Time: 25 minutes| Difficulty: Easy| Serving 2

1 cup quinoa
2 cups water or vegetable broth
2 tablespoons olive oil
2 cloves garlic, minced
1 onion, diced
2 carrots, julienned
1 red bell pepper, sliced
1 cup broccoli florets
1 cup snap peas
1/4 cup soy sauce or tamari
1 tablespoon rice vinegar
1 tablespoon sesame oil
Salt and pepper to taste

Optional: *sliced green onions and sesame seeds for garnish*

1. Rinse quinoa under cold water, and then combine with water or vegetable broth in a saucepan. Bring to a boil, then reduce heat to low, cover, and simmer for 15-20 minutes, or until quinoa is cooked and liquid is absorbed.
2. In a large skillet or wok, heat olive oil over medium-high heat. Add minced garlic and diced onion, and cook until softened and fragrant.
3. Add julienned carrots, sliced red bell pepper, broccoli florets, and snap peas to the skillet. Stir-fry for 5-7 minutes, or until vegetables are tender-crisp.
4. In a small bowl, mix together soy sauce or tamari, rice vinegar, and sesame oil. Pour the sauce over the vegetables in the skillet and stir to combine.
5. Add cooked quinoa to the skillet and toss everything together until well combined.
6. Season with salt and pepper to taste.
7. Serve hot, garnished with sliced green onions and sesame seeds if desired.

Per serving
Calories: 200| Protein: 5g| Carbs: 25g| Fat: 8g| Fiber: 5g

Cauliflower Fried Rice with Tofu

Time: 30 minutes| Difficulty: Easy| Serving 2
1 head cauliflower, riced
2 tablespoons olive oil
1 block (14 ounces) firm tofu, drained and pressed
2 cloves garlic, minced
1 onion and 2 carrots, diced
1 cup frozen peas
2 tablespoons soy sauce and 1 tablespoon sesame oil
Optional: *sliced green onions for garnish*

1. Cut cauliflower into florets, and then place them in a food processor. Pulse until cauliflower resembles rice grains.
2. Heat olive oil in a large skillet or wok over medium-high heat. Add riced cauliflower to the skillet and cook for 5-7 minutes, or until cauliflower is tender.
3. Cut pressed tofu into cubes and add them to the skillet with cauliflower. Cook for an additional 5-7 minutes, or until tofu is golden brown.
4. Push cauliflower and tofu to one side of the skillet, then add minced garlic, diced onion, and diced carrots to the other side. Sauté until vegetables are softened.
5. Add frozen peas to the skillet and cook until heated through.
6. In a small bowl, whisk together soy sauce or tamari and sesame oil. Pour the sauce over the cauliflower and tofu mixture in the skillet.
7. Toss everything together until well combined. Season with salt and pepper to taste.
8. Serve hot, garnished with sliced green onions if desired.

Per serving
Calories: 300| Carbs: 20g| Fats: 15g| Protein: 20g

Grilled Portobello Mushroom Burgers

Time: 30 minutes| Difficulty: Easy| Serving 2
4 large Portobello mushroom caps
2 tbs. balsamic vinegar and 2 tbs. olive oil
2 cloves garlic, minced
4 whole wheat burger buns
Lettuce leaves, tomato slices, and avocado slices for topping

1. In a shallow dish, whisk together balsamic vinegar, olive oil, minced garlic, salt, and pepper to make the marinade.
2. Place Portobello mushroom caps in the marinade and let them marinate for 15-20 minutes.
3. Preheat grill or grill pan to medium-high heat. Remove mushroom caps from the marinade and discard excess marinade.
4. Grill mushroom caps for 4-5 minutes on each side, or until tender.
5. Toast whole wheat burger buns on the grill for 1-2 minutes, or until lightly browned.
6. Assemble grilled Portobello mushroom burgers by placing a grilled mushroom cap on each burger bun.
7. Top with lettuce leaves, tomato slices, and avocado slices.

Per serving (1 mushroom burger):
Calories: 250| Carbs: 30g| Fats: 10g| Protein: 10g

Quinoa Stuffed Bell Peppers

Time: 45 minutes| Difficulty: Moderate| Serving 2
3 bell peppers (any color), halved and seeds removed
1 cup quinoa and 2 cups vegetable broth
1 tablespoon olive oil
1 onion and 2 cloves garlic, minced
1 zucchini and 1 carrot, diced
1 cup diced tomatoes
1 teaspoon dried oregano and 1 teaspoon dried basil
Optional: *shredded vegan cheese for topping*

1. Preheat oven to 375°F (190°C). Place halved bell peppers in a baking dish.
2. Rinse quinoa under cold water, and then combine with vegetable broth in a saucepan. Bring to a boil, then reduce heat to low, cover, and simmer for 15-20 minutes, or until quinoa is cooked and liquid is absorbed.
3. Heat olive oil in a skillet over medium heat. Add diced onion and minced garlic, and sauté until softened and fragrant.
4. Add diced zucchini, diced carrot, diced tomatoes, dried oregano, dried basil, salt, and pepper to the skillet. Cook until vegetables are tender.
5. Stir cooked quinoa into the vegetable mixture until well combined.
6. Spoon quinoa mixture into each bell peppers half, pressing down gently to pack the filling.
7. Cover the baking dish with foil and bake in the preheated oven for 25-30 minutes, or until bell peppers are tender.
8. Optional: Remove foil, sprinkle shredded vegan cheese over the stuffed bell peppers, and bake for an additional 5 minutes until cheese is melted and bubbly.

Per serving

Calories: 250| Carbs: 35g| Fats: 7g| Protein: 10g

Eggplant Parmesan with Whole Wheat Pasta

Time: 1 hour| Difficulty: Moderate| Serving 2

8 ounces whole wheat spaghetti
1 large eggplant, sliced into rounds
1 cup whole wheat breadcrumbs
1/4 cup grated Parmesan cheese
2 eggs, beaten
2 cups marinara sauce
1 cup shredded mozzarella cheese
Salt and pepper to taste
Fresh basil leaves for garnish

1. Preheat oven to 400°F (200°C). Cook whole wheat spaghetti according to package instructions.
2. Place sliced eggplant rounds on a paper towel and sprinkle with salt. Let them sit for 10-15 minutes to release excess moisture.
3. In a shallow dish, combine whole wheat breadcrumbs and grated Parmesan cheese.
4. Dip eggplant rounds into beaten eggs, then coat them with breadcrumb mixture.
5. Place breaded eggplant rounds on a baking sheet lined with parchment paper. Bake in the preheated oven for 20-25 minutes, or until golden brown and crispy.
6. Spread marinara sauce evenly in the bottom of a baking dish. Arrange baked eggplant rounds on top of the sauce.
7. Top eggplant rounds with shredded mozzarella cheese.
8. Bake in the oven for an additional 10-15 minutes, or until cheese is melted and bubbly.
9. Serve eggplant Parmesan over cooked whole wheat spaghetti.
10. Garnish with fresh basil leaves before serving.

Per serving
Calories: 400| Carbs: 50g| Fats: 15g| Protein: 20g

Vegan Lentil Shepherd's Pie

Time: 1 hour| Difficulty: Moderate| Serving 2

1 cup dried green lentils
3 cups vegetable broth
2 tablespoons olive oil
1 onion, diced
2 carrots, diced
2 celery stalks, diced
2 cloves garlic, minced
1 teaspoon dried thyme
1 teaspoon dried rosemary
Salt and pepper to taste
4 cups mashed potatoes (prepared in advance)
Fresh parsley for garnish

1. Rinse lentils under cold water, and then combine with vegetable broth in a saucepan. Bring to a boil, then reduce heat to low, cover, and simmer for 20-25 minutes, or until lentils are tender and most of the liquid is absorbed.
2. Preheat oven to 375°F (190°C).
3. Heat olive oil in a skillet over medium heat. Add diced onion, diced carrots, diced celery, and minced garlic. Sauté until vegetables are softened.
4. Stir in cooked lentils, dried thyme, dried rosemary, salt, and pepper. Cook for an additional 5 minutes to allow flavors to meld together.
5. Transfer lentil mixture to a baking dish and spread it out evenly.
6. Spread mashed potatoes over the lentil mixture, creating an even layer.
7. Bake in the preheated oven for 25-30 minutes, or until the mashed potatoes are golden brown and the filling is bubbly.
8. Serve hot, garnished with fresh parsley.

Per serving (1/2 of the pie)
Calories: 300| Carbs: 45g| Fats: 7g| Protein: 12g

2.7 Side Dishes

Roasted Brussels Sprouts

Time: 30 minutes| Difficulty: Easy| Serving 2

1 pound Brussels sprouts, trimmed and halved
2 tablespoons olive oil
Salt and pepper to taste

1. Preheat oven to 400°F (200°C).
2. Toss Brussels sprouts with olive oil, salt, and pepper in a bowl until evenly coated.
3. Spread Brussels sprouts in a single layer on a baking sheet.
4. Roast in the preheated oven for 20-25 minutes, or until Brussels sprouts are tender and caramelized, stirring halfway through.
5. Serve hot.

Per serving
Calories: 50| Carbs: 6g| Fats: 3g| Protein: 2g

Quinoa Pilaf

Time: 30 minutes| Difficulty: Easy| Serving 2

1 cup quinoa
2 cups vegetable broth
1 tablespoon olive oil
1 onion, diced
2 cloves garlic, minced
1 carrot, diced
1 bell pepper, diced
1/2 cup frozen peas
Salt and pepper to taste
Fresh parsley for garnish

1. Rinse quinoa under cold water, and then combine with vegetable broth in a saucepan. Bring to a boil, then reduce heat to low, cover, and simmer for 15-20 minutes, or until quinoa is cooked and liquid is absorbed.
2. Heat olive oil in a skillet over medium heat. Add diced onion and minced garlic, and sauté until softened and fragrant.
3. Add diced carrot and diced bell pepper to the skillet. Cook until vegetables are tender.
4. Stir cooked quinoa and frozen peas into the skillet. Cook for an additional 2-3 minutes, or until peas are heated through.
5. Season with salt and pepper to taste.
6. Garnish with fresh parsley before serving.

Per serving
Calories: 100| Carbs: 16g| Fats: 3g| Protein: 4g

Balsamic Glazed Roasted Carrots

Time: 30 minutes| Difficulty: Easy| Serving 2

1 pound carrots, peeled and halved lengthwise
2 tablespoons olive oil
2 tablespoons balsamic vinegar
1 tablespoon honey or maple syrup
Salt and pepper to taste
Fresh parsley for garnish

1. Preheat oven to 400°F (200°C).
2. In a small bowl, whisk together olive oil, balsamic vinegar, honey or maple syrup, salt, and pepper.
3. Place halved carrots on a baking sheet lined with parchment paper.
4. Drizzle balsamic glaze over the carrots, tossing to coat evenly.
5. Roast in the preheated oven for 20-25 minutes, or until carrots are tender and caramelized, stirring halfway through.
6. Garnish with fresh parsley before serving.
7. Serve hot.

Per serving
Calories: 60| Carbs: 8g| Fats: 3g| Protein: 1g

Lemon Herb Quinoa Salad

Time: 25 minutes| Difficulty: Easy| Serving 2

1 cup quinoa
2 cups vegetable broth
1 lemon, juiced and zest
2 tablespoons olive oil
1/4 cup chopped fresh parsley
1/4 cup chopped fresh mint
Salt and pepper to taste

1. Rinse quinoa under cold water, then combine with vegetable broth in a saucepan. Bring to a boil, then reduce heat to low, cover, and simmer for 15-20 minutes, or until quinoa is cooked and liquid is absorbed.
2. In a small bowl, whisk together lemon juice, lemon zest, olive oil, chopped fresh parsley, and chopped fresh mint.
3. Transfer cooked quinoa to a large bowl. Pour the lemon herb dressing over the quinoa and toss until evenly coated.
4. Season with salt and pepper to taste.
5. Serve chilled or at room temperature.

Per serving
Calories: 100| Carbs: 16g| Fats: 4g| Protein: 3g

Garlic Mashed Cauliflower

Time: 25 minutes| Difficulty: Easy| Serving 2

1 head cauliflower, chopped into florets
2 cloves garlic, minced
2 tablespoons olive oil
Salt and pepper to taste
Fresh chives for garnish (optional)

1. Steam cauliflower florets until tender, about 10-12 minutes.
2. Heat olive oil in a skillet over medium heat. Add minced garlic and sauté until fragrant, about 1-2 minutes.
3. Transfer steamed cauliflower to a food processor. Add sautéed garlic, olive oil, salt, and pepper. Blend until smooth and creamy.
4. Adjust seasoning to taste.
5. Garnish with fresh chives if desired.
6. Serve hot.

Per serving
Calories: 40| Carbs: 4g| Fats: 3g| Protein: 2g

Lemon Garlic Roasted Broccoli

Time: 20 minutes| Difficulty: Easy| Serving 2

1 pound broccoli florets
2 tablespoons olive oil
2 cloves garlic, minced
1 lemon, juiced and zest
Salt and pepper to taste

1. Preheat oven to 425°F (220°C).
2. Toss broccoli florets with olive oil, minced garlic, lemon juice, lemon zest, salt, and pepper in a bowl until evenly coated.
3. Spread broccoli florets in a single layer on a baking sheet lined with parchment paper.
4. Roast in the preheated oven for 15-20 minutes, or until broccoli is tender and slightly browned, stirring halfway through.
5. Serve hot.

Per serving
Calories: 40| Carbs: 6g| Fats: 2g| Protein: 2g

Steamed Asparagus

Time: 15 minutes| Difficulty: Easy| Serving 2

1 bunch asparagus, trimmed
Salt and pepper to taste
Lemon wedges for serving (optional)

1. Bring a pot of water to a boil.
2. Place trimmed asparagus in a steamer basket over the boiling water. Cover and steam for 5-7 minutes, or until asparagus is tender-crisp.
3. Season with salt and pepper to taste.
4. Serve hot with lemon wedges if desired.

Per serving
Calories: 20| Carbs: 4g| Fats: 0g| Protein: 2g

Grilled Portobello Mushroom Caps

Time: 20 minutes| Difficulty: Easy| Serving 2

4 large Portobello mushroom caps
2 tablespoons balsamic vinegar
2 tablespoons olive oil
2 cloves garlic, minced
Salt and pepper to taste
Fresh parsley for garnish

1. Preheat grill or grill pan to medium-high heat.
2. In a small bowl, whisk together balsamic vinegar, olive oil, minced garlic, salt, and pepper.
3. Brush both sides of Portobello mushroom caps with the balsamic mixture.
4. Grill mushroom caps for 5-7 minutes on each side, or until tender and grill marks appear.
5. Garnish with fresh parsley before serving.
6. Serve hot.

Per serving
Calories: 40| Carbs: 3g| Fats: 3g| Protein: 2g

Sauteed Spinach with Garlic and Lemon

Time: 15 minutes| Difficulty: Easy| Serving 2
8 ounces baby spinach
2 cloves garlic, minced
1 tablespoon olive oil
1 lemon, juiced and zest
1. Heat olive oil in a large skillet over medium heat. Add minced garlic and sauté until fragrant, about 1-2 minutes.
2. Add baby spinach to the skillet in batches, tossing until wilted.
3. Once all the spinach is wilted, add lemon juice and zest to the skillet. Stir well to combine.

Per serving
Calories: 20| Carbs: 2g| Fats: 1g| Protein: 2g

Garlic Roasted Cauliflower

Time: 25 minutes| Difficulty: Easy| Serving 2
1 head cauliflower, chopped into florets
2 tablespoons olive oil
2 cloves garlic, minced
1. Preheat oven to 425°F (220°C).
2. Toss cauliflower florets with olive oil, minced garlic, salt, and pepper in a bowl until evenly coated.
3. Spread cauliflower florets in a single layer on a baking sheet lined with parchment paper.
4. Roast in the preheated oven for 20-25 minutes, or until cauliflower is tender and caramelized, stirring halfway through.

Per serving
Calories: 40| Carbs: 6g| Fats: 2g| Protein: 2g

Baked Sweet Potato Fries

Time: 30 minutes| Difficulty: Easy| Serving 2
2 large sweet potatoes, cut into fries
2 tablespoons olive oil
1 teaspoon paprika
1/2 teaspoon garlic powder
1. Preheat oven to 425°F (220°C).
2. In a large bowl, toss sweet potato fries with olive oil, paprika, garlic powder, salt, and pepper until evenly coated.
3. Spread sweet potato fries in a single layer on a baking sheet lined with parchment paper.
4. Bake in the preheated oven for 25-30 minutes, or until fries are crispy and golden brown, flipping halfway through.

Per serving
Calories: 50| Carbohydrates: 8g| Fats: 2g| Protein: 1g

Steamed Green Beans with Almonds

Time: 20 minutes| Difficulty: Easy| Serving 2

1 pound green beans, trimmed
2 tablespoons sliced almonds
1 tablespoon olive oil
Salt and pepper to taste
Lemon wedges for serving (optional)

1. Bring a pot of water to a boil.
2. Place trimmed green beans in a steamer basket over the boiling water. Cover and steam for 5-7 minutes, or until green beans are tender-crisp.
3. While the green beans are steaming, heat olive oil in a skillet over medium heat. Add sliced almonds and toast until golden brown and fragrant, about 2-3 minutes.
4. Transfer steamed green beans to a serving dish. Drizzle with toasted almond slices.
5. Season with salt and pepper to taste.
6. Serve hot with lemon wedges if desired.

Per serving
Calories: 50| Carbs: 6g| Fats: 3g| Protein: 2g

Herb Roasted Potatoes

Time: 40 minutes| Difficulty: Easy| Serving 2

1 pound baby potatoes, halved
2 tablespoons olive oil
2 cloves garlic, minced
1 teaspoon dried rosemary
1 teaspoon dried thyme

1. Preheat oven to 400°F (200°C).
2. Toss halved baby potatoes with olive oil, minced garlic, dried rosemary, dried thyme, salt, and pepper in a bowl until evenly coated.
3. Spread potatoes in a single layer on a baking sheet lined with parchment paper.
4. Roast in the preheated oven for 30-35 minutes, or until potatoes are golden brown and crispy, stirring halfway through.

Per serving
Calories: 60| Carbs: 10g| Fats: 3g| Protein: 1g

Grilled Eggplant Slices

Time: 20 minutes| Difficulty: Easy| Serving 2

1 large eggplant, sliced into rounds
2 tablespoons olive oil
1 teaspoon dried oregano
1 teaspoon dried thyme
Salt and pepper to taste

1. Preheat grill or grill pan to medium-high heat.
2. Brush eggplant slices with olive oil on both sides.
3. Sprinkle dried oregano, dried thyme, salt, and pepper on both sides of eggplant slices.
4. Grill eggplant slices for 3-4 minutes on each side, or until tender and grill marks appear.
5. Serve hot.

Per serving
Calories: 40| Carbs: 6g| Fats: 2g| Protein: 1g

Lemon Garlic Green Beans

Time: 20 minutes| Difficulty: Easy| Serving 2

1 pound green beans, trimmed
2 cloves garlic, minced
2 tablespoons olive oil
1 lemon, juiced and zest
Salt and pepper to taste

1. Bring a pot of water to a boil.
2. Place trimmed green beans in a steamer basket over the boiling water. Cover and steam for 5-7 minutes, or until green beans are tender-crisp.
3. While the green beans are steaming, heat olive oil in a skillet over medium heat. Add minced garlic and sauté until fragrant, about 1-2 minutes.
4. Once the green beans are cooked, transfer them to the skillet with the garlic.
5. Add lemon juice and zest to the skillet. Stir well to combine.
6. Season with salt and pepper to taste.

Per serving
Calories: 30| Carbs: 4g| Fats: 2g| Protein: 1g

Oven-Roasted Tomatoes

Time: 35 minutes| Difficulty: Easy| Serving 2

1 pound cherry tomatoes
2 tablespoons olive oil
2 cloves garlic, minced
1 teaspoon dried basil
Salt and pepper to taste
Fresh basil for garnish

1. Preheat oven to 375°F (190°C).
2. Toss cherry tomatoes with olive oil, minced garlic, dried basil, salt, and pepper in a bowl until evenly coated.
3. Spread cherry tomatoes in a single layer on a baking sheet lined with parchment paper.
4. Roast in the preheated oven for 25-30 minutes, or until tomatoes are soft and caramelized, stirring halfway through.
5. Garnish with fresh basil before serving.
6. Serve hot or at room temperature.

Per serving
Calories: 40| Carbohydrates: 4g| Fats: 3g| Protein: 1g

Sauteed Mushrooms with Garlic and Herbs

Time: 20 minutes| Difficulty: Easy| Serving 2

8 ounces mushrooms, sliced
2 cloves garlic, minced
2 tablespoons olive oil
1 tablespoon chopped fresh parsley
1 tablespoon chopped fresh thyme
Salt and pepper to taste

1. Heat olive oil in a large skillet over medium heat. Add minced garlic and sauté until fragrant, about 1-2 minutes.
2. Add sliced mushrooms to the skillet. Cook until mushrooms are tender and golden brown, stirring occasionally.
3. Stir in chopped fresh parsley and chopped fresh thyme. Cook for an additional 1-2 minutes.
4. Season with salt and pepper to taste.
5. Serve hot.

Per serving
Calories: 30| Carbs: 2g| Fats: 3g| Protein: 1g

Herbed Roasted Carrots and Parsnips

Time: 30 minutes| Difficulty: Easy| Serving 2

1 pound carrots, peeled and cut into sticks
1 pound parsnips, peeled and cut into sticks
2 tablespoons olive oil
1 tablespoon chopped fresh rosemary
1 tablespoon chopped fresh thyme
Salt and pepper to taste

1. Preheat oven to 400°F (200°C).
2. Toss carrot sticks and parsnip sticks with olive oil, chopped fresh rosemary, chopped fresh thyme, salt, and pepper in a bowl until evenly coated.
3. Spread carrot and parsnip sticks in a single layer on a baking sheet lined with parchment paper.
4. Roast in the preheated oven for 25-30 minutes, or until vegetables are tender and caramelized, stirring halfway through.
5. Serve hot.

Per serving
Calories: 60| Carbs: 8g| Fats: 3g| Protein: 1g

Roasted Butternut Squash with Cinnamon

Time: 40 minutes| Difficulty: Easy| Serving 2

1 medium butternut squash, peeled, seeded, and cut into cubes
2 tablespoons olive oil
1 teaspoon ground cinnamon
Salt and pepper to taste

1. Preheat oven to 400°F (200°C).
2. Toss butternut squash cubes with olive oil, ground cinnamon, salt, and pepper in a bowl until evenly coated.
3. Spread butternut squash cubes in a single layer on a baking sheet lined with parchment paper.
4. Roast in the preheated oven for 30-35 minutes, or until squash is tender and caramelized, stirring halfway through.
5. Serve hot.

Per serving
Calories: 60| Carbs: 10g| Fats: 3g| Protein: 1g

Garlic Herb Roasted Potatoes

Time: 35 minutes| Difficulty: Easy| Serving 2

1 pound baby potatoes, halved
2 tablespoons olive oil
2 cloves garlic, minced
1 tablespoon chopped fresh rosemary
1 tablespoon chopped fresh thyme
Salt and pepper to taste

1. Preheat oven to 425°F (220°C).
2. Toss halved baby potatoes with olive oil, minced garlic, chopped fresh rosemary, chopped fresh thyme, salt, and pepper in a bowl until evenly coated.
3. Spread potatoes in a single layer on a baking sheet lined with parchment paper.
4. Roast in the preheated oven for 30-35 minutes, or until potatoes are golden brown and crispy, stirring halfway through.
5. Serve hot.

Per serving
Calories: 60| Carbs: 10g| Fats: 3g| Protein: 1g

Sauteed Kale with Garlic and Lemon

Time: 15 minutes| Difficulty: Easy| Serving 2

1 bunch kale, stems removed and leaves chopped
2 cloves garlic, minced
2 tablespoons olive oil
1 lemon, juiced and zest
Salt and pepper to taste

1. Heat olive oil in a large skillet over medium heat. Add minced garlic and sauté until fragrant, about 1-2 minutes.
2. Add chopped kale to the skillet. Cook until kale is wilted and tender, stirring occasionally.
3. Once the kale is cooked, add lemon juice and zest to the skillet. Stir well to combine.
4. Season with salt and pepper to taste.
5. Serve hot.

Per serving
Calories: 30| Carbs: 4g| Fats: 2g| Protein: 2g

Roasted Beet Salad with Goat Cheese and Walnuts

Time: 50 minutes| Difficulty: Intermediate| Serving 2

2 large beets, peeled and diced
2 tablespoons olive oil
Salt and pepper to taste
2 cups mixed greens
1/4 cup crumbled goat cheese
1/4 cup chopped walnuts
Balsamic glaze for drizzling

1. Preheat oven to 400°F (200°C).
2. Toss diced beets with olive oil, salt, and pepper in a bowl until evenly coated.
3. Spread beets in a single layer on a baking sheet lined with parchment paper.
4. Roast in the preheated oven for 40-45 minutes, or until beets are tender and caramelized, stirring halfway through.
5. In a serving bowl, arrange mixed greens. Top with roasted beets, crumbled goat cheese, and chopped walnuts.
6. Drizzle balsamic glaze over the salad before serving.
7. Serve warm or at room temperature.

Per serving:
Calories: 70| Carbs: 6g| Fats: 5g| Protein: 2g

Grilled Asparagus with Lemon and Parmesan

Time: 15 minutes| Difficulty: Easy| Serving 2

1 pound asparagus, trimmed
2 tablespoons olive oil
1 lemon, juiced and zest
1/4 cup grated Parmesan cheese
Salt and pepper to taste

1. Preheat grill or grill pan to medium-high heat.
2. Toss trimmed asparagus with olive oil, lemon juice, lemon zest, salt, and pepper in a bowl until evenly coated.
3. Grill asparagus spears for 3-4 minutes on each side, or until tender and grill marks appear.
4. Transfer grilled asparagus to a serving platter. Sprinkle grated Parmesan cheese on top.
5. Serve hot.

Per serving:
Calories: 50| Carbs: 4g| Fats: 4g| Protein: 3g

Roasted Brussels Sprouts with Balsamic Glaze

Time: 30 minutes| Difficulty: Easy| Serving 2

1 pound Brussels sprouts, trimmed and halved
2 tablespoons olive oil
Salt and pepper to taste
2 tablespoons balsamic glaze

1. Preheat oven to 400°F (200°C).
2. Toss halved Brussels sprouts with olive oil, salt, and pepper in a bowl until evenly coated.
3. Spread Brussels sprouts in a single layer on a baking sheet lined with parchment paper.
4. Roast in the preheated oven for 25-30 minutes, or until Brussels sprouts are tender and caramelized, stirring halfway through.
5. Drizzle roasted Brussels sprouts with balsamic glaze before serving.
6. Serve hot.

Per serving:
Calories: 50| Carbs: 6g| Fats: 3g| Protein: 2g

2.8 Snacks and Appetizers

Roasted Chickpeas

Time: 40 minutes| Difficulty: Easy| Serving 2
1 can (15 ounces) chickpeas, drained and rinsed
1 tablespoon olive oil
1 teaspoon ground cumin and 1 teaspoon paprika
1/2 teaspoon garlic powder
1. Preheat oven to 400°F (200°C).
2. Pat chickpeas dry with paper towels to remove excess moisture.
3. In a bowl, toss chickpeas with olive oil, ground cumin, paprika, garlic powder, salt, and pepper until evenly coated.
4. Spread chickpeas in a single layer on a baking sheet lined with parchment paper.
5. Roast in the preheated oven for 30-35 minutes, or until chickpeas are crispy, stirring halfway through.
6. Allow roasted chickpeas to cool before serving.

Per serving
Calories: 60| Carbs: 10g| Fats: 2g| Protein: 3g

Caprese Skewers with Balsamic Glaze

Time: 15 minutes| Difficulty: Easy| Serving 2

Cherry tomatoes and Fresh basil leaves
Fresh mozzarella balls
Balsamic glaze
1. Thread one cherry tomato, one mozzarella-ball, and one fresh basil leaf onto each skewer.
2. Arrange the skewers on a serving platter.
3. Drizzle with balsamic glaze just before serving.

Per serving
Calories: 30| Carbs: 2g| Fats: 2g| Protein: 2g

Stuffed Mini Bell Peppers

Time: 20 minutes| Difficulty: Easy| Serving 2
Mini bell peppers, halved and seeds removed
Hummus
Cherry tomatoes, halved
Fresh parsley, chopped
1. Fill each mini bell pepper half with a spoonful of hummus.
2. Top with a halved cherry tomato.
3. Garnish with chopped fresh parsley.
4. Serve chilled or at room temperature.

Per serving (2 stuffed pepper halves)
Calories: 50| Carbs: 6g| Fats: 2g| Protein: 2g

Avocado Hummus with Whole Wheat Pita Chips

Time: 15 minutes| Difficulty: Easy| Serving 2

1 ripe avocado, peeled and pitted
1 can (15 ounces) chickpeas, drained and rinsed
2 tablespoons tahini
2 tablespoons lemon juice
1 clove garlic, minced
2 tablespoons olive oil
Salt and pepper to taste
Whole wheat pita bread, cut into wedges and toasted

1. In a food processor, combine ripe avocado, chickpeas, tahini, lemon juice, minced garlic, olive oil, salt, and pepper.
2. Blend until smooth and creamy.
3. Serve the avocado hummus with toasted whole wheat pita wedges for dipping.

Per serving
Calories: 80| Carbs: 10g| Fats: 4g| Protein: 3g

Cauliflower Buffalo Bites

Time: 30 minutes| Difficulty: Intermediate| Serving 2

1 head cauliflower, cut into florets
1/2 cup buffalo sauce
1 tablespoon melted butter or olive oil
1/2 teaspoon garlic powder
Ranch or blue cheese dressing for dipping

1. Preheat oven to 425°F (220°C). Line a baking sheet with parchment paper.
2. In a bowl, whisk together buffalo sauce, melted butter or olive oil, and garlic powder.
3. Toss cauliflower florets in the buffalo sauce mixture until evenly coated.
4. Spread coated cauliflower florets in a single layer on the prepared baking sheet.
5. Bake for 20-25 minutes, or until cauliflower is tender and edges are crispy.
6. Serve hot with ranch or blue cheese dressing for dipping.

Per serving
Calories: 50| Carbs: 5g| Fats: 3g| Protein: 2g

Guacamole Stuffed Mini Peppers

Time: 15 minutes| Difficulty: Easy| Serving 2

Mini sweet peppers, halved and seeded
Ripe avocado, mashed
Cherry tomatoes, diced
Red onion, finely chopped
Jalapeño, seeded and minced (optional)
Lime juice
Salt and pepper to taste
Fresh cilantro for garnish

1. In a bowl, combine mashed avocado, diced cherry tomatoes, finely chopped red onion, minced jalapeño (if using), lime juice, salt, and pepper.
2. Fill each mini pepper half with the guacamole mixture.
3. Garnish with fresh cilantro before serving.

Per serving: (2 stuffed mini peppers)
Calories:60| Carbs: 4g| Fats: 4g| Protein: 2g

Mediterranean Stuffed Dates

Time: 10 minutes| Difficulty: Easy| Serving 2

Medjool dates, pitted
Soft goat cheese
Walnut halves

1. Stuff each pitted date with a small amount of soft goat cheese.
2. Press a walnut half on top of the goat cheese.
3. Arrange stuffed dates on a serving platter.

Per serving (2 stuffed dates)
Calories: 80| Carbs: 12g| Fats: 3g| Protein: 2g

Smoked Salmon Cucumber Bites

Time: 10 minutes| Difficulty: Easy| Serving 2

English cucumber, sliced into rounds
Smoked salmon slices
Cream cheese
Fresh dill for garnish

1. Spread a thin layer of cream cheese on each cucumber round.
2. Top with a piece of smoked salmon.
3. Garnish with fresh dill before serving.

Per serving (2 cucumber bites)
Calories: 40| Carbs: 2g| Fats: 3g| Protein: 3g

Greek Yogurt Dip with Veggies

Time: 10 minutes| Difficulty: Easy| Serving 2

1 cup Greek yogurt
1 tablespoon lemon juice
1 clove garlic, minced
1 tablespoon chopped fresh dill
Salt and pepper to taste
Assorted vegetables for dipping (carrots, cucumber, bell peppers, etc.)

1. In a mixing bowl, combine Greek yogurt, lemon juice, minced garlic, chopped fresh dill, salt, and pepper.
2. Stir until well combined.
3. Serve the yogurt dip with assorted vegetables for dipping.

Per serving
Calories: 50| Carbs: 4g| Fats: 1g| Protein: 6g

Cucumber Slices with Herbed Cream Cheese

Time: 10 minutes| Difficulty: Easy| Serving 2

English cucumber, sliced into rounds
Cream cheese
Fresh herbs (dill, chives, parsley, etc.)
Salt and pepper to taste

1. Spread a thin layer of cream cheese on each cucumber round.
2. Sprinkle with chopped fresh herbs.
3. Season with salt and pepper to taste.
4. Serve chilled.

Per serving
Calories: 50| Carbs: 2g| Fats: 4g| Protein: 2g

Apple Slices with Low-Fat Cheese

Time: 5 minutes| Difficulty: Easy| Serving 2

1 medium apple, sliced
2 slices of low-fat cheese (such as mozzarella or cheddar)

1. Wash and slice the apple into thin slices.
2. Cut the low-fat cheese slices into smaller pieces or strips.
3. Arrange the apple slices and cheese on a plate or in a portable container.
4. Serve and enjoy as a simple and satisfying snack.

Per serving
Calories: 120| Protein: 6g| Carbs: 15g| Fat: 4g| Fiber: 3g

Baked Zucchini Fries

Time: 30 minutes| Difficulty: Intermediate| Serving 2
2 medium zucchinis, cut into fries
1/2 cup breadcrumbs
1/4 cup grated Parmesan cheese
1 teaspoon Italian seasoning
Salt and pepper to taste
1 egg, beaten
Cooking spray

1. Preheat oven to 425°F (220°C). Line a baking sheet with parchment paper and lightly coat with cooking spray.
2. In a shallow dish, combine breadcrumbs, Parmesan cheese, Italian seasoning, salt, and pepper.
3. Dip zucchini fries into beaten egg, then coat with breadcrumb mixture.
4. Place coated zucchini fries on the prepared baking sheet in a single layer.
5. Bake for 20-25 minutes, or until golden brown and crispy.
6. Serve hot with your favorite dipping sauce.

Per serving (6 zucchini fries)
Calories: 70| Carbs: 10g| Fats: 2g| Protein: 4g

Cucumber Avocado Rolls

Time: 15 minutes| Difficulty: Easy| Serving 2
English cucumber
Avocado
Red bell pepper, thinly sliced
Carrot, thinly sliced
Alfalfa sprouts
Hummus
Sesame seeds for garnish (optional)

1. Using a vegetable peeler, slice the cucumber lengthwise into thin strips.
2. Spread a thin layer of hummus on each cucumber strip.
3. Place a few slices of avocado, red bell pepper, carrot, and a small handful of alfalfa sprouts at one end of the cucumber strip.
4. Roll up the cucumber strip tightly, enclosing the filling.
5. Secure with a toothpick if necessary.
6. Sprinkle with sesame seeds for garnish if desired.
7. Serve chilled.

Per serving (2 cucumber rolls)
Calories: 60| Carbs: 5g| Fats: 4g| Protein: 2g

Quinoa and Black Bean Stuffed Mushrooms

Time: 30 minutes| Difficulty: Intermediate| Serving 2

Large mushrooms, stems removed
Cooked quinoa
Black beans, drained and rinsed
Salsa
Shredded cheese (optional)
Fresh cilantro for garnish

1. Preheat oven to 375°F (190°C). Line a baking sheet with parchment paper.
2. In a bowl, combine cooked quinoa, black beans, and salsa.
3. Stuff each mushroom cap with the quinoa and black bean mixture.
4. If desired, sprinkle shredded cheese on top of each stuffed mushroom.
5. Place stuffed mushrooms on the prepared baking sheet.
6. Bake for 20-25 minutes, or until mushrooms are tender and filling is heated through.
7. Garnish with fresh cilantro before serving.

Per serving (2 stuffed mushrooms)
Calories: 70| Carbs: 10g|Fats: 2g| Protein: 4g

Hummus with Veggie Sticks

Time: 15 minutes| Difficulty: Easy| Serving 2

1 cup shelled hummus, cooked and cooled
1 tablespoon tahini
2 cloves garlic, minced
2 tablespoons lemon juice
2 tablespoons olive oil
Salt and pepper to taste
Assorted veggie sticks (carrots, celery, bell peppers, etc.)
for dipping

1. In a food processor, combine cooked hummus, tahini, minced garlic, lemon juice, olive oil, salt, and pepper.
2. Blend until smooth and creamy, adding water as needed to reach desired consistency.
3. Transfer hummus to a serving bowl.
4. Serve with assorted veggie sticks for dipping.

Per serving (2 tablespoons hummus with veggies)
Calories: 50| Carbs: 4g| Fats: 3g| Protein: 3g

Spinach and Artichoke Dip with Whole Wheat Pita Chips

Time: 30 minutes| Difficulty: Intermediate | Serving 2

1 cup frozen chopped spinach, thawed and drained
1 can (14 ounces) artichoke hearts, drained and chopped
1/2 cup plain Greek yogurt
1/4 cup grated Parmesan cheese
1/4 cup shredded mozzarella cheese
1/4 teaspoon garlic powder
Salt and pepper to taste
Whole wheat pita bread, cut into wedges and toasted

1. Preheat oven to 375°F (190°C).
2. In a mixing bowl, combine chopped spinach, chopped artichoke hearts, Greek yogurt, grated Parmesan cheese, shredded mozzarella cheese, garlic powder, salt, and pepper.
3. Transfer the mixture to a baking dish.
4. Bake for 20-25 minutes, or until bubbly and golden brown on top.
5. Serve hot with whole wheat pita chips for dipping

Per serving (2 tablespoons dip with pita chips)
Calories: 80| Carbs: 10g| Fats: 3g| Protein: 5g

Trail Mix

Time: 5 minutes| Difficulty: Easy| Serving 2

1/2 cup almonds
1/2 cup cashews
1/4 cup dried cranberries
1/4 cup pumpkin seeds
1/4 cup dark chocolate chips (optional)

1. In a mixing bowl, combine all the ingredients.
2. Toss gently to mix evenly.
3. Divide the trail mix into two servings and transfer to portable containers.
4. Enjoy as a convenient and energizing snack on the go.

Per serving
Calories: 300| Protein: 8g| Carbs: 20g| Fat: 20g| Fiber: 5g

Avocado Cucumber Rolls

Time: 15 minutes| Difficulty: Easy| Serving 2
English cucumber
Avocado
Red bell pepper, thinly sliced
Carrot, thinly sliced
Alfalfa sprouts
Hummus
Sesame seeds for garnish (optional)

1. Using a vegetable peeler, slice the cucumber lengthwise into thin strips.
2. Spread a thin layer of hummus on each cucumber strip.
3. Place a few slices of avocado, red bell pepper, carrot, and a small handful of alfalfa sprouts at one end of the cucumber strip.
4. Roll up the cucumber strips tightly, enclosing the filling.
5. Secure with a toothpick if necessary.
6. Sprinkle with sesame seeds for garnish if desired.
7. Serve chilled.

Per serving (2 cucumber rolls)
Calories: 60| Carbs: 5g| Fats: 4g| Protein: 2g

Greek Yogurt with Berries and Almonds

Time: 5 minutes| Difficulty: Easy| Serving 2
1 cup Greek yogurt
1/2 cup mixed berries (such as strawberries, blueberries, and raspberries)
1/4 cup almonds, sliced or chopped

1. In serving bowls or jars, divide the Greek yogurt evenly.
2. Top each portion of Greek yogurt with mixed berries and almonds.
3. Serve immediately or store in the refrigerator until ready to eat.

Per serving
Calories: 200| Protein: 15g| Carbs: 15g| Fat: 10g\ Fiber: 4g

Banana Slices with Almond Butter

Time: 5 minutes| Difficulty: Easy| Serving 2

1 banana, sliced
2 tablespoons almond butter

1. Spread almond butter on banana slices.
2. Arrange the banana slices on a plate or in a portable container.
3. Serve immediately for a delicious and satisfying snack.

Per serving
Calories: 220| Protein: 5g| Carbs: 25g| Fat: 12g| Fiber: 4g

Cherry Tomatoes with Cottage Cheese

Time: 5 minutes| Difficulty: Easy| Serving 2

1 cup cherry tomatoes
1/2 cup cottage cheese

1. Wash the cherry tomatoes and place them in a bowl.
2. Serve the cherry tomatoes with cottage cheese on the side.
3. Enjoy this refreshing and protein-rich snack option.

Per serving
Calories: 120| Protein: 10g| Carbs: 10g| Fat: 4g| Fiber: 2g

Cucumber Slices with Tzatziki

Time: 5 minutes| Difficulty: Easy| Serving 2

1 cucumber, sliced
1/2 cup tzatziki sauce

1. Wash and slice the cucumber.
2. Serve the cucumber slices with tzatziki sauce for dipping.
3. Enjoy this refreshing and flavorful snack option.

Per serving
Calories: 70| Protein: 2g| Carbs: 8g| Fat: 4g| Fiber: 1g

2.9 Desserts Recipes

Whole Wheat Banana Pancakes

Time: 15 minutes| Difficulty: Easy| Serving 2

1 ripe banana, mashed
2 eggs
1/2 cup whole wheat flour
1/4 cup almond milk
1/2 teaspoon baking powder
1/4 teaspoon cinnamon
1/4 teaspoon vanilla extract
Butter or oil for cooking

1. In a mixing bowl, whisk together mashed banana, eggs, whole wheat flour, almond milk, baking powder, cinnamon, and vanilla extract until smooth.
2. Heat a non-stick skillet over medium heat and add butter or oil.
3. Pour pancake batter onto the skillet to form small pancakes.
4. Cook for 2-3 minutes on each side, until golden brown and cooked through.
5. Serve warm with your favorite toppings, such as sliced fruit or a drizzle of honey.

Per serving
Calories: 250| Protein: 10g| Carbs: 30g| Fat: 10g| Fiber: 4g

Almond Flour Pancakes

Time: 15 minutes| Difficulty: Easy| Serving 2

1 cup almond flour and 1/4 cup almond milk
2 eggs
1 tablespoon honey (optional)
1/2 teaspoon baking powder
Pinch of salt and Oil for cooking

1. In a mixing bowl, whisk almond flour, eggs, almond milk, honey (if using), baking powder, and salt until well combined.
2. Heat a non-stick skillet over medium heat and add oil.
3. Pour pancake batter onto the skillet to form small pancakes.
4. Cook for 2-3 minutes on each side, until golden brown and cooked through.
5. Serve warm with your favourite toppings, such as fresh berries or a drizzle of honey.

Per serving
Calories: 250| Protein: 8g| Carbs: 15g| Fat: 18g| Fiber: 3g

Mixed Berry Parfait

Time: 10 minutes| Difficulty: Easy| Serving 2

1 cup Greek yogurt (unsweetened)
1 cup mixed berries (strawberries, blueberries, raspberries)
2 tablespoons granola and 1 tablespoon honey (optional)

1. In two serving glasses, layer Greek yogurt, mixed berries, and granola (if using), repeating until glasses are filled.
2. Drizzle honey or maple syrup over the top if desired.

Per serving
Calories: 120| Carbs: 15g| Fats: 3g| Protein: 10g

Berry Chia Seed Pudding

Time: 10 minutes (plus chilling time)|Difficulty: Easy| For 2

1/4 cup chia seeds
1 cup unsweetened almond milk
1 tablespoon maple syrup or honey
1/2 teaspoon vanilla extract
Mixed berries for topping

1. In a bowl, whisk together chia seeds, almond milk, maple syrup or honey, and vanilla extract.
2. Cover and refrigerate for at least 2 hours or overnight, until the mixture thickens to a pudding-like consistency.
3. Serve topped with mixed berries.

Per serving
Calories: 120| Carbs: 15g| Fats: 5g| Protein: 4g

Whole Wheat Banana Bread

Time: 1 hour| Difficulty: Moderate| Serving 2

2 ripe bananas, mashed
1/4 cup honey or maple syrup
1/4 cup olive oil
2 eggs
1 teaspoon vanilla extract
1 1/2 cups whole wheat flour
1 teaspoon baking powder
1/2 teaspoon baking soda
1/2 teaspoon cinnamon
Pinch of salt
Chopped nuts or chocolate chips for topping (optional)

1. Preheat the oven to 350°F (175°C) and grease a loaf pan with olive oil.
2. In a mixing bowl, whisk together mashed bananas, honey or maple syrup, olive oil, eggs, and vanilla extract until well combined.
3. In a separate bowl, combine whole wheat flour, baking powder, baking soda, cinnamon, and salt.
4. Gradually add the dry ingredients to the wet ingredients, stirring until just combined.
5. Pour the batter into the prepared loaf pan and smooth the top with a spatula.
6. If desired, sprinkle chopped nuts or chocolate chips over the top of the batter.
7. Bake for 45-50 minutes, or until a toothpick inserted into the center comes out clean.
8. Allow the banana bread to cool in the pan for 10 minutes before transferring it to a wire rack to cool completely.
9. Slice and serve warm or at room temperature.

Per serving
Calories: 200| Protein: 6g| Carbs: 30g|Fat: 7g| Fiber: 4g

Mediterranean Egg Muffins

Time: 20 minutes| Difficulty: Easy| Serving 2

6 large eggs
1/2 cup chopped spinach
1/4 cup diced tomatoes
1/4 cup crumbled feta cheese
2 tablespoons chopped olives
Salt and pepper to taste
Olive oil for greasing muffin tin

1. Preheat the oven to 350°F (175°C) and grease a muffin tin with olive oil.
2. In a mixing bowl, whisk together eggs, salt, and pepper until well beaten.
3. Stir in chopped spinach, diced tomatoes, crumbled feta cheese, and chopped olives.
4. Pour the egg mixture into the prepared muffin tin, filling each cup about two-thirds full.
5. Bake for 15-20 minutes, or until the egg muffins are set and golden brown on top.
6. Remove from the oven and let them cool slightly before serving.
7. Serve warm or at room temperature, and enjoy these protein-packed egg muffins!

Per serving
Calories: 180| Protein: 12g| Carbs: 4g| Fat: 12g| Fiber: 2g

Lemon Coconut Bliss Balls

Time: 15 minutes (plus chilling time)| Difficulty: Easy| for 2

1/2 cup raw cashews
1/2 cup unsweetened shredded coconut
2 tablespoons coconut oil, melted
Zest and juice of 1 lemon
1 tablespoon maple syrup or honey
Pinch of salt

1. In a food processor, combine raw cashews, shredded coconut, melted coconut oil, lemon zest, lemon juice, maple syrup or honey, and a pinch of salt.
2. Process until mixture comes together and forms dough.
3. Roll the dough into small balls.
4. Place bliss balls on a plate and chill in the refrigerator for at least 30 minutes before serving.

Per serving (2 bliss balls)
Calories: 120|Carbs: 7g| Fats: 10g| Protein: 2g

Banana Oatmeal Muffins

Time: 25 minutes| Difficulty: Easy| Serving 2

2 ripe bananas, mashed
1 cup rolled oats
1/4 cup almond flour
2 eggs
1/4 cup honey or maple syrup
1 teaspoon baking powder
1/2 teaspoon cinnamon
Pinch of salt

1. Preheat the oven to 350°F (175°C) and line a muffin tin with paper liners.
2. In a large mixing bowl, combine mashed bananas, rolled oats, almond flour, eggs, honey or maple syrup, baking powder, cinnamon, and salt. Mix until well combined.
3. Spoon the batter into the prepared muffin tin, filling each cup about two-thirds full.
4. Bake for 20-25 minutes, until the muffins are golden brown and a toothpick inserted into the center comes out clean.
5. Allow the muffins to cool in the tin for 5 minutes, then transfer to a wire rack to cool completely.

Per serving
Calories: 200| Protein: 6g| Carbs: 30g| Fat: 7g| Fiber: 4g

Coconut Mango Popsicles

Time: 10 minutes (plus freezing time)| Difficulty: Easy| For 2

1 ripe mango, peeled and diced
1/2 cup coconut milk (canned or homemade)
1 tablespoon maple syrup or honey
Unsweetened shredded coconut for topping (optional)

1. In a blender, combine diced mango, coconut milk, and maple syrup or honey.
2. Blend until smooth.
3. Pour the mixture into popsicle molds.
4. Insert popsicle sticks and freeze for at least 4 hours or until firm.
5. Before serving, sprinkle with shredded coconut if desired.

Per serving (1 popsicle)
Calories: Approximately 70| Carbs: 10g| Fats: 4g| Protein: 1g

Coconut Chia Seed Pudding

Time: 10 minutes (plus chilling time)| Difficulty: Easy| For 2
1/4 cup chia seeds
1 cup coconut milk (canned or homemade)
1 tablespoon maple syrup or honey
1/2 teaspoon vanilla extract
Shredded coconut for topping

1. In a bowl, whisk together chia seeds, coconut milk, maple syrup or honey, and vanilla extract.
2. Cover and refrigerate for at least 2 hours or overnight, until the mixture thickens to a pudding-like consistency.
3. Serve topped with shredded coconut.

Per serving
Calories: 130| Carbs: 10g| Fats: 10g| Protein: 3g

Zucchini and Carrot Breakfast Muffins

Time: 25 minutes| Difficulty: Easy| Serving 2
1 cup grated zucchini
1 cup grated carrot
1/4 cup chopped nuts (such as walnuts or pecans)
1/4 cup raisins or dried cranberries
2 eggs
1/4 cup honey or maple syrup
1/4 cup olive oil
1 teaspoon vanilla extract
1 cup whole wheat flour
1 teaspoon baking powder
1/2 teaspoon baking soda
1/2 teaspoon cinnamon

1. Preheat the oven to 350°F (175°C) and line a muffin tin with paper liners.
2. In a mixing bowl, combine grated zucchini, grated carrot, chopped nuts, and raisins or dried cranberries.
3. In a separate bowl, whisk together eggs, honey or maple syrup, olive oil, and vanilla extract.
4. Gradually add the wet ingredients to the dry ingredients, stirring until just combined.
5. Spoon the batter into the prepared muffin tin, filling each cup about two-thirds full.
6. Bake for 20-25 minutes, or until the muffins are golden brown and a toothpick inserted into the center comes out clean.
7. Allow the muffins to cool in the tin for 5 minutes before transferring them to a wire rack to cool completely.

Per serving
Calories: 220|Protein: 6g| Carbs: 30g| Fat: 10g| Fiber: 5g

Banana Oat Cookies

Time: 20 minutes| Difficulty: Easy| Serving 2

1 ripe banana, mashed
1 cup rolled oats
2 tablespoons almond butter
1 tablespoon maple syrup or honey
1/2 teaspoon vanilla extract
Pinch of cinnamon (optional)

1. Preheat oven to 350°F (175°C) and line a baking sheet with parchment paper.
2. In a bowl, combine mashed banana, rolled oats, almond butter, maple syrup or honey, vanilla extract, and cinnamon (if using).
3. Drop spoonful of the mixture onto the prepared baking sheet and flatten slightly with the back of a spoon.
4. Bake for 12-15 minutes, or until cookies are golden brown around the edges.
5. Let cool before serving.

Per serving (2 cookies)
Calories: 100| Carbs: 15g| Fats: 3g| Protein: 2g

Baked Apples with Cinnamon

Time: 30 minutes| Difficulty: Easy| Serving 2

2 apples, cored
2 tablespoons almond butter
1 tablespoon maple syrup or honey
1/2 teaspoon cinnamon
Chopped nuts for topping (optional)

1. Preheat oven to 375°F (190°C) and line a baking dish with parchment paper.
2. Place cored apples in the prepared baking dish.
3. In a small bowl, mix together almond butter, maple syrup or honey, and cinnamon.
4. Stuff each apple with the almond butter mixture.
5. Bake for 20-25 minutes, or until apples are tender.
6. Serve hot, sprinkled with chopped nuts if desired.

Per serving
Calories: 150| Carbs: 20g| Fats: 7g| Protein: 2g

Chocolate Avocado Mousse

Time: 15 minutes| Difficulty: Easy| Serving 2
1 ripe avocado
2 tablespoons cocoa powder
2 tablespoons maple syrup or honey
1/2 teaspoon vanilla extract and Pinch of salt
Berries or chopped nuts for topping (optional)

1. Scoop the flesh of the avocado into a blender or food processor.
2. Add cocoa powder, maple syrup or honey, vanilla extract, and a pinch of salt.
3. Blend until smooth and creamy, scraping down the sides as needed.
4. Divide the mousse into serving dishes and chill in the refrigerator for at least 30 minutes.
5. Serve topped with berries or chopped nuts if desired.

Per serving
Calories:150| Carbs: 15g| Fats: 10g| Protein: 2g

Apple Nachos

Time: 10 minutes| Difficulty: Easy| Serving 2
1 apple, thinly sliced
2 tablespoons almond butter
2 tablespoons dark chocolate chips
Chopped nuts for topping (optional)
Shredded coconut for topping (optional)

1. Arrange apple slices on a serving plate.
2. Drizzle almond butter over the apple slices.
3. Sprinkle dark chocolate chips, chopped nuts, and shredded coconut over the top if desired.

Per serving
Calories: 120| Carbs: 15g| Fats: 7g| Protein: 2g

Vanilla Coconut Rice Pudding

Time: 40 minutes| Difficulty: Easy| Serving 2
1/2 cup white rice
2 cups coconut milk (canned or homemade)
1/4 cup maple syrup or honey
1 teaspoon vanilla extract and Pinch of salt
Ground cinnamon for topping (optional)

1. In a saucepan, combine rice, coconut milk, maple syrup or honey, vanilla extract, and a pinch of salt.
2. Bring to a boil, then reduce heat and simmer, stirring occasionally, for 30-35 minutes, or until rice is cooked and mixture thickens.
3. Remove from heat and let cool slightly.
4. Serve warm or chilled, optionally topped with ground cinnamon.

Per serving
Calories: 200| Carbs: 25g| Fats: 10g| Protein: 2g

Cinnamon Baked Pears

Time: 30 minutes| Difficulty: Easy| Serving 2
2 ripe pears, halved and cored, 1 tbs. coconut oil, melted
1 tbs. maple syrup and 1/2 teaspoon cinnamon
1. Preheat oven to 375°F (190°C) and line a baking dish with parchment paper.
2. Place pear halves in the prepared baking dish.
3. In a small bowl, mix together melted coconut oil, maple syrup or honey, and cinnamon.
4. Drizzle the mixture over the pear halves.
5. Bake for 20-25 minutes, or until pears are tender.

Per serving
Calories: 120| Carbs: 20g| Fats: 5g| Protein: 1g

Chocolate Almond Date Balls

Time: 15 min (plus chilling time)| Difficulty: Easy| Serving 2
1/2 cup almonds and 1/2 cup pitted dates
2 tablespoons cocoa powder
1 tablespoon almond butter and Pinch of salt
1. In a food processor, pulse almonds until finely chopped.
2. Add pitted dates, cocoa powder, almond butter, and a pinch of salt.
3. Process until mixture comes together and forms dough.
4. Roll the dough into small balls.
5. Place date balls on a plate and chill in the refrigerator for at least 30 minutes before serving.

Per serving (2 date balls)
Calories: 100|Carbs: 12g| Fats: 6g|Protein: 3g

Blueberry Oatmeal Cookies

Time: 20 min (plus chilling time)| Difficulty: Easy| Serving 2
1/2 cup rolled oats
1/4 cup almond flour and 1/4 cup dried blueberries
2 tbs. honey and 1 tbs. coconut oil, melted
1/2 teaspoon vanilla extract and Pinch of cinnamon
1. Preheat oven to 350°F (175°C) and line a baking sheet with parchment paper.
2. In a bowl, mix together rolled oats, almond flour, dried blueberries, maple syrup or honey, melted coconut oil, vanilla extract, and cinnamon (if using).
3. Form the mixture into small cookies and place them on the prepared baking sheet.
4. Flatten each cookie slightly with the back of a spoon.
5. Bake for 12-15 minutes, or until cookies are golden brown.

Per serving (2 cookies)
Calories: 120| Carbs: 15g| Fats: 6g| Protein: 2g

Pumpkin Spice Energy Balls

Time: 20 min (plus chilling time) | Difficulty: Easy | Serving 2
1/2 cup rolled oats and 1/4 cup pumpkin puree
2 tablespoons almond butter
1 tablespoon maple syrup and
Unsweetened shredded coconut for rolling (optional)
1. In a mixing bowl, combine rolled oats, pumpkin puree, almond butter, maple syrup, and pumpkin pie spice.
2. Mix until well combined.
3. Roll the mixture into small balls.
4. Roll each ball in shredded coconut if desired.
5. Place energy balls on a plate and chill in the refrigerator for at least 30 minutes before serving.

Per serving (2 energy balls)
Calories: 100| Carbs: 12g| Fats: 5g| Protein: 2g

Chocolate Covered Strawberries

Time: 15 min (plus chilling time)| Difficulty: Easy| Serving 2
1 cup strawberries, washed and dried
2 ounces dark chocolate, chopped and 1 tsp. coconut oil
1. In a microwave-safe bowl, combine chopped dark chocolate and coconut oil.
2. Microwave in 30-second intervals, stirring between each interval, until chocolate is melted and smooth.
3. Dip each strawberry into the melted chocolate, coating evenly.
4. Place dipped strawberries on a parchment-lined baking sheet.
5. Chill in the refrigerator for at least 30 minutes, or until chocolate is set.

Per serving (5 strawberries)
Calories: 100| Carbs: 12g| Fats: 6g| Protein: 2g

Peach and Almond Crisp

Time: 45 minutes| Difficulty: Easy| Serving 2
2 ripe peaches, sliced and 1/4 cup almond flour
1/4 cup rolled oats
2 tbs. coconut oil, melted and 2 tbs. honey
1/2 teaspoon cinnamon and Pinch of salt
1. Preheat oven to 350°F (175°C) and grease a baking dish.
2. Place sliced peaches in the prepared baking dish.
3. In a bowl, combine almond flour, rolled oats, melted coconut oil, maple syrup or honey, cinnamon, and a pinch of salt.
4. Sprinkle the mixture over the peaches.
5. Bake for 25-30 minutes, or until topping is golden brown and peaches are bubbly.

Per serving
Calories: 180| Carbs: 20g| Fats: 10g| Protein: 2g

2.10 Sauces

Lemon Herb Sauce

Time: 10 minutes| Difficulty: Easy| Serving 2
Juice of 2 lemons
1/4 cup olive oil
1/4 cup fresh parsley, finely chopped
1 tbsp. fresh chives, finely chopped
1 clove garlic, minced and Salt and pepper to taste
1. In a bowl, combine lemon juice, olive oil, parsley, chives, and garlic.
2. Whisk together until well blended.
3. Season with salt and pepper to taste.
4. Serve with grilled or steamed vegetables, fish, or chicken.

Per serving
Calories: 125| Protein: 0g| Fat: 14g| Carbs: 2g

Avocado Cilantro Sauce

Time: 10 minutes| Difficulty: Easy| Serving 2
1 ripe avocado, peeled and pitted
1/4 cup cilantro, chopped
Juice of 1 lime
1 clove garlic, minced
1/4 cup water (or more for desired consistency)
Salt to taste
1. Place avocado, cilantro, lime juice, garlic, and water in a blender.
2. Blend until smooth, adding more water if needed to reach desired consistency.
3. Season with salt.
4. Serve as a dip or drizzle over tacos, salads, or grilled meats.

Per serving
Calories: 80| Protein: 1g| Fat: 7g| Carbs: 4g

Ginger Soy Dressing

Time: 10 minutes| Difficulty: Easy| Serving 2
2 tbsp. soy sauce (low sodium)
1 tbsp. sesame oil
1 tbsp. rice vinegar
1 tbsp. honey
1 tsp. fresh ginger, grated
1 clove garlic, minced
1. In a small bowl, whisk together soy sauce, sesame oil, rice vinegar, honey, ginger, and garlic.
2. Mix until well combined.
3. Use as a dressing for salads or as a sauce for steamed or stir-fried vegetables.

Per serving
Calories: 60| Protein: 1g| Fat: 5g| Carbs: 4g

Mint Yogurt Sauce

Time: 10 minutes| Difficulty: Easy| Serving 2
Ingredients:
1 cup low-fat Greek yogurt
1/4 cup fresh mint, chopped
1 tablespoon lemon juice and Salt and pepper to taste
1. Combine yogurt, mint, and lemon juice in a bowl.
2. Season with salt and pepper, mix well.
3. Chill before serving with grilled lamb or vegetables.

Per serving
Calories: 30| Protein: 4g| Fat: 1g| Carbs: 3g

Carrot Ginger Sauce

Time: 20 minutes| Difficulty: Easy| Serving 2
1 cup carrot juice
1 tablespoon fresh ginger, grated
1 tablespoon honey
1 tablespoon apple cider vinegar
1. Combine all ingredients in a saucepan.
2. Simmer over low heat for 15 minutes.
3. Allow to cool and serve as a dressing or sauce for salads and meats.

Per serving
Calories: 45| Protein: 0g| Fat: 0g| Carbs: 11g

Cucumber Dill Sauce

Time: 10 minutes| Difficulty: Easy| Serving 2
1 cucumber, grated and drained
1 cup low-fat Greek yogurt
2 tablespoons fresh dill, chopped
1 tablespoon lemon juice
Salt and pepper to taste
1. Mix grated cucumber, yogurt, dill, and lemon juice in a bowl.
2. Season with salt and pepper.
3. Chill and serve with fish or as a dip.

Per serving
Calories: 25| Protein: 3g| Fat: 0g| Carbs: 4g

Balsamic Reduction

Time: 15 minutes| Difficulty: Easy| Serving 2
1 cup balsamic vinegar
1. Pour vinegar into a small saucepan.
2. Simmer over low heat until reduced by half.
3. Cool and drizzle over salads or roasted vegetables.

Per serving
Calories: 43| Protein: 0g|Fat: 0g| Carbs: 10g

Tomato Basil Sauce

Time: 30 minutes| Difficulty: Easy| Serving 2

1 can (14 oz.) diced tomatoes, no salt added
1/4 cup fresh basil, chopped
1 tbsp. olive oil
1 onion, finely chopped
2 cloves garlic, minced
Salt and pepper to taste

1. In a saucepan, heat olive oil over medium heat.
2. Add onion and garlic, sauté until soft.
3. Stir in diced tomatoes and simmer for 20 minutes.
4. Add chopped basil, salt, and pepper.
5. Blend with an immersion blender until smooth.
6. Serve over pasta or as a base for other dishes.

Per serving
Calories: 70| Protein: 1g| Fat: 5g| Carbs: 6g

Dill Yogurt Sauce

Time: 10 minutes| Difficulty: Easy| Serving 2

1 cup Greek yogurt, low-fat
1/4 cup fresh dill, finely chopped
Juice of 1 lemon
1 clove garlic, minced and Salt and pepper to taste

1. In a mixing bowl, combine Greek yogurt, dill, lemon juice, and garlic.
2. Stir well until all ingredients are evenly distributed.
3. Season with salt and pepper.
4. Chill for at least 30 minutes before serving.
5. Ideal as a sauce for fish, potatoes, or as a vegetable dip.

Per serving
Calories: 35| Protein: 6g| Fat: 0.5g| Carbs: 2g

Greek Tzatziki

Time: 10 minutes| Difficulty: Easy| Serving 2

1 cup low-fat Greek yogurt
1 cucumber, peeled, seeded, and grated
2 cloves garlic, minced and 1 tablespoon olive oil
1 tablespoon dill, chopped
Juice of 1/2 lemon and Salt to taste

1. Squeeze excess water from grated cucumber.
2. Mix cucumber with yogurt, garlic, olive oil, dill, and lemon juice.
3. Season with salt.
4. Chill for at least 1 hour before serving.
5. Serve as a dip or over grilled meats.

Per serving
Calories: 35| Protein: 5g| Fat: 1.5g| Carbs: 3g

Chimichurri Sauce

Time: 10 minutes| Difficulty: Easy| Serving 2

1/2 cup parsley, finely chopped
2 tablespoons oregano, finely chopped
3 cloves garlic, minced
2 tablespoons red wine vinegar
1/4 cup olive oil and Salt and pepper to taste

1. Mix parsley, oregano, garlic, vinegar, and olive oil in a bowl.
2. Season with salt and pepper.
3. Let it sit for at least 10 minutes before serving.
4. Serve with grilled meats or vegetables.

Per serving
Calories: 120| Protein: 0g| Fat: 14g| Carbs: 1g

Sesame Ginger Sauce

Time: 10 minutes| Difficulty: Easy| Serving 2

2 tablespoons sesame oil
1 tablespoon soy sauce
1 tablespoon rice vinegar
1 tablespoon honey and 1 teaspoon grated ginger

1. Combine all ingredients in a small bowl.
2. Whisk until well combined.
3. Serve with Asian-inspired dishes like dumplings or stir-fry.

Per serving
Calories: 70| Protein: 0g| Fat: 7g| Carbs: 3g

Orange Rosemary Sauce

Time: 15 minutes| Difficulty: Easy| Serving 2

Juice of 1 orange and 1 teaspoon orange zest
1 tablespoon fresh rosemary, finely chopped
1 tablespoon honey

1. Combine orange juice, zest, rosemary, and honey in a saucepan.
2. Simmer over medium heat for 10 minutes.
3. Serve with poultry or pork.

Per serving
Calories: 30| Protein: 0g| Fat: 0g| Carbs: 8g

Pineapple Salsa

Time: 10 minutes| Difficulty: Easy| Serving 2

1 cup pineapple, finely chopped
1/4 cup red onion, finely chopped
1 jalapeño, seeded and finely chopped
1/4 cup cilantro, chopped and Juice of 1 lime

1. Combine pineapple, onion, jalapeño, cilantro, and lime juice in a bowl.
2. Mix well and chill before serving.
3. Serve with grilled chicken or fish.

Per serving
Calories: 35| Protein: 0g| Fat: 0g| Carbs: 9g

Roasted Red Pepper Sauce

Time: 15 minutes| Difficulty: Easy| Serving 2
1 cup roasted red peppers, drained and chopped
1 tablespoon olive oil
1 clove garlic, minced
1/4 teaspoon smoked paprika
1. Blend all ingredients until smooth.
2. Serve as a sauce for pasta, a spread for sandwiches, or a dip.
Per serving
Calories: 50| Protein: 0g| Fat: 3.5g| Carbs: 4g

Caramelized Onion Sauce

Time: 25 minutes| Difficulty: Medium| Serving 2
1 large onion, thinly sliced
1 tablespoon olive oil
1/2 cup beef or vegetable broth
Salt and pepper to taste
1. Heat olive oil in a pan, add onions, and cook on low heat until caramelized (about 20 minutes).
2. Add broth and simmer until reduced by half.
3. Blend until smooth, season with salt and pepper.
4. Serve with meat or vegetables.
Per serving
Calories: 60| Protein: 1g| Fat: 3.5g| Carbs: 6g

Coconut Curry Sauce

Time: 20 minutes| Difficulty: Easy| Serving 2
1 cup coconut milk (light)
1 tablespoon curry powder
1 teaspoon honey
1 clove garlic, minced and Salt to taste
1. Combine all ingredients in a saucepan.
2. Bring to a simmer and cook for 15 minutes.
3. Adjust seasoning and serve with rice or vegetables.
Per serving
Calories: 50| Protein: 1g| Fat: 4g| Carbs: 3g

Pesto Sauce

Time: 10 minutes| Difficulty: Easy| Serving 2
1 cup fresh basil leaves
1/4 cup pine nuts
2 tablespoons olive oil
1 garlic clove and Salt to taste
1. Blend basil, pine nuts, olive oil, and garlic until smooth.
2. Season with salt.
3. Serve with pasta, spread on sandwiches, or drizzle over roasted vegetables.
Per serving
Calories: 130| Protein: 2g| Fat: 13g| Carbs: 2g

Ginger Soy Sauce

Time: 10 minutes| Difficulty: Easy| Serving 2
1/4 cup soy sauce (low sodium)
1 tablespoon ginger, finely grated
1 tablespoon honey and 1 clove garlic, minced
1. Combine all ingredients in a small bowl.
2. Serve as a marinade or dipping sauce for sushi and other Asian dishes.
Per serving
Calories: 35| Protein: 1g| Fat: 0g| Carbs: 8g

Creamy Mustard Sauce

Time: 10 minutes| Difficulty: Easy| Serving 2
2 tablespoons Dijon mustard
1/4 cup low-fat Greek yogurt
1 tablespoon honey and 1 tablespoon lemon juice
1. Whisk together mustard, yogurt, honey, and lemon juice until smooth.
2. Serve with steamed vegetables or grilled meats.
Per serving
Calories: 35| Protein: 2g| Fat: 1g| Carbs: 6g

Lemon Tahini Dressing

Time: 10 minutes| Difficulty: Easy| Serving 2
1/4 cup tahini
Juice of 1 lemon and 2 tablespoons water
1 clove garlic, minced and Salt to taste
1. Whisk tahini, lemon juice, water, and garlic until smooth.
2. Add water as needed to reach desired consistency.
3. Season with salt.
4. Serve as a dressing for salads or as a dip for raw vegetables.
Per serving
Calories: 90| Protein: 3g| Fat: 8g| Carbs: 3g

Mango Coconut Salsa

Time: 15 minutes| Difficulty: Easy| Serving 2
1 ripe mango, diced and 1/2 cup diced red bell pepper
1/4 cup diced red onion and 1/4 cup shredded coconut
Juice of 1 lime and Salt to taste
2 tablespoons chopped fresh cilantro
1. In a bowl, combine diced mango, red bell pepper, red onion, shredded coconut, lime juice, and chopped cilantro.
2. Season with salt to taste.
3. Let the flavors meld for about 10 minutes before serving.
4. Serve as a topping for grilled chicken or fish.
Per serving
Calories: 50| Protein: 1g| Fat: 1g| Carbs: 10g

Cilantro Lime Dressing

Time: 10 minutes| Difficulty: Easy| Serving 2

1/2 cup fresh cilantro, chopped
Juice of 2 limes and 1 tablespoon honey
1/4 cup olive oil and Salt and pepper to taste

1. Blend cilantro, lime juice, honey, and olive oil until smooth.
2. Season with salt and pepper.
3. Serve as a dressing for salads or as a marinade for chicken or fish.

Per serving
Calories: 120| Protein: 0g| Fat: 14g| Carbs: 4g

Orange Ginger Sauce

Time: 10 minutes| Difficulty: Easy| Serving 2

1/4 cup orange juice and 1 tablespoon honey
1 tablespoon soy sauce (low sodium)
1 teaspoon fresh ginger, grated
1 teaspoon cornstarch mixed with 1 tablespoon water

1. Combine orange juice, soy sauce, honey, and ginger in a small saucepan.
2. Bring to a simmer and add the cornstarch mixture.
3. Cook until thickened, stirring constantly.
4. Cool slightly and serve over chicken or fish.

Per serving
Calories: 30| Protein: 0g| Fat: 0g| Carbs: 7g

Creamy Avocado Sauce

Time: 10 minutes| Difficulty: Easy| Serving 2

1 ripe avocado, peeled and pitted
1/4 cup plain low-fat yogurt
1 clove garlic, minced
Juice of 1 lime and Salt and pepper to taste

1. Blend all ingredients until smooth.
2. Season with salt and pepper.
3. Serve as a spread for sandwiches or as a dip.

Per serving
Calories: 70| Protein: 2g| Fat: 5g| Carbs: 4g

Spicy Pineapple Sauce

Time: 15 minutes| Difficulty: Easy | Serving 2

1 cup pineapple, finely chopped
1 jalapeño, seeded and minced
Juice of 1 lime
1 tablespoon honey and Salt to taste

1. Combine all ingredients and simmer over medium heat for 10 minutes.
2. Allow to cool and adjust seasoning.
3. Serve with grilled chicken or pork.

Per serving
Calories: 35 | Protein: 0g| Fat: 0g| Carbs: 9g

Lemon Caper Sauce

Time: 10 minutes| Difficulty: Easy| Serving 2

1/4 cup lemon juice
2 tablespoons capers, rinsed
1 clove garlic, minced
1 tablespoon olive oil
Salt and pepper to taste

1. Combine lemon juice, capers, garlic, and olive oil in a small saucepan.
2. Warm over low heat just until heated through.
3. Season with salt and pepper.
4. Serve over fish or chicken.

Per serving
Calories: 50| Protein: 0g| Fat: 4.5g| Carbs: 2g

Garlic Herb Aioli

Time: 10 minutes| Difficulty: Easy| Serving 2

1/2 cup low-fat mayonnaise
2 cloves garlic, minced
1 tablespoon lemon juice
1/4 cup mixed herbs (parsley, chives), finely chopped
Salt and pepper to taste

1. Mix all ingredients in a bowl until well combined.
2. Chill before serving.
3. Ideal for sandwiches or as a vegetable dip.

Per serving
Calories: 90| Protein: 0g| Fat: 9g| Carbs: 2g

Cucumber Mint Chutney

Time: 10 minutes| Difficulty: Easy| Serving 2

1 cucumber, peeled and diced
1/4 cup mint leaves
2 tablespoons yogurt
1 tablespoon lemon juice
Salt to taste

1. Blend all ingredients until smooth.
2. Chill before serving.
3. Serve with grilled meats or as a dip.

Per serving
Calories: 20| Protein: 1g| Fat: 0g| Carbs: 3g

Lemon Dill Yogurt Sauce

Time: 5 minutes| Difficulty: Easy| Serving 2
1 cup low-fat Greek yogurt
2 tablespoons fresh dill, chopped
Zest and juice of 1 lemon and Salt to taste
1. Combine all ingredients in a bowl.
2. Chill before serving.
3. Perfect for fish or as a salad dressing.

Per serving
Calories: 35| Protein: 6g| Fat: 0g| Carbs: 3g

Mango Chutney

Time: 30 minutes| Difficulty: Easy| Serving 2
1 ripe mango, peeled and diced
1/4 cup apple cider vinegar
1 tablespoon honey
1/4 teaspoon cinnamon
1 small red chili, finely chopped (optional)
1. Combine all ingredients in a saucepan.
2. Bring to a simmer over medium heat.
3. Reduce heat and simmer for 20 minutes or until thickened.
4. Cool and serve with curries or grilled meats.

Per serving
Calories: 40| Protein: 0g| Fat: 0g| Carbs: 10g

Blueberry Compote

Time: 20 minutes| Difficulty: Easy| Serving 2
1 cup fresh blueberries
2 tablespoons water
1 tablespoon honey and 1 teaspoon lemon juice
1. Combine blueberries, water, and honey in a small saucepan.
2. Cook over medium heat until berries burst and sauce thickens, about 10 minutes.
3. Stir in lemon juice.
4. Serve over pancakes, yogurt, or oatmeal.

Per serving
Calories: 50| Protein: 0g| Fat: 0g| Carbs: 13g

Honey Mustard Dressing

Time: 5 minutes| Difficulty: Easy| Serving 2

2 tablespoons mustard
1 tablespoon honey
1 tablespoon apple cider vinegar
2 tablespoons water to thin
1. Whisk all ingredients together until smooth.
2. Adjust consistency with water.
3. Serve over salads or as a dip for vegetables.

Per serving
Calories: 35| Protein: 0g| Fat: 0g| Carbs: 8g

Lime Coriander Sauce

Time: 10 minutes| Difficulty: Easy| Serving 2

Juice of 2 limes
1/4 cup fresh coriander, finely chopped
1 tablespoon honey
1 clove garlic, minced
1. Whisk together lime juice, coriander, honey, and garlic in a bowl.
2. Let it sit for 10 minutes to blend the flavors.
3. Serve with seafood or chicken.

Per serving
Calories: 30| Protein: 0g| Fat: 0g| Carbs: 8g

Tomato Coulis

Time: 25 minutes| Difficulty: Easy| Serving 2

2 cups cherry tomatoes
1 clove garlic, minced
1 tablespoon olive oil
Salt and pepper to taste

1. Heat olive oil in a pan over medium heat.
2. Add garlic and tomatoes, cook until tomatoes burst.
3. Blend until smooth and season.
4. Serve with fish or pasta.

Per serving
Calories: 45| Protein: 1g| Fat: 3.5g| Carbs: 4g

Green Goddess Dressing

Time: 10 minutes| Difficulty: Easy| Serving 2

1/2 cup plain Greek yogurt
1/4 cup chopped fresh parsley
2 tablespoons chopped fresh chives
2 tablespoons chopped fresh basil
1 tablespoon chopped fresh tarragon
1 garlic clove, minced
Juice of 1 lemon
Salt and pepper to taste

1. In a blender or food processor, combine Greek yogurt, parsley, chives, basil, tarragon, garlic, and lemon juice.
2. Blend until smooth.
3. Season with salt and pepper to taste.
4. Serve over salads or grilled chicken.

Per serving
Calories: 50| Protein: 3g| Fat: 3g| Carbs: 4g

Balsamic Herb Vinaigrette

Time: 5 minutes| Difficulty: Easy| Serving 2

1/4 cup balsamic vinegar
1/4 cup extra virgin olive oil
1 teaspoon Dijon mustard
1 garlic clove, minced
1 tablespoon fresh herbs (such as basil, thyme, or oregano), chopped
Salt and pepper to taste
1. Whisk together balsamic vinegar, olive oil, Dijon mustard, and minced garlic.
2. Stir in fresh herbs and season with salt and pepper.
3. Serve over salads or grilled vegetables.

Per serving
Calories: 120| Protein: 0g| Fat: 14g| Carbs: 2g

Chipotle Yogurt Sauce

Time: 10 minutes| Difficulty: Easy| Serving 2

1/2 cup plain Greek yogurt
1 chipotle pepper in adobo sauce, minced
1 tablespoon adobo sauce
1 tablespoon lime juice
Salt to taste
1. In a bowl, combine Greek yogurt, minced chipotle pepper, adobo sauce, and lime juice.
2. Season with salt to taste.
3. Serve as a spicy dip for sweet potato fries or grilled vegetables.

Per serving
Calories: 30| Protein: 2g| Fat: 0g| Carbs: 3g

Sun-Dried Tomato Pesto

Time: 15 minutes| Difficulty: Easy| Serving 2
1/2 cup sun-dried tomatoes (packed in oil), drained

1/4 cup pine nuts
1 garlic clove
2 tablespoons grated Parmesan cheese
2 tablespoons extra virgin olive oil
Salt and pepper to taste
1. In a food processor, combine sun-dried tomatoes, pine nuts, garlic, and Parmesan cheese.
2. Pulse until finely chopped.
3. With the processor running, drizzle in olive oil until smooth.
4. Season with salt and pepper to taste.
5. Serve tossed with pasta or as a spread on crostini.

Per serving
Calories: 100| Protein: 2g| Fat: 9g| Carbs: 4g

Avocado Lime Dressing

Time: 10 minutes| Difficulty: Easy| Serving 2

1 ripe avocado
Juice of 2 limes
2 tablespoons Greek yogurt
1 tablespoon honey
Salt and pepper to taste
1. In a blender, combine avocado, lime juice, Greek yogurt, and honey.
2. Blend until smooth.
3. Season with salt and pepper to taste.
4. Serve over salads or grilled chicken.

Per serving
Calories: 90| Protein: 2g| Fat: 6g| Carbs: 10g

Cashew Cream Sauce

Time: 15 minutes| Difficulty: Easy| Serving 2
1 cup raw cashews, soaked in water for 2 hours
1 cup vegetable broth
2 tablespoons nutritional yeast
1 clove garlic
Juice of 1 lemon
Salt and pepper to taste
1. Drain soaked cashews and rinse under cold water.
2. In a blender, combine cashews, vegetable broth, nutritional yeast, garlic, and lemon juice.
3. Blend until smooth, adding more broth if needed to reach desired consistency.
4. Season with salt and pepper to taste.
5. Serve over pasta or steamed vegetables.

Per serving
Calories: 120| Protein: 5g| Fat: 8g| Carbs: 8g

Sweet Onion Relish

Time: 20 minutes| Difficulty: Easy| Serving 2

2 large sweet onions, thinly sliced
1/4 cup apple cider vinegar
2 tablespoons honey
1/4 teaspoon ground cinnamon
Salt to taste
1. In a saucepan, combine sliced onions, apple cider vinegar, honey, and ground cinnamon.
2. Cook over medium heat, stirring occasionally, until onions are soft and mixture has thickened (about 15-20 minutes).
3. Season with salt to taste.
4. Serve as a condiment for grilled meats or sandwiches.

Per serving
Calories: 50| Protein: 1g| Fat: 0g| Carbs: 13g

Teriyaki Sauce

Time: 15 minutes| Difficulty: Easy| Serving 2
1/4 cup soy sauce (or tamari for gluten-free)
2 tablespoons honey
1 tablespoon rice vinegar
1 garlic clove, minced and 1 teaspoon grated ginger
1 teaspoon cornstarch (optional, for thickening)
2 tablespoons water (if using cornstarch)

1. In a small saucepan, combine soy sauce, honey, rice vinegar, minced garlic, and grated ginger.
2. If desired, mix cornstarch with water to form a slurry and add to the saucepan.
3. Heat over medium heat, stirring constantly until the sauce thickens.
4. Remove from heat and let cool slightly before serving.
5. Serve as a sauce for stir-fries, grilled salmon, or chicken.

Per serving
Calories: 50| Protein: 1g|Fat: 0g| Carbs: 12g

Tomato Basil Marinara Sauce

Time: 30 minutes| Difficulty: Intermediate| Serving 2
2 tablespoons olive oil
1 onion, finely chopped and 2 garlic cloves, minced
1 can (14 oz.) crushed tomatoes
2 tablespoons tomato paste
1/4 cup chopped fresh basil
1 teaspoon dried oregano/ Salt and pepper to taste

1. In a saucepan, heat olive oil over medium heat.
2. Add chopped onion and minced garlic. Cook until softened.
3. Stir in crushed tomatoes, tomato paste, chopped basil, dried oregano, salt, and pepper.
4. Simmer for about 20 minutes, stirring occasionally, until the sauce thickens.
5. Adjust seasoning to taste.
6. Serve hot over pasta or use as a pizza sauce.

Per serving
Calories: 60| Protein: 2g| Fat: 4g| Carbs: 7g

Balsamic Dijon Dressing

Time: 5 minutes| Difficulty: Easy| Serving 2
2 tablespoons balsamic vinegar
1 tablespoon Dijon mustard and 1 garlic clove, minced
1/4 cup extra virgin olive oil/ Salt and pepper to taste

1. In a small bowl, whisk together balsamic vinegar, Dijon mustard, minced garlic, and olive oil.
2. Season with salt and pepper to taste.
3. Serve as a dressing for salads or drizzle over grilled vegetables.

Per serving
Calories: 90| Protein: 0g| Fat: 10g| Carbs: 1g

Creamy Mushroom Sauce

Time: 20 minutes| Difficulty: Intermediate| Serving 2
2 tablespoons butter
8 oz. mushrooms, sliced
2 garlic cloves, minced
2 tablespoons all-purpose flour (or cornstarch for gluten-free)
1 cup chicken or vegetable broth
1/2 cup heavy cream
1/4 cup grated Parmesan cheese
Salt and pepper to taste

1. In a skillet, melt butter over medium heat.
2. Add sliced mushrooms and minced garlic. Cook until mushrooms are golden brown and tender.
3. Sprinkle flour over the mushroom mixture and stir to combine.
4. Gradually pour in chicken or vegetable broth, stirring constantly until thickened.
5. Stir in heavy cream and grated Parmesan cheese.
6. Simmer for a few more minutes until the sauce thickens.
7. Season with salt and pepper to taste.
8. Serve hot over grilled chicken or pasta.

Per serving
Calories: 120| Protein: 3g| Fat: 10g| Carbs: 4g

Mushroom Gravy

Time: 20 minutes| Difficulty: Intermediate| Serving 2
2 cups sliced mushrooms
1 onion, finely chopped
2 garlic cloves, minced
2 tablespoons butter
2 tablespoons all-purpose flour (or cornstarch for gluten-free)
2 cups vegetable broth
1 tablespoon soy sauce (or tamari for gluten-free)
Salt and pepper to taste

1. In a skillet, melt butter over medium heat.
2. Add sliced mushrooms, chopped onion, and minced garlic. Cook until mushrooms are tender and onions are translucent.
3. Sprinkle flour over the mushroom mixture and stir to combine.
4. Gradually pour in vegetable broth, stirring constantly until thickened.
5. Stir in soy sauce and season with salt and pepper to taste.
6. Simmer for a few more minutes until flavors meld.
7. Serve hot over mashed potatoes or roasted vegetables.

Per serving
Calories: 70| Protein: 2g| Fat: 4g| Carbs: 8g

Spicy Peanut Sauce

Time: 15 minutes| Difficulty: Easy| Serving 2
1/4 cup creamy peanut butter
2 tablespoons soy sauce (or tamari for gluten-free)
1 tablespoon rice vinegar and 1 tablespoon honey
1 teaspoon sriracha sauce (adjust to taste)
1 garlic clove, minced and Water (as needed to thin)
1. In a bowl, whisk together peanut butter, soy sauce, rice vinegar, honey, sriracha sauce, and minced garlic.
2. Add water gradually until desired consistency is reached.
3. Adjust seasoning to taste.
4. Serve as a dipping sauce for spring rolls or grilled chicken skewers.

Per serving
Calories: 70| Protein: 3g| Fat: 5g| Carbs: 5g

Creamy Herb Gravy

Time: 25 minutes| Difficulty: Intermediate| Serving 2
2 tablespoons butter and 1/2 cup heavy cream
2 tablespoons all-purpose flour
1 cup chicken or vegetable broth
1 tablespoon chopped fresh herbs (such as thyme, rosemary, and sage)and Salt and pepper to taste
1. Melt butter in a saucepan over medium heat.
2. Stir in flour and cook until golden brown.
3. Gradually whisk in broth, stirring constantly until smooth.
4. Pour in heavy cream and chopped herbs, simmer until thickened.
5. Season with salt and pepper to taste.

Per serving
Calories: 120| Protein: 1g| Fat: 10g| Carbs: 5g

Sage and Onion Gravy

2 tablespoons butter
1 onion, finely chopped and 1 garlic clove, minced
2 tablespoons all-purpose flour
1 cup vegetable broth and Salt and pepper to taste
1 tablespoon chopped fresh sage leaves
1. Melt butter in a saucepan over medium heat.
2. Add chopped onion and minced garlic, sauté until softened.
3. Sprinkle flour over the onion mixture and cook for a minute.
4. Gradually pour in vegetable broth, stirring constantly until thickened.
5. Stir in chopped sage leaves, simmer for a few minutes.
6. Season with salt and pepper to taste.

Per serving
Calories: 70| Protein: 1g| Fat: 4g| Carbs: 8g

Rich Red Wine Mushroom Gravy

Time: 40 minutes| Difficulty: Intermediate| Serving 2
2 tablespoons olive oil and 1 onion, finely chopped
2 garlic cloves, minced and 8 oz. mushrooms, sliced
2 tablespoons all-purpose flour
1 cup vegetable broth and 1/2 cup red wine
Salt and pepper to taste
1. Heat olive oil in a skillet over medium heat.
2. Add chopped onion and minced garlic, sauté until softened.
3. Stir in sliced mushrooms and cook until they release their moisture and become golden brown.
4. Sprinkle flour over the mushroom mixture and cook for a minute.
5. Gradually pour in vegetable broth and red wine, stirring constantly until thickened.
6. Season with salt and pepper to taste.

Per serving
Calories: 80| Protein: 2g| Fat: 4g| Carbs: 8g

Maple Glazed Onion Gravy

Time: 35 minutes| Difficulty: Intermediate| Serving 2
2 tablespoons olive oil
2 large onions, thinly sliced
2 tablespoons maple syrup
2 tablespoons all-purpose flour
1 cup vegetable broth and Salt and pepper to taste
1. Heat olive oil in a skillet over medium-low heat.
2. Add thinly sliced onions and maple syrup, cook until caramelized and golden brown.
3. Sprinkle flour over the onions and cook for a minute.
4. Gradually pour in vegetable broth, stirring constantly until thickened.
5. Season with salt and pepper to taste.

Per serving
Calories: 80| Protein: 1g| Fat: 4g| Carbs: 11g

Spicy Cajun Gravy

Time: 20 minutes| Difficulty: Intermediate| Serving 2
2 tablespoons butter
2 tablespoons all-purpose flour
1 cup chicken or vegetable broth and 1/2 cup milk
1 teaspoon Cajun seasoning and Salt and pepper to taste
1. Melt butter in a saucepan over medium heat.
2. Stir in flour and cook until lightly browned.
3. Gradually whisk in broth and milk, stirring constantly until thickened.
4. Add Cajun seasoning, salt, and pepper, simmer for a few minutes.
5. Adjust seasoning according to taste.

Per serving
Calories: 90| Protein: 2g| Fat: 5g| Carbs: 8g

2.11 Pies and Quiches

Crustless Spinach and Feta Quiche

Time: 45 minutes| Difficulty: Easy| Serving 2
1 tablespoon olive oil
1 onion, diced
2 cups fresh spinach, chopped
4 large eggs
1 cup milk (or non-dairy milk)
1/2 cup crumbled feta cheese

1. Preheat the oven to 375°F (190°C) and grease a pie dish.
2. Heat olive oil in a skillet over medium heat. Add diced onion and cook until translucent.
3. Add chopped spinach to the skillet and cook until wilted. Remove from heat and let cool.
4. In a mixing bowl, whisk together eggs, milk, salt, and pepper.
5. Stir in cooked spinach mixture and crumbled feta cheese.
6. Pour the mixture into the greased pie dish.
7. Bake for 30-35 minutes, or until the quiche is set and golden on top.

Per serving
Calories: 180|Protein: 12g|Fat: 10g|Carbs: 10g

Sweet Potato Shepherd's Pie

Time: 1 hour| Difficulty: Moderate| Serving 2
2 large sweet potatoes, peeled and cubed
1 tablespoon olive oil
1 onion, diced and 2 cloves garlic, minced
1 pound ground turkey
1 cup mixed vegetables (carrots, peas, corn)
1 cup low-sodium chicken broth

1. Preheat the oven to 375°F (190°C) and grease a pie dish.
2. Boil sweet potato cubes in a pot of water until tender. Drain and mash.
3. In a skillet, heat olive oil over medium heat. Add diced onion and minced garlic, cook until softened.
4. Add ground turkey to the skillet and cook until browned.
5. Stir in mixed vegetables and chicken broth. Simmer for 5 minutes.
6. Season with salt and pepper to taste.
7. Transfer the turkey mixture to the greased pie dish.
8. Spread mashed sweet potatoes over the top.
9. Bake for 25-30 minutes, or until the sweet potatoes are golden.

Per serving
Calories: 250| Protein: 20g| Fat: 8g| Carbs: 25g

Tomato Basil Pie

Time: 50 minutes| Difficulty: Easy| Serving 2
1 pre-made pie crust (or homemade)
4 large tomatoes, sliced
1 cup fresh basil leaves, chopped
1 cup shredded mozzarella cheese
1/4 cup grated Parmesan cheese
2 cloves garlic, minced

1. Preheat the oven to 375°F (190°C).
2. Place the pre-made pie crust in a pie dish and crimp the edges.
3. Layer sliced tomatoes and chopped basil in the pie crust.
4. Sprinkle minced garlic, salt, and pepper over the tomatoes.
5. Top with shredded mozzarella cheese and grated Parmesan cheese.
6. Bake for 30-35 minutes, or until the crust is golden and the cheese is bubbly.

Per serving
Calories: 280|Protein: 10g| Fat: 15g| Carbs: 25g

Chicken Pot Pie

Time: 1 h 15 min| Difficulty: Moderate| Serving 2
1 pre-made pie crust (or homemade)
2 boneless, skinless chicken breasts, cooked and shredded
1 tablespoon olive oil
1 onion, 2 carrots and 2 celery stalks, diced
2 cloves garlic, minced
1/4 cup all-purpose flour
1 cup low-sodium chicken broth and 1 cup frozen peas
1/2 cup milk (or non-dairy milk)

1. Preheat the oven to 375°F (190°C).
2. In a skillet, heat olive oil over medium heat. Add diced onion, carrots, celery, and minced garlic. Cook until softened.
3. Sprinkle flour over the vegetable mixture and stir to coat.
4. Slowly pour in chicken broth and milk, stirring constantly until thickened.
5. Stir in cooked shredded chicken and frozen peas. Season with salt and pepper to taste.
6. Pour the mixture into a pie dish lined with the pre-made pie crust.
7. Cover with another pie crust and crimp the edges to seal. Cut slits in the top crust for ventilation.
8. Bake for 35-40 minutes, or until the crust is golden brown.

Per serving
Calories: 320| Protein: 20g| Fat: 15g| Carbs: 25g

Vegetable and Lentil Pie

Time: 1 hour| Difficulty: Moderate| Serving 2

1 pre-made pie crust (or homemade)
1 cup dry green lentils, cooked
1 tablespoon olive oil
1 onion, diced
2 carrots, diced
2 celery stalks, diced
2 cloves garlic, minced
1 cup diced tomatoes
1 cup vegetable broth
1 teaspoon dried thyme

1. Preheat the oven to 375°F (190°C).
2. In a skillet, heat olive oil over medium heat. Add diced onion, carrots, celery, and minced garlic. Cook until softened.
3. Stir in cooked green lentils, diced tomatoes, vegetable broth, dried thyme, salt, and pepper. Simmer for 10-15 minutes.
4. Roll out the pie crust and line a pie dish.
5. Pour the vegetable and lentil mixture into the pie crust.
6. Cover with another pie crust and crimp the edges to seal. Cut slits in the top crust for ventilation.
7. Bake for 30-35 minutes, or until the crust is golden brown.

Per serving
Calories: 290| Protein: 15g| Fat: 12g| Carbs: 30g

Mushroom and Spinach Quiche

Time: 1 hour| Difficulty: Moderate| Serving 2

1 pre-made pie crust (or homemade)
2 cups sliced mushrooms and 2 cups fresh spinach
1 onion, diced
4 large eggs
1 cup milk (or non-dairy milk)
1/2 cup shredded Swiss cheese

1. Preheat the oven to 375°F (190°C) and grease a pie dish.
2. In a skillet, sauté sliced mushrooms and diced onion until tender.
3. Add fresh spinach to the skillet and cook until wilted. Remove from heat and let cool.
4. In a mixing bowl, whisk together eggs, milk, salt, and pepper.
5. Stir in cooked mushroom and spinach mixture, and shredded Swiss cheese.
6. Pour the mixture into the greased pie dish.
7. Bake for 35-40 minutes, or until the quiche is set and golden on top.

Per serving
Calories: 220| Protein: 12g| Fat: 14g| Carbs: 15g

Savory Potato Pie

Time: 1 h15 min| Difficulty: Moderate| Serving 2

1 pre-made pie crust (or homemade)
3 large potatoes, peeled and thinly sliced
1 onion, thinly sliced
2 cloves garlic, minced
1 cup shredded cheddar cheese
1 cup milk (or non-dairy milk)
4 large eggs
Salt and pepper to taste

1. Preheat the oven to 375°F (190°C) and grease a pie dish.
2. Layer thinly sliced potatoes, onion, and minced garlic in the pie dish.
3. Sprinkle shredded cheddar cheese over the potato mixture.
4. In a mixing bowl, whisk together eggs, milk, salt, and pepper.
5. Pour the egg mixture over the potato mixture in the pie dish.
6. Bake for 45-50 minutes, or until the potatoes are tender and the top is golden brown.

Per serving
Calories: 280| Protein: 15g| Fat: 12g| Carbs: 25g

Cheesy Broccoli Pie

Time: 1 hour| Difficulty: Easy| Serving 2

1 pre-made pie crust (or homemade)
2 cups chopped broccoli florets
1 onion, diced
2 cloves garlic, minced
1 cup shredded cheddar cheese
4 large eggs
1 cup milk (or non-dairy milk)
Salt and pepper to taste

1. Preheat the oven to 375°F (190°C) and grease a pie dish.
2. In a skillet, sauté diced onion and minced garlic until softened.
3. Add chopped broccoli florets to the skillet and cook until tender. Remove from heat and let cool.
4. Sprinkle shredded cheddar cheese over the bottom of the pie crust.
5. In a mixing bowl, whisk together eggs, milk, salt, and pepper.
6. Stir in cooked broccoli mixture.
7. Pour the egg and broccoli mixture into the pie crust.
8. Bake for 35-40 minutes, or until the quiche is set and golden on top.

Per serving
Calories: 250| Protein: 14g| Fat: 15g| Carbs: 18g

Turkey and Vegetable Pie

Time: 1 h30 min| Difficulty: Moderate| Serving 2

1 pre-made pie crust (or homemade)
1 tablespoon olive oil
1 onion, diced
2 carrots, diced
2 celery stalks, diced
2 cloves garlic, minced
1 pound ground turkey
1 cup frozen peas
1 cup low-sodium chicken broth
2 tablespoons all-purpose flour

1. Preheat the oven to 375°F (190°C) and grease a pie dish.
2. In a skillet, heat olive oil over medium heat. Add diced onion, carrots, celery, and minced garlic. Cook until softened.
3. Add ground turkey to the skillet and cook until browned.
4. Stir in frozen peas and cook for 2-3 minutes.
5. Sprinkle flour over the turkey mixture and stir to coat.
6. Slowly pour in chicken broth, stirring constantly until thickened.
7. Season with salt and pepper to taste.
8. Transfer the turkey mixture to the greased pie dish.
9. Cover with the pre-made pie crust and crimp the edges to seal. Cut slits in the top crust for ventilation.
10. Bake for 35-40 minutes, or until the crust is golden brown.

Per serving
Calories: 320| Protein: 20g| Fat: 15g| Carbs: 25g

Tomato and Basil Tart

Time: 40 minutes| Difficulty: Easy| Serving 2

1 pre-made pie crust
3 large tomatoes, sliced
1/2 cup fresh basil leaves
1/4 cup mozzarella cheese, shredded
1/4 cup low-fat ricotta cheese
1 tablespoon olive oil

1. Preheat oven to 375°F (190°C).
2. Lay the pie crust in a tart pan.
3. Spread ricotta cheese on the base of the crust.
4. Arrange tomato slices and basil over ricotta.
5. Sprinkle with mozzarella cheese, salt, and pepper.
6. Drizzle with olive oil.
7. Bake for 25-30 minutes until crust is golden.

Per serving
Calories: 270| Protein: 7g| Fat: 17g| Carbs: 20g

Shrimp and Spinach Pie

Time: 1 hour| Difficulty: Moderate| Serving 2

1 pre-made pie crust (or homemade)
1 cup cooked shrimp, chopped
2 cups fresh spinach
1 onion, diced
2 cloves garlic, minced
1 cup shredded mozzarella cheese
4 large eggs
1 cup milk (or non-dairy milk)
Salt and pepper to taste

1. Preheat the oven to 375°F (190°C) and grease a pie dish.
2. In a skillet, sauté diced onion and minced garlic until softened.
3. Add fresh spinach to the skillet and cook until wilted. Remove from heat and let cool.
4. Sprinkle shredded mozzarella cheese over the bottom of the pie crust.
5. Arrange chopped cooked shrimp on top of the cheese.
6. In a mixing bowl, whisk together eggs, milk, salt, and pepper.
7. Stir in cooked spinach mixture.
8. Pour the egg and spinach mixture into the pie crust.
9. Bake for 35-40 minutes, or until the quiche is set and golden on top.

Per serving
Calories: 280| Protein: 16g| Fat: 14g| Carbs: 20g

Chicken and Sweet Potato Pie

Time: 1 h 10 min| Difficulty: Moderate| Serving 2

1 pre-made pie crust
2 cups cooked chicken breast, shredded
1 large sweet potato, peeled and diced
1 onion, chopped
1/2 cup low-sodium chicken broth
1/4 cup skim milk
1 tablespoon olive oil
1 teaspoon dried thyme
Salt and pepper to taste

1. Preheat oven to 375°F (190°C).
2. Sauté onion in olive oil until soft.
3. Add sweet potato, thyme, salt, and pepper. Cook until tender.
4. Stir in chicken, broth, and milk. Cook until thickened.
5. Pour mixture into pie crust.
6. Bake for 35 minutes until crust is golden.

Per serving
Calories: 330| Protein: 18g| Fat: 14g| Carbs: 29g

Crab and Corn Pie

Time: 1 hour| Difficulty: Moderate| Serving 2

1 pre-made pie crust (or homemade)
1 cup lump crab meat
1 cup corn kernels
1 onion, diced
2 cloves garlic, minced
1 cup shredded cheddar cheese
4 large eggs
1 cup milk (or non-dairy milk)
Salt and pepper to taste

1. Preheat the oven to 375°F (190°C) and grease a pie dish.
2. In a skillet, sauté diced onion and minced garlic until softened.
3. Add corn kernels to the skillet and cook until slightly caramelized.
4. Stir in lump crab meat and cook until heated through. Remove from heat and let cool.
5. Sprinkle shredded cheddar cheese over the bottom of the pie crust.
6. Arrange the crab and corn mixture on top of the cheese.
7. In a mixing bowl, whisk together eggs, milk, salt, and pepper.
8. Pour the egg mixture over the crab and corn mixture in the pie dish.
9. Bake for 35-40 minutes, or until the quiche is set and golden on top.

Per serving
Calories: 310| Protein: 16g| Fat: 16g| Carbs: 22g

Tuna and Olive Pie

Time: 50 minutes| Difficulty: Easy| Serving 2

1 pre-made pie crust
1 can tuna, drained
1/2 cup black olives, sliced
1/4 cup low-fat cream cheese
1/4 cup low-fat milk
2 eggs
Salt and pepper to taste

1. Preheat oven to 375°F (190°C).
2. In a bowl, mix tuna, olives, cream cheese, milk, eggs, salt, and pepper.
3. Pour into pie crust.
4. Bake for 30-35 minutes until set.

Per serving
Calories: 280| Protein: 18g| Fat: 16g| Carbs: 18g

Cod and Vegetable Pie

Time: 1 hour| Difficulty: Moderate| Serving 2

1 pre-made pie crust (or homemade)
2 cod fillets, cooked and flaked
1 cup diced potatoes
1 onion, diced
2 carrots, diced
1 cup frozen peas
1 cup low-sodium chicken broth
2 tablespoons all-purpose flour
1/2 cup heavy cream

1. Preheat the oven to 375°F (190°C) and grease a pie dish.
2. In a skillet, sauté diced onion until softened.
3. Add diced potatoes and carrots to the skillet and cook until slightly tender.
4. Stir in cooked and flaked cod fillets and frozen peas.
5. Sprinkle flour over the cod and vegetable mixture and stir to coat.
6. Slowly pour in chicken broth and heavy cream, stirring constantly until thickened.
7. Season with salt and pepper to taste.
8. Transfer the cod and vegetable mixture to the greased pie dish.
9. Cover with the pre-made pie crust and crimp the edges to seal. Cut slits in the top crust for ventilation.
10. Bake for 35-40 minutes, or until the crust is golden brown.

Per serving
Calories: 340| Protein: 18g| Fat: 18g| Carbs: 25g

Mushroom and Leek Quiche

Time: 1 hour| Difficulty: Moderate| Serving 2

1 pre-made pie crust
1 cup leeks, chopped and cleaned
2 cups mushrooms, sliced
1/2 cup skim milk
4 eggs
1/2 cup grated low-fat cheddar cheese
1 tablespoon olive oil

1. Preheat oven to 375°F (190°C).
2. Sauté leeks and mushrooms in olive oil until soft.
3. In a bowl, whisk together eggs and milk. Season with salt and pepper.
4. Spread the vegetable mix into the pie crust.
5. Pour the egg mixture over the vegetables.
6. Sprinkle with cheese.
7. Bake for 35-40 minutes until set.

Per serving
Calories: 260| Protein: 12g| Fat: 16g| Carbs: 18g

Spinach and Feta Phyllo Pie

Time: 50 minutes| Difficulty: Moderate| Serving 2
8 sheets phyllo dough
2 cups fresh spinach, chopped
1/2 cup feta cheese, crumbled
1 onion, finely chopped and 2 cloves garlic, minced
2 eggs, beaten
1/4 cup non-fat Greek yogurt
2 tablespoons olive oil

1. Preheat the oven to 375°F (190°C).
2. Sauté onion and garlic in one tablespoon of olive oil until translucent.
3. Add spinach and cook until wilted. Let cool slightly.
4. In a bowl, mix the spinach mixture, feta cheese, eggs, yogurt, and seasonings.
5. Layer 4 phyllo sheets in a greased pie pan, brushing each sheet with olive oil.
6. Pour the spinach mixture over the phyllo base.
7. Cover with the remaining 4 phyllo sheets, oiling each layer.
8. Bake for 30-35 minutes until golden brown.

Per serving
Calories: 250| Protein: 8g| Fat: 12g| Carbs: 26g

Salmon and Broccoli Pie

Time: 1 hour| Difficulty: Moderate| Serving 2
1 pre-made pie crust (or homemade)
2 salmon fillets, cooked and flaked
2 cups chopped broccoli florets
1 onion, diced and 2 cloves garlic, minced
1 cup shredded cheddar cheese
4 large eggs and 1 cup milk (or non-dairy milk)

1. Preheat the oven to 375°F (190°C) and grease a pie dish.
2. In a skillet, sauté diced onion and minced garlic until softened.
3. Add chopped broccoli florets to the skillet and cook until tender. Remove from heat and let cool.
4. Sprinkle shredded cheddar cheese over the bottom of the pie crust.
5. Arrange cooked and flaked salmon on top of the cheese.
6. In a mixing bowl, whisk together eggs, milk, salt, and pepper.
7. Stir in cooked broccoli mixture.
8. Pour the egg and broccoli mixture into the pie crust.
9. Bake for 35-40 minutes, or until the quiche is set and golden on top.

Per serving
Calories: 300| Protein: 18g| Fat: 16g| Carbs: 20g

Zucchini Ricotta Galette

Time: 1 hour| Difficulty: Moderate| Serving 2
1 pre-made pie crust
2 zucchinis, thinly sliced
1/2 cup ricotta cheese
1/4 cup Parmesan cheese, grated
1 garlic clove, minced
2 tablespoons olive oil
1 egg (for egg wash)

1. Preheat oven to 400°F (205°C).
2. Roll out pie crust on a baking sheet.
3. Mix ricotta, Parmesan, garlic, salt, and pepper. Spread over crust, leaving a border.
4. Arrange zucchini slices on top.
5. Fold edges of crust over, partially covering zucchini.
6. Brush crust with beaten egg.
7. Drizzle olive oil over zucchini.
8. Bake for 30-35 minutes until golden.

Per serving
Calories: 300| Protein: 10g| Fat: 18g| Carbs: 24g

Tuna and Mushroom Pie

Time: 1 hour| Difficulty: Moderate| Serving 2
1 pre-made pie crust (or homemade)
1 can tuna, drained and flaked
2 cups sliced mushrooms
1 onion, diced
2 cloves garlic, minced
1 cup shredded Swiss cheese
4 large eggs
1 cup milk (or non-dairy milk)
Salt and pepper to taste

1. Preheat the oven to 375°F (190°C) and grease a pie dish.
2. In a skillet, sauté diced onion and minced garlic until softened.
3. Add sliced mushrooms to the skillet and cook until tender. Remove from heat and let cool.
4. Sprinkle shredded Swiss cheese over the bottom of the pie crust.
5. Arrange flaked tuna and cooked mushroom mixture on top of the cheese.
6. In a mixing bowl, whisk together eggs, milk, salt, and pepper.
7. Pour the egg mixture over the tuna and mushroom mixture in the pie dish.
8. Bake for 35-40 minutes, or until the quiche is set and golden on top.

Per serving
Calories: 290| Protein: 16g| Fat: 15g| Carbs: 20g

Pumpkin and Spinach Pie

Time: 1 h15 min| Difficulty: Moderate| Serving 2

1 pre-made pie crust
2 cups pumpkin, cubed
2 cups spinach, fresh
1 onion, chopped
2 cloves garlic, minced
1/2 cup feta cheese, crumbled
1/4 cup skim milk
2 eggs
1 tablespoon olive oil
Salt and pepper to taste

1. Preheat oven to 375°F (190°C).
2. Sauté onion and garlic in olive oil until soft.
3. Add pumpkin and cook until tender.
4. Stir in spinach until wilted.
5. In a bowl, whisk eggs and milk. Season with salt and pepper.
6. Mix in the vegetables and feta.
7. Pour into pie crust.
8. Bake for 35-40 minutes until set.

Per serving
Calories: 270| Protein: 9g| Fat: 15g| Carbs: 24g

Roasted Vegetable Medley Pie

Time: 1 hour| Difficulty: Moderate| Serving 2

1 pre-made pie crust
1 cup bell peppers, assorted colors, chopped
1 cup zucchini, chopped
1 cup eggplant, chopped
1 onion, chopped
2 cloves garlic, minced
1/2 cup tomato sauce
1/4 cup Parmesan cheese, grated
2 tablespoons olive oil
Salt and pepper to taste

1. Preheat oven to 400°F (205°C).
2. Toss vegetables with olive oil, salt, and pepper.
3. Roast in the oven for 20-25 minutes until tender.
4. Reduce oven temperature to 375°F (190°C).
5. Spread roasted vegetables in pie crust.
6. Pour tomato sauce over vegetables.
7. Sprinkle with Parmesan.
8. Bake for 30-35 minutes until crust is golden.

Per serving
Calories: 260| Protein: 6g| Fat: 15g| Carbs: 24g

Shrimp and Asparagus Quiche

Time: 1 hour| Difficulty: Moderate| Serving 2
1 pre-made pie crust
1 cup asparagus, chopped
1 cup shrimp, cooked and chopped
1/2 cup low-fat cream cheese
1/4 cup low-fat milk
4 eggs
1 tablespoon olive oil
Salt and pepper to taste

1. Preheat oven to 375°F (190°C).
2. Sauté asparagus in olive oil until tender.
3. In a bowl, whisk together eggs, milk, cream cheese, salt, and pepper.
4. Stir in asparagus and shrimp.
5. Pour into pie crust.
6. Bake for 35-40 minutes until set.

Per serving
Calories: 280| Protein: 16g| Fat: 16g| Carbs: 18g

Sweet Corn and Chicken Pie

Time: 1 hour| Difficulty: Moderate| Serving 2
1 pre-made pie crust
2 cups cooked chicken, shredded
1 cup sweet corn
1/2 cup low-fat cheddar cheese, shredded
1/4 cup skim milk
4 eggs
1 tablespoon olive oil

1. Preheat oven to 375°F (190°C).
2. In a bowl, whisk together eggs, milk, salt, and pepper.
3. Stir in chicken, corn, and cheese.
4. Pour into pie crust.
5. Bake for 35-40 minutes until set.

Per serving
Calories: 300| Protein: 18g| Fat: 16g| Carbs: 20g

Broccoli and Cheddar Quiche

Time: 1 hour| Difficulty: Easy| Serving 2
1 pre-made pie crust
2 cups broccoli, chopped and blanched
1/2 cup low-fat cheddar cheese, shredded
1/4 cup skim milk
4 eggs

1. Preheat oven to 375°F (190°C).
2. Spread broccoli and cheese in pie crust.
3. In a bowl, whisk together eggs, milk, salt, and pepper.
4. Pour over broccoli.
5. Bake for 35-40 minutes until set.

Per serving
Calories: 250| Protein: 12g| Fat: 14g| Carbs: 18g

Beef and Mushroom Pie

Time: 1 h20 min| Difficulty: Moderate| Serving 2

1 pre-made pie crust
2 cups lean ground beef, cooked
1 cup mushrooms, sliced
1 onion, chopped
1/2 cup low-sodium beef broth
1/4 cup skim milk
2 tablespoons all-purpose flour
1 tablespoon Worcestershire sauce
1 tablespoon olive oil
Salt and pepper to taste

1. Preheat oven to 375°F (190°C).
2. Sauté onion and mushrooms in olive oil until soft.
3. Add cooked beef, Worcestershire sauce, and flour. Stir until well combined.
4. Slowly add broth and milk, stirring until thickened.
5. Pour into pie crust.
6. Bake for 35-40 minutes until crust is golden.

Per serving
Calories: 320| Protein: 20g| Fat: 17g| Carbs: 20g

Peach and Berry Cobbler

Time: 50 minutes| Difficulty: Easy| Serving 2

2 cups fresh peaches, sliced
1 cup mixed berries (blueberries, raspberries)
1/2 cup whole wheat flour
1/2 cup rolled oats
1/4 cup brown sugar
1/4 cup unsalted butter, melted
1/2 teaspoon cinnamon
1/4 teaspoon nutmeg

1. Preheat oven to 375°F (190°C).
2. Arrange fruit in a baking dish.
3. In a bowl, mix flour, oats, sugar, cinnamon, nutmeg, and butter until crumbly.
4. Sprinkle over fruit.
5. Bake for 30-35 minutes until topping is golden.

Per serving
Calories: 210| Protein: 3g| Fat: 8g| Carbs: 34g

Lemon and Herb Salmon Pie

Time: 50 minutes| Difficulty: Moderate| Serving 2
1 pre-made pie crust
2 salmon fillets, cooked and flaked
1/4 cup low-fat cream cheese
1 lemon, zest and juice
1 tablespoon dill, chopped
1 tablespoon parsley, chopped
2 green onions, chopped
Salt and pepper to taste
1. Preheat oven to 375°F (190°C).
2. In a bowl, mix flaked salmon, cream cheese, lemon zest, lemon juice, dill, parsley, green onions, salt, and pepper.
3. Spread salmon mixture into pie crust.
4. Bake for 30-35 minutes until crust is golden.

Per serving
Calories: 290| Protein: 18g| Fat: 15g| Carbs: 20g

Lobster Pot Pie

Time: 1 h 30 min| Difficulty: Moderate| Serving 2
1 pre-made pie crust (or homemade)
1 cup cooked lobster meat, chopped
2 cups diced potatoes
1 onion, diced
2 cloves garlic, minced
1 cup frozen peas
1 cup low-sodium chicken broth
2 tablespoons all-purpose flour
1/2 cup heavy cream
Salt and pepper to taste
1. Preheat the oven to 375°F (190°C) and grease a pie dish.
2. In a skillet, sauté diced onion and minced garlic until softened.
3. Add diced potatoes to the skillet and cook until slightly tender.
4. Stir in chopped cooked lobster meat and frozen peas.
5. Sprinkle flour over the lobster mixture and stir to coat.
6. Slowly pour in chicken broth and heavy cream, stirring constantly until thickened.
7. Season with salt and pepper to taste.
8. Transfer the lobster mixture to the greased pie dish.
9. Cover with the pre-made pie crust and crimp the edges to seal. Cut slits in the top crust for ventilation.
10. Bake for 35-40 minutes, or until the crust is golden brown.

Per serving
Calories: 350| Protein: 18g| Fat: 20g| Carbs: 25g

Turkey and Sweet Potato Shepherd's Pie

Time: 50 minutes| Difficulty: Easy| Serving 2

2 cups cooked, ground turkey breast
2 sweet potatoes, mashed
1 cup frozen mixed vegetables (carrots, peas, corn)
1 onion, chopped
1 clove garlic, minced and 1 tbsp. olive oil
1/2 cup low-sodium chicken broth

1. Preheat oven to 375°F (190°C).
2. Sauté onion and garlic in olive oil until translucent.
3. Add ground turkey and vegetables. Cook for 5 minutes.
4. Add broth and simmer until mostly absorbed.
5. Place turkey mixture in a baking dish, top with mashed sweet potatoes.
6. Bake for 20 minutes until topping is slightly crispy.

Per serving
Calories: 280| Protein: 21g| Fat: 10g| Carbs: 25g

Spinach and Ricotta Pie

Time: 40 minutes| Difficulty: Easy| Serving 2

1 pre-made pie crust
2 cups fresh spinach, chopped
1 cup ricotta cheese, low-fat
1/4 cup Parmesan cheese, grated
2 eggs, beaten
1/4 tsp. nutmeg

1. Preheat oven to 375°F (190°C).
2. Blanch spinach, drain well, and mix with ricotta, Parmesan, eggs, nutmeg, salt, and pepper.
3. Pour mixture into pie crust.
4. Bake for 25-30 minutes until set and golden.

Per serving
Calories: 250| Protein: 14g| Fat: 15g| Carbs: 15g

Chicken and Leek Pie

Time: 1 hour| Difficulty: Moderate| Serving 2

1 pre-made pie crust
2 cups cooked chicken breast, shredded
2 leeks, cleaned and sliced
1/2 cup low-fat cream cheese
1/4 cup low-fat milk
1 tbsp. olive oil

1. Preheat oven to 375°F (190°C).
2. Sauté leeks in olive oil until soft.
3. Mix leeks, chicken, cream cheese, milk, salt, and pepper.
4. Pour mixture into pie crust.
5. Bake for 30-35 minutes until crust is golden.

Per serving
Calories: 290\ Protein: 19g| Fat: 16g| Carbs: 18g

Zucchini and Tomato Tart

Time: 45 minutes| Difficulty: Easy| Serving 2

1 pre-made pie crust
2 zucchinis, thinly sliced
2 tomatoes, thinly sliced
1/2 cup feta cheese, crumbled
1/4 cup basil leaves, chopped
2 tbsp. olive oil

1. Preheat oven to 375°F (190°C).
2. Arrange zucchini and tomato slices in pie crust, alternating layers.
3. Sprinkle with feta, basil, olive oil, salt, and pepper.
4. Bake for 30-35 minutes until vegetables are tender and crust is golden.

Per serving
Calories: 260| Protein: 6g| Fat: 18g| Carbs: 20g

Creamy Mushroom and Thyme Pie

Time: 50 minutes| Difficulty: Moderate| Serving 2

1 pre-made pie crust
2 cups mushrooms, sliced
1 onion, chopped
1/2 cup low-fat sour cream
1/4 cup low-fat milk
1 tbsp. fresh thyme, chopped
1 tbsp. olive oil

1. Preheat oven to 375°F (190°C).
2. Sauté mushrooms and onion in olive oil until tender.
3. Mix sour cream, milk, thyme, salt, and pepper with the mushrooms.
4. Pour into pie crust.
5. Bake for 35 minutes until set and crust is golden.

Per serving
Calories: 240| Protein: 5g| Fat: 15g| Carbs: 20g

Salmon and Asparagus Quiche

Time: 1 hour| Difficulty: Moderate| Serving 2

1 pre-made pie crust
1 cup cooked salmon, flaked
1 cup asparagus, chopped
1/2 cup low-fat cream cheese
1/4 cup skim milk
4 eggs

1. Preheat oven to 375°F (190°C).
2. Spread salmon and asparagus in pie crust.
3. In a bowl, whisk together eggs, cream cheese, milk, salt, and pepper.
4. Pour over salmon and asparagus.
5. Bake for 35-40 minutes until set.

Per serving
Calories: 280| Protein: 20g| Fat: 16g| Carbs: 12g

Beef and Potato Pie

Time: 1 h20 min| Difficulty: Moderate| Serving 2
1 pre-made pie crust
2 cups lean ground beef
2 potatoes, boiled and mashed
1 carrot and 1 onion, finely chopped
1/2 cup peas
1/2 cup low-sodium beef broth
1 tbsp. olive oil
1. Preheat oven to 375°F (190°C).
2. Cook beef and onion in olive oil until browned.
3. Add carrots, peas, and broth, simmer until veggies are tender.
4. Place beef mixture in pie crust, top with mashed potatoes.
5. Bake for 40 minutes until topping is golden.

Per serving
Calories: 300| Protein: 20g| Fat: 15g| Carbs: 20g

Ratatouille Tart

Time: 1 h10 min| Difficulty: Moderate| Serving 2
1 pre-made pie crust
1/2 cup each of sliced zucchini, yellow squash, and eggplant
1/4 cup red bell pepper, sliced
1/4 cup tomato sauce
1/4 cup Parmesan cheese, grated
2 tbsp. olive oil and 1 tsp. dried herbs (thyme, rosemary)
1. Preheat oven to 375°F (190°C).
2. Toss all vegetables with olive oil, salt, pepper, and dried herbs.
3. Layer vegetables over tomato sauce in pie crust.
4. Top with Parmesan cheese.
5. Bake for 40-45 minutes until vegetables are tender and crust is golden.

Per serving
Calories: 270| Protein: 8g| Fat: 16g| Carbs: 24g

Pumpkin and Goat Cheese Pie

Time: 1 hour| Difficulty: Moderate| Serving 2
1 pre-made pie crust
2 cups pumpkin puree
1/2 cup goat cheese, softened
1/4 cup low-fat milk
2 eggs
1/4 tsp. cinnamon and 1/4 tsp. nutmeg
1. Preheat oven to 375°F (190°C).
2. In a bowl, mix pumpkin, goat cheese, milk, eggs, cinnamon, nutmeg, and salt.
3. Pour mixture into pie crust.
4. Bake for 35-40 minutes until set.

Per serving
Calories: 260| Protein: 10g| Fat: 14g| Carbs: 24g

Apple and Cinnamon Tart

Time: 45 minutes| Difficulty: Easy| Serving 2
1 pre-made pie crust
3 apples, peeled, cored, and sliced
1/4 cup brown sugar
1 tsp. cinnamon
1 tbsp. lemon juice
1 tbsp. cornstarch
1. Preheat oven to 375°F (190°C).
2. Toss apple slices with lemon juice, brown sugar, cinnamon, and cornstarch.
3. Arrange apples in pie crust.
4. Bake for 30-35 minutes until apples are tender and crust is golden.

Per serving
Calories: 250| Protein: 2g| Fat: 12g| Carbs: 34g

Roasted Vegetable Pie

Time: 1 hour| Difficulty: Easy| Serving 2
1 pre-made pie crust
1/2 cup each of chopped zucchini, bell peppers, and eggplant
1/4 cup cherry tomatoes
1/4 cup feta cheese, crumbled
2 tbsp. olive oil
Salt and pepper to taste
1 tsp. dried oregano
1. Preheat oven to 375°F (190°C).
2. Toss vegetables with olive oil, salt, pepper, and oregano.
3. Roast vegetables for 25 minutes.
4. Arrange roasted vegetables in pie crust, top with feta cheese.
5. Bake for 25-30 minutes until crust is golden.

Per serving
Calories: 260| Protein: 6g| Fat: 16g| Carbs: 24g

Chicken and Broccoli Pie

Time: 1 hour| Difficulty: Moderate| Serving 2
1 pre-made pie crust
2 cups cooked chicken breast, chopped
1 cup broccoli florets
1/2 cup low-fat cream cheese
1/4 cup skim milk
Salt and pepper to taste
1. Preheat oven to 375°F (190°C).
2. Blanch broccoli until just tender.
3. Mix chicken, broccoli, cream cheese, and milk. Season with salt and pepper.
4. Pour into pie crust.
5. Bake for 35-40 minutes until golden and set.

Per serving
Calories: 280| Protein: 25g| Fat: 14g| Carbs: 12g

Spinach and Mushroom Quiche

Time: 50 minutes| Difficulty: Easy| Serving 2

1 pre-made pie crust
2 cups fresh spinach
1 cup mushrooms, sliced
4 eggs
1/2 cup skim milk
1/4 cup low-fat cheese, grated
Salt and pepper to taste

1. Preheat oven to 375°F (190°C).
2. Sauté mushrooms until browned, add spinach until wilted.
3. Whisk eggs and milk in a bowl. Season with salt and pepper.
4. Spread vegetable mix in pie crust, pour egg mixture over.
5. Sprinkle cheese on top.
6. Bake for 30-35 minutes until set.

Per serving
Calories: 220| Protein: 12g| Fat: 14g| Carbs: 14g

Crustless Spinach and Feta Pie

Time: 45 minutes| Difficulty: Easy| Serving 2

2 cups fresh spinach
1/4 cup crumbled feta cheese
4 eggs
1/4 cup skim milk
1/4 cup low-fat cheese, grated
Salt and pepper to taste

1. Preheat oven to 375°F (190°C).
2. Sauté spinach until wilted.
3. Spread spinach and feta in a greased pie dish.
4. Whisk eggs and milk in a bowl. Season with salt and pepper.
5. Pour egg mixture over spinach and feta.
6. Sprinkle grated cheese on top.
7. Bake for 25-30 minutes until set and golden.

Per serving
Calories: 180| Protein: 14g| Fat: 10g| Carbs: 8g

Turkey and Vegetable Pot Pie

Time: 1 h15 min| Difficulty: Moderate| Serving 2
1 pre-made pie crust
1 cup cooked turkey breast, diced
1 cup mixed vegetables (carrots, peas, corn)
1/2 cup low-sodium chicken broth
1/4 cup skim milk and 2 tbsp all-purpose flour
1. Prehcat ovcn to 375°F (190°C).
2. In a saucepan, mix chicken broth, milk, flour, salt, and pepper over medium heat until thickened.
3. Add turkey and mixed vegetables, stir until heated through.
4. Pour mixture into pie crust.
5. Cover with second pie crust, seal edges, and cut slits in the top for ventilation.
6. Bake for 35-40 minutes until crust is golden.

Per serving
Calories: 280| Protein: 18g| Fat: 12g| Carbs: 24g

Salmon and Broccoli Quiche

Time: 50 minutes| Difficulty: Easy| Serving 2
1 pre-made pie crust
1 cup cooked salmon fillet, flaked
1 cup broccoli florets, blanched
4 eggs
1/2 cup skim milk and 1/4 cup low-fat cheese, grated
1. Preheat oven to 375°F (190°C).
2. Whisk eggs and milk in a bowl. Season with salt and pepper.
3. Spread salmon and broccoli in pie crust, pour egg mixture over.
4. Sprinkle cheese on top.
5. Bake for 30-35 minutes until set.

Per serving
Calories: 240| Protein: 18g| Fat: 12g| Carbs: 16g

Butternut Squash and Caramelized Onion Tart

Time: 1 hour| Difficulty: Moderate| Serving 2
1 pre-made pie crust
2 cups butternut squash, cubed
1 large onion, sliced
1/4 cup goat cheese, crumbled and 1 tbsp olive oil
1. Preheat oven to 375°F (190°C).
2. Roast butternut squash until tender, about 25 minutes.
3. Caramelize onions in olive oil over low heat.
4. Combine squash, onions, and goat cheese in pie crust.
5. Season with salt and pepper.
6. Bake for 30 minutes until crust is golden.

Per serving
Calories: 290| Protein: 6g| Fat: 16g| Carbs: 28g

2.12 Smoothies and Beverages Recipes

Green Smoothie Bowl

Time: 5 minutes| Difficulty: Easy| Serving 2
2 cups baby spinach
1 ripe banana
1 cup frozen mixed berries
1/2 cup almond milk
2 tablespoons chia seeds
Toppings: sliced fruit, nuts, seeds, granola (optional)

1. In a blender, combine baby spinach, banana, frozen mixed berries, almond milk, and chia seeds.
2. Blend until smooth and creamy.
3. Divide the smoothie mixture between two serving bowls.
4. Top with sliced fruit, nuts, seeds, or granola, if desired.
5. Enjoy this nutrient-packed and refreshing breakfast bowl!

Per serving
Calories: 200| Protein: 5g| Carbs: 30g| Fat: 8g| Fiber: 8g

Strawberry Banana Smoothie

Time: 5 minutes| Difficulty: Easy| Serving 2
1 cup strawberries, hulled
1 banana
1 cup Greek yogurt
1/2 cup almond milk
Honey, to taste (optional)

1. Place all the ingredients in a blender.
2. Blend until smooth and creamy.
3. Taste and adjust sweetness with honey if desired.
4. Pour into glasses and serve immediately.

Per serving
Calories: 150| Protein: 10g| Carbs: 20g| Fat: 3g| Fiber: 4g

Banana Almond Milkshake

Time: 5 minutes| Difficulty: Easy| Serving 2
2 ripe bananas
1 cup unsweetened almond milk
2 tablespoons almond butter
1 tablespoon honey or maple syrup
1/2 teaspoon vanilla extract and Ice cubes

1. Combine bananas, almond milk, almond butter, honey or maple syrup, vanilla extract, and ice cubes in a blender.
2. Blend until smooth and creamy.
3. Pour into glasses and serve immediately.

Per serving
Calories: 180| Carbs: 25g| Fats: 7g| Protein: 5g

Turmeric Ginger Smoothie

Time: 5 minutes| Difficulty: Easy| Serving 2

1 ripe banana
1 cup frozen mango chunks
1 cup spinach leaves
1/2 cup Greek yogurt
1 teaspoon grated fresh ginger
1/2 teaspoon ground turmeric
1 cup almond milk
Honey or maple syrup for sweetening (optional)

1. In a blender, combine banana, frozen mango chunks, spinach leaves, Greek yoghurt, grated fresh ginger, ground turmeric, and almond milk.
2. Blend until smooth and creamy.
3. Sweeten with honey or maple syrup, if desired.
4. Pour into glasses and serve immediately.
5. Enjoy this vibrant and immune-boosting smoothie!

Per serving
Calories: 250| Protein: 10g| Carbs: 40g| Fat: 5g| Fiber: 6g

Matcha Green Tea Latte

Time: 5 minutes| Difficulty: Easy| Serving 2

2 teaspoons matcha green tea powder
1 cup hot water
1 cup unsweetened almond milk
Honey or stevia (optional, to taste)

1. Whisk matcha powder into hot water until dissolved.
2. Heat almond milk in a saucepan until hot but not boiling.
3. Froth almond milk using a frother or whisk.
4. Pour matcha mixture into mugs.
5. Top with frothed almond milk.
6. Sweeten with honey or stevia if desired.

Per serving
Calories: 15| Carbs: 2g| Fats: 1g| Protein: 1g

Berry Blast Smoothie

Time: 5 minutes| Difficulty: Easy| Serving 2

1 cup mixed berries (such as strawberries, blueberries, raspberries)
1/2 cup plain Greek yogurt
1 ripe banana
1 tablespoon chia seeds
1 cup almond milk
Handful of ice cubes

1. Place all ingredients in a blender.
2. Blend until smooth and well combined.
3. Pour into glasses and serve immediately.

Per serving
Calories: 150| Carbs: 20g| Fats: 5g| Protein: 7g

Creamy Almond Butter Smoothie

Time: 5 minutes| Difficulty: Easy| Serving 2

2 tablespoons almond butter
1 ripe banana
1 cup unsweetened almond milk
1 tablespoon honey or maple syrup
1/2 teaspoon vanilla extract
Handful of spinach (optional)
Handful of ice cubes

1. Combine all ingredients in a blender.
2. Blend until smooth and creamy.
3. Pour into glasses and serve immediately.

Per serving
Calories: 200| Carbs: 25g| Fats: 10g| Protein: 5g

Ginger Lemon Detox Drink

Time: 5 minutes| Difficulty: Easy| Serving 2

2 cups water
1-inch piece of fresh ginger, thinly sliced
Juice of 1 lemon
Honey or stevia (optional, to taste)
Ice cubes

1. Bring water to a boil in a saucepan.
2. Add ginger slices and let simmer for 5 minutes.
3. Remove from heat and stir in lemon juice.
4. Sweeten with honey or stevia if desired.
5. Let cool, then pour over ice cubes and serve.

Per serving
Calories: 10| Carbs: 3g| Fats: 0g| Protein: 0g

Tropical Paradise Smoothie

Time: 5 minutes| Difficulty: Easy| Serving 2
1/2 cup frozen pineapple chunks
1/2 cup frozen mango chunks and 1/2 banana
1/2 cup coconut milk and 1/2 cup orange juice
Handful of spinach (optional)
Handful of ice cubes

1. Add all ingredients to a blender.
2. Blend until smooth and creamy.
3. Pour into glasses and enjoy immediately.

Per serving
Calories: 160| Carbs: 30g| Fats: 5g| Protein: 2g

Peaches and Cream Smoothie

Time: 5 minutes| Difficulty: Easy| Serving 2
1 cup frozen peach slices
1/2 cup plain Greek yogurt
1/2 cup unsweetened almond milk
1 tablespoon honey or maple syrup
1/2 teaspoon vanilla extract
Handful of ice cubes

1. Place all ingredients in a blender.
2. Blend until smooth and creamy.
3. Pour into glasses and serve immediately.

Per serving
Calories: 150| Carbs: 20g| Fats: 3g| Protein: 8g

Pineapple Coconut Smoothie

Time: 5 minutes| Difficulty: Easy| Serving 2

1 cup frozen pineapple chunks
1/2 cup coconut milk
1/2 cup plain Greek yogurt
Honey or stevia (optional, to taste)and Ice cubes

1. Place all ingredients in a blender.
2. Blend until smooth and creamy.
3. Sweeten with honey or stevia if desired.
4. Pour into glasses and serve immediately.

Per serving
Calories: 150| Carbs: 20g|Fats: 3g| Protein: 8g

Green Goddess Smoothie

Time: 5 minutes| Difficulty: Easy| Serving 2
2 cups spinach and 1 ripe banana
1/2 cup cucumber, chopped
1/2 avocado
1 cup coconut water and Juice of 1/2 lime
Handful of ice cubes

1. Combine all ingredients in a blender.
2. Blend until smooth and creamy.
3. Pour into glasses and serve immediately.

Per serving
Calories: 120|Carbs: 20g| Fats: 5g| Protein: 3g

Banana Nut Smoothie

Time: 5 minutes| Difficulty: Easy| Serving 2

2 ripe bananas
2 tablespoons almond butter
1 cup unsweetened almond milk
1 tablespoon honey or maple syrup
1/2 teaspoon cinnamon
Handful of ice cubes

1. Add all ingredients to a blender.
2. Blend until smooth and creamy.
3. Pour into glasses and enjoy immediately.

Per serving
Calories: 220| Carbs: 30g| Fats: 10g| Protein: 5g

Peanut Butter Banana Smoothie

Time: 5 minutes| Difficulty: Easy| Serving 2

2 ripe bananas
2 tablespoons peanut butter
1 cup unsweetened almond milk
1 tablespoon honey or maple syrup
Handful of ice cubes

1. Place all ingredients in a blender.
2. Blend until smooth and creamy.
3. Pour into glasses and enjoy immediately.

Per serving
Calories: 220| Carbs: 25g| Fats: 10g| Protein: 5g

Peach Green Tea Smoothie

Time: 5 minutes| Difficulty: Easy| Serving 2

1 cup frozen peach slices
1 cup brewed green tea, chilled
1/2 cup plain Greek yogurt
Honey or stevia (optional, to taste)
Ice cubes

1. Combine peach slices, green tea, Greek yogurt, and honey or stevia in a blender.
2. Blend until smooth and creamy.
3. Add ice cubes and blend until desired consistency.
4. Pour into glasses and serve immediately.

Per serving
Calories: 120| Carbs: 20g| Fats: 1g| Protein: 8g

Mango Coconut Smoothie

Time: 5 minutes| Difficulty: Easy| Serving 2

1 cup frozen mango chunks
1/2 cup coconut milk
1/2 cup plain Greek yogurt
1 tablespoon honey or maple syrup
Juice of 1/2 lime
Handful of ice cubes

1. Add all ingredients to a blender.
2. Blend until smooth and creamy.
3. Pour into glasses and serve immediately.

Per serving
Calories: 160| Carbs: 20g| Fats: 7g| Protein: 7g

Vanilla Berry Smoothie

Time: 5 minutes| Difficulty: Easy| Serving 2

1 cup mixed berries (such as strawberries, raspberries, blueberries)
1/2 cup plain Greek yogurt
1/2 cup unsweetened almond milk
1 tablespoon honey or maple syrup
1/2 teaspoon vanilla extract
Handful of ice cubes

1. Combine all ingredients in a blender.
2. Blend until smooth and creamy.
3. Pour into glasses and serve immediately.

Per serving
Calories: 150| Carbs: 20g| Fats: 3g| Protein: 8g

Mixed Berry Smoothie Bowl

Time: 10 minutes| Difficulty: Easy| Serving 2

1 cup mixed berries (such as strawberries, blueberries, raspberries)
1/2 banana
1/2 cup plain Greek yogurt
1/4 cup almond milk
1 tablespoon chia seeds
***Toppings:** sliced fruit, granola, shredded coconut*

1. Place mixed berries, banana, Greek yogurt, almond milk, and chia seeds in a blender.
2. Blend until smooth and creamy.
3. Pour into bowls.
4. Top with sliced fruit, granola, and shredded coconut.
5. Serve immediately.

Per serving
Calories: 150|Carbs: 20g| Fats: 3g| Protein: 8g

Raspberry Chia Seed Smoothie

Time: 5 minutes| Difficulty: Easy| Serving 2

1 cup frozen raspberries
1/2 cup plain Greek yogurt
1/2 cup unsweetened almond milk
1 tablespoon chia seeds
Honey or stevia (optional, to taste)
Ice cubes

1. Combine raspberries, Greek yogurt, almond milk, and chia seeds in a blender.
2. Blend until smooth and creamy.
3. Sweeten with honey or stevia if desired.
4. Add ice cubes and blend until desired consistency.
5. Pour into glasses and serve immediately.

Per serving
Calories: 130| Carbs: 15g|Fats: 4g| Protein: 8g

Vanilla Almond Protein Shake

Time: 5 minutes| Difficulty: Easy| Serving 2

1 cup unsweetened almond milk
1 scoop vanilla protein powder
1 tablespoon almond butter
1/2 teaspoon vanilla extract
Honey or stevia (optional, to taste)
Ice cubes

1. Combine almond milk, protein powder, almond butter, vanilla extract, and honey or stevia in a blender.
2. Blend until smooth and creamy.
3. Add ice cubes and blend until desired consistency.
4. Pour into glasses and serve immediately.

Per serving
Calories: 160| Carbs: 5g| Fats: 7g|Protein: 8g

Chapter 3: Special Occasion Recipes

3.1 Festive and holiday dishes

Herb-Roasted Potatoes

Time: 45 minutes| Difficulty: Easy| Serving 2

2 cups baby potatoes, halved
2 tablespoons olive oil
1 teaspoon dried rosemary
1 teaspoon dried thyme
1 teaspoon dried oregano
Salt and pepper to taste

1. Preheat the oven to 400°F (200°C).
2. In a large bowl, toss the halved baby potatoes with olive oil, dried rosemary, dried thyme, dried oregano, salt, and pepper until evenly coated.
3. Spread the potatoes in a single layer on a baking sheet lined with parchment paper.
4. Roast in the preheated oven for 30-35 minutes, or until the potatoes are golden brown and crispy.
5. Remove from the oven and serve hot as a festive side dish.

Per serving
Calories: 200|Carbs: 25g| Fats: 10g| Protein: 3g

Quinoa Stuffed Acorn Squash

Time: 1h15min| Difficulty: Moderate| Serving 2
2 acorn squash, halved and seeds removed
1 cup cooked quinoa
1/2 cup diced apple
1/4 cup dried cranberries
1/4 cup chopped pecans
1 tbs. maple syrup and 1 teaspoon cinnamon

1. Preheat the oven to 400°F (200°C).
2. Place the acorn squash halves cut side down on a baking sheet lined with parchment paper.
3. Roast in the preheated oven for 30-40 minutes, or until tender.
4. In a large bowl, combine the cooked quinoa, diced apple, dried cranberries, chopped pecans, maple syrup, cinnamon, salt, and pepper.
5. Once the squash halves are tender, flip them over and fill each half with the quinoa mixture.
6. Return to the oven and bake for an additional 15 minutes.

Per serving
Calories: 350| Carbs: 65g| Fats: 7g| Protein: 9g

Herb-Roasted Vegetables

Time: 30 minutes| Difficulty: Easy| Serving 2

2 cups mixed vegetables (such as carrots, Brussels sprouts, and cauliflower), chopped
2 tablespoons olive oil
2 cloves garlic, minced
1 teaspoon dried thyme
1 teaspoon dried rosemary
Salt and pepper to taste

1. Preheat the oven to 400°F (200°C).
2. In a large bowl, toss the chopped vegetables with olive oil, minced garlic, dried thyme, dried rosemary, salt, and pepper until evenly coated.
3. Spread the vegetables in a single layer on a baking sheet lined with parchment paper.
4. Roast in the preheated oven for 30-35 minutes, or until the vegetables are tender and slightly caramelized.
5. Remove from the oven and serve hot as a festive side dish.

Per serving
Calories: 150| Carbs: 10g| Fats: 10g| Protein: 2g

Garlic Butter Roasted Rack of Lamb

Time: 1 hour| Difficulty: Moderate| Serving 2

1 rack of lamb (about 1 lb)
4 cloves garlic, minced
2 tablespoons fresh rosemary, chopped
2 tablespoons unsalted butter, melted
Salt and pepper to taste

1. Preheat the oven to 400°F (200°C).
2. In a small bowl, mix together minced garlic, chopped rosemary, melted butter, salt, and pepper.
3. Rub the garlic butter mixture all over the rack of lamb.
4. Place the rack of lamb in a roasting pan.
5. Roast in the preheated oven for about 25-30 minutes, or until the lamb is cooked to your desired doneness (medium-rare is recommended), with an internal temperature of 145°F (63°C).
6. Let the lamb rest for 10 minutes before slicing.
7. Serve hot as a festive main dish.

Per serving
Calories: 350| Carbs: 0g| Fats: 25g| Protein: 30g

Brussels Sprouts and Bacon

Time: 30 minutes| Difficulty: Easy| Serving 2

2 cups Brussels sprouts, trimmed and halved
2 slices bacon, chopped
1 tablespoon olive oil
2 cloves garlic, minced
Salt and pepper to taste

1. In a large skillet, cook the chopped bacon over medium heat until crispy.
2. Remove the bacon from the skillet and set aside.
3. In the same skillet, add olive oil and minced garlic. Cook until fragrant.
4. Add Brussels sprouts to the skillet and cook until tender and caramelized.
5. Season with salt and pepper to taste.
6. Stir in the cooked bacon pieces.
7. Serve hot as a festive side dish.

Per serving
Calories: 150| Carbs: 10g| Fats: 10g| Protein: 5g

Maple Mustard Glazed Salmon

Time: 30 minutes| Difficulty: Easy| Serving 2

2 salmon fillets
1/4 cup maple syrup
2 tablespoons Dijon mustard
1 tablespoon olive oil
Salt and pepper to taste

1. Preheat the oven to 400°F (200°C).
2. In a small bowl, mix together maple syrup, Dijon mustard, olive oil, salt, and pepper.
3. Place the salmon fillets on a baking sheet lined with parchment paper.
4. Brush the maple mustard glaze all over the salmon fillets.
5. Roast in the preheated oven for about 12-15 minutes, or until the salmon is cooked through and flakes easily with a fork.
6. Serve hot as a festive main dish.

Per serving
Calories: 300| Carbs: 20g| Fats: 15g| Protein: 30g

Roasted Root Vegetables with Maple Glaze

Time: 1 hour| Difficulty: Easy| Serving 2

2 cups mixed root vegetables (such as carrots, parsnips, and sweet potatoes), peeled and chopped
2 tablespoons olive oil
2 tablespoons maple syrup
1 teaspoon dried thyme
Salt and pepper to taste

1. Preheat the oven to 400°F (200°C).
2. In a large bowl, toss the chopped root vegetables with olive oil, maple syrup, dried thyme, salt, and pepper until evenly coated.
3. Spread the vegetables in a single layer on a baking sheet lined with parchment paper.
4. Roast in the preheated oven for 30-40 minutes, or until the vegetables are tender and caramelized.
5. Remove from the oven and serve hot as a festive side dish.

Per serving
Calories: 200| Carbs: 30g| Fats: 8g| Protein: 2g

Cauliflower Stuffing

Time: 45 minutes| Difficulty: Moderate| Serving 2

1 head cauliflower, chopped into small pieces
1 tablespoon olive oil
1 onion, diced
2 celery stalks, diced
2 cloves garlic, minced
1/2 cup chopped mushrooms
1/4 cup chopped fresh parsley
1 teaspoon dried sage
1 teaspoon dried thyme
Salt and pepper to taste

1. In a large skillet, heat olive oil over medium heat.
2. Add diced onion, celery, and minced garlic. Cook until softened, about 5 minutes.
3. Add chopped mushrooms and cook until they release their moisture and start to brown, about 5 minutes.
4. Stir in chopped cauliflower, dried sage, dried thyme, salt, and pepper. Cook until cauliflower is tender, about 10-15 minutes.
5. Remove from heat and stir in chopped fresh parsley.
6. Serve hot as a festive stuffing alternative.

Per serving
Calories: 150| Carbs: 20g| Fats: 6g| Protein: 5g

Roasted Turkey Breast with Herbs

Time: 1 hour| Difficulty: Moderate| Serving 2

1 turkey breast (about 1.5 lbs.)
2 tablespoons olive oil
2 cloves garlic, minced
1 teaspoon dried thyme
1 teaspoon dried rosemary
Salt and pepper to taste

1. Preheat the oven to 375°F (190°C).
2. In a small bowl, mix together the olive oil, minced garlic, dried thyme, dried rosemary, salt, and pepper.
3. Rub the mixture all over the turkey breast.
4. Place the turkey breast on a baking sheet lined with parchment paper.
5. Roast in the preheated oven for about 45-50 minutes, or until the internal temperature reaches 165°F (74°C).
6. Remove from the oven and let it rest for 10 minutes before slicing.
7. Serve with your favorite side dishes.

Per serving
Calories: 250| Carbs: 1g| Fats: 11g| Protein: 35g

Garlic Herb Mashed Cauliflower

Time: 30 minutes| Difficulty: Easy| Serving 2

1 head cauliflower, chopped into florets
2 cloves garlic, minced
2 tablespoons olive oil
2 tablespoons chopped fresh parsley
Salt and pepper to taste

1. Steam or boil the cauliflower florets until tender.
2. In a skillet, sauté the minced garlic in olive oil until fragrant.
3. Transfer the cooked cauliflower and garlic to a food processor.
4. Add chopped fresh parsley, salt, and pepper to the food processor.
5. Blend until smooth and creamy, adding more olive oil if needed.
6. Season with additional salt and pepper to taste.
7. Serve hot as a festive side dish.

Per serving
Calories: 100| Carbs: 10g| Fats: 7g| Protein: 3g

Rosemary Garlic Roast Chicken

Time: 1 h 30 min| Difficulty: Moderate| Serving 2
1 whole chicken (about 3-4 lbs.)
4 cloves garlic, minced
2 tablespoons fresh rosemary, chopped
2 tablespoons olive oil
Salt and pepper to taste
1. Preheat the oven to 375°F (190°C).
2. In a small bowl, mix together minced garlic, chopped rosemary, olive oil, salt, and pepper to form a paste.
3. Rub the garlic-rosemary paste all over the chicken, including under the skin.
4. Place the chicken in a roasting pan or on a baking sheet.
5. Roast in the preheated oven for about 1 hour and 15 minutes, or until the chicken is golden brown and the internal temperature reaches 165°F (75°C).
6. Let the chicken rest for 10 minutes before carving.
7. Serve hot as a festive main dish.

Per serving
Calories: 300| Carbs: 0g| Fats: 15g| Protein: 40g

Garlic Herb Roasted Pork Tenderloin

Time: 1 hour| Difficulty: Moderate| Serving 2

1 pork tenderloin (about 1 lb.)
4 cloves garlic, minced
2 tablespoons fresh herbs (such as rosemary, thyme, or sage), chopped
2 tablespoons olive oil
Salt and pepper to taste
1. Preheat the oven to 400°F (200°C).
2. In a small bowl, mix together minced garlic, chopped fresh herbs, olive oil, salt, and pepper.
3. Rub the garlic-herb mixture all over the pork tenderloin.
4. Place the pork tenderloin in a roasting pan or on a baking sheet.
5. Roast in the preheated oven for about 25-30 minutes, or until the pork is cooked through and the internal temperature reaches 145°F (63°C).
6. Let the pork tenderloin rest for 10 minutes before slicing.
7. Serve hot as a festive main dish.

Per serving
Calories: 280| Carbs: 1g| Fats: 10g| Protein: 45g

Cranberry Glazed Turkey Breast

Time: 2 hours| Difficulty: Moderate| Serving 2
1 turkey breast (about 2 lbs.)
1/2 cup cranberry juice
1/4 cup honey
2 tablespoons balsamic vinegar
1 tablespoon olive oil
Salt and pepper to taste
1. Preheat the oven to 375°F (190°C).
2. In a small saucepan, combine cranberry juice, honey, balsamic vinegar, olive oil, salt, and pepper. Bring to a boil, then reduce heat and simmer until slightly thickened, about 10-15 minutes.
3. Place the turkey breast in a roasting pan or on a baking sheet.
4. Brush the cranberry glaze all over the turkey breast.
5. Roast in the preheated oven for about 1 hour and 30 minutes, or until the turkey is cooked through and the internal temperature reaches 165°F (75°C), basting with the glaze every 30 minutes.
6. Let the turkey breast rest for 10 minutes before slicing.
7. Serve hot as a festive main dish.

Per serving
Calories: 250| Carbs: 20g|Fats: 5g| Protein: 35g

Balsamic Glazed Ham

Time: 2 hours| Difficulty: Moderate| Serving 2
1 small boneless ham (about 2 lbs.)
1/4 cup balsamic vinegar
2 tablespoons honey
1 tablespoon Dijon mustard
1 tablespoon olive oil
Salt and pepper to taste
1. Preheat the oven to 350°F (175°C).
2. In a small saucepan, combine balsamic vinegar, honey, Dijon mustard, olive oil, salt, and pepper. Bring to a boil, then reduce heat and simmer until slightly thickened, about 10-15 minutes.
3. Place the ham in a roasting pan.
4. Brush the balsamic glaze all over the ham.
5. Roast in the preheated oven for about 1 hour, or until the ham is heated through.
6. Baste the ham with the glaze every 20 minutes.
7. Serve hot as a festive main dish.

Per serving
Calories: 300| Carbs: 10g| Fats: 10g| Protein: 45g

Apple Cider Glazed Pork Chops

Time: 1 hour| Difficulty: Moderate| Serving 2
2 pork chops
1/2 cup apple cider
2 tablespoons apple cider vinegar
2 tablespoons honey
1 tablespoon Dijon mustard
1 tablespoon olive oil
Salt and pepper to taste

1. In a small saucepan, combine apple cider, apple cider vinegar, honey, Dijon mustard, olive oil, salt, and pepper. Bring to a boil, then reduce heat and simmer until slightly thickened, about 10-15 minutes.
2. Preheat a skillet over medium-high heat and add a little olive oil.
3. Season the pork chops with salt and pepper on both sides.
4. Sear the pork chops in the skillet for about 3-4 minutes on each side, until golden brown.
5. Reduce heat to medium-low and pour the apple cider glaze over the pork chops.
6. Continue to cook for another 5-7 minutes, or until the pork chops are cooked through and the glaze is caramelized.

Per serving
Calories: 280| Carbs: 20g| Fats: 10g| Protein: 30g

Cider Glazed Pork Roast

Time: 2 hours| Difficulty: Moderate| Serving 2
1 pork shoulder roast (about 2 lbs.)
1 cup apple cider
1/4 cup apple cider vinegar
2 tablespoons brown sugar
1 tablespoon Dijon mustard
1 tablespoon olive oil

1. Preheat the oven to 325°F (160°C).
2. In a small saucepan, combine apple cider, apple cider vinegar, brown sugar, Dijon mustard, olive oil, salt, and pepper. Heat over medium heat until well combined.
3. Place the pork shoulder roast in a roasting pan.
4. Pour the cider glaze over the pork shoulder roast.
5. Roast in the preheated oven for about 2 hours, or until the pork is tender and pulls apart easily.
6. Baste the pork shoulder roast with the glaze every 30 minutes.

Per serving
Calories: 300| Carbs: 25g| Fats: 15g| Protein: 35g

Lemon Herb Roasted Cornish Hens

Time: 1 h 30 min| Difficulty: Moderate| Serving 2
2 Cornish hens
2 tablespoons lemon juice
2 tablespoons olive oil
2 cloves garlic, minced
1 tablespoon fresh rosemary, chopped
1 tablespoon fresh thyme leaves
Salt and pepper to taste

1. Preheat the oven to 375°F (190°C).
2. In a small bowl, mix together lemon juice, olive oil, minced garlic, chopped rosemary, chopped thyme, salt, and pepper.
3. Rub the lemon-herb mixture all over the Cornish hens, inside and out.
4. Place the Cornish hens in a roasting pan or on a baking sheet.
5. Roast in the preheated oven for about 1 hour and 15 minutes, or until the hens are golden brown and the internal temperature reaches 165°F (75°C).
6. Let the hens rest for 10 minutes before serving.

Per serving
Calories: 350| Carbs: 0g| Fats: 20g| Protein: 40g

Herb Crusted Beef Tenderloin

Time: 1 h 30 min| Difficulty: Moderate| Serving 2
1 beef tenderloin (about 1 lb.)
2 tablespoons fresh thyme leaves
2 tablespoons fresh rosemary, chopped
2 tablespoons fresh parsley, chopped
2 tablespoons Dijon mustard
2 tablespoons olive oil
Salt and pepper to taste

1. Preheat the oven to 425°F (220°C).
2. In a small bowl, mix together fresh thyme leaves, chopped rosemary, chopped parsley, Dijon mustard, olive oil, salt, and pepper.
3. Rub the herb mixture all over the beef tenderloin.
4. Place the beef tenderloin on a baking sheet.
5. Roast in the preheated oven for about 25-30 minutes, or until the beef tenderloin reaches your desired level of doneness (medium-rare is recommended), with an internal temperature of 145°F (63°C).
6. Let the beef tenderloin rest for 10 minutes before slicing.

Per serving
Calories: 350| Carbs: 0g| Fats: 20g| Protein: 40g

Apricot Glazed Pork Loin

Time: 1 h30 min| Difficulty: Moderate| Serving 2

1 pork loin roast (about 2 lbs.)
1/2 cup apricot preserves
2 tablespoons soy sauce
2 tablespoons olive oil
2 cloves garlic, minced
Salt and pepper to taste

1. Preheat the oven to 375°F (190°C).
2. In a small saucepan, combine apricot preserves, soy sauce, olive oil, minced garlic, salt, and pepper. Heat over medium heat until melted and well combined.
3. Place the pork loin roast in a roasting pan.
4. Brush the apricot glaze all over the pork loin.
5. Roast in the preheated oven for about 1 hour and 15 minutes, or until the pork loin is cooked through and the internal temperature reaches 145°F (63°C), basting with the glaze every 20 minutes.
6. Let the pork loin rest for 10 minutes before slicing.
7. Serve hot as a festive main dish.

Per serving
Calories: 320| Carbs: 20g| Fats: 15g| Protein: 35g

Baked Chicken with Spinach and Pine Nuts

Time: 40 minutes| Difficulty: Easy| Serving 2
2 chicken breasts (6 oz each)
2 cups fresh spinach
2 tablespoons pine nuts
1 lemon, juiced and zested
2 cloves garlic, minced
Salt and pepper to taste
1 tablespoon olive oil

1. Preheat the oven to 400°F.
2. In a pan, sauté spinach with garlic until wilted.
3. Mix in pine nuts, lemon zest, and juice.
4. Slice chicken breasts halfway to create a pocket, stuff with spinach mixture.
5. Place on a baking sheet, drizzle with olive oil, and season with salt and pepper.
6. Bake for 25-30 minutes until chicken is cooked through.

Per serving
Calories: 310| Protein: 35g| Fat: 14g| Carbs: 8g

Cranberry Pecan Stuffed Pork Chops

Time: 1 h 30 min| Difficulty: Moderate| Serving 2
2 pork chops
1/4 cup dried cranberries, chopped
1/4 cup pecans, chopped
2 tablespoons breadcrumbs
2 tablespoons olive oil
Salt and pepper to taste

1. Preheat the oven to 375°F (190°C).
2. In a small bowl, mix together chopped dried cranberries, chopped pecans, breadcrumbs, olive oil, salt, and pepper.
3. Using a sharp knife, cut a slit horizontally in each pork chop to create a pocket.
4. Stuff each pork chop with the cranberry pecan mixture, pressing gently to seal.
5. Heat a skillet over medium-high heat and add a little olive oil.
6. Sear the stuffed pork chops for about 3-4 minutes on each side, until golden brown.
7. Transfer the seared pork chops to a baking dish and bake in the preheated oven for about 20-25 minutes, or until cooked through.
8. Serve hot as a festive main dish.

Per serving
Calories: 350| Carbs: 15g| Fats: 20g| Protein: 30g

Beef Stew with Root Vegetables

Time: 2 hours| Difficulty: Medium| Serving 2
1 lb lean beef stew meat, cut into cubes
1 tbsp olive oil
2 carrots, diced
2 parsnips, diced
1 turnip, diced
4 cups beef broth (low-fat)
1 onion, chopped
2 cloves garlic, minced
1 tsp dried thyme
Salt and pepper, to taste

1. Heat olive oil in a large pot and brown the beef on all sides.
2. Add onions and garlic, cook until softened.
3. Add carrots, parsnips, turnip, thyme, and beef broth.
4. Bring to a boil, then reduce to a simmer.
5. Cover and simmer for 1.5 hours or until meat is tender.

Per serving
Calories: 280| Protein: 25g| Fat: 10g| Carbs: 22g

Herb-Crusted Rack of Lamb
Time: 45 minutes| Difficulty: Medium| Serving 2

1 rack of lamb (about 1 lb., trimmed of fat)
1 tablespoon Dijon mustard
1/4 cup breadcrumbs
1 tablespoon chopped fresh rosemary
1 tablespoon chopped fresh thyme
2 cloves garlic, minced
Salt and pepper to taste
1 tablespoon olive oil

1. Preheat the oven to 400°F.
2. Season the lamb with salt and pepper.
3. Rub Dijon mustard all over the lamb.
4. Mix breadcrumbs, rosemary, thyme, and garlic, then press onto the lamb.
5. Heat olive oil in an ovenproof skillet, sear lamb on all sides.
6. Transfer skillet to the oven and roast for 20-25 minutes for medium-rare.
7. Let rest before carving.

Per serving
Calories: 320| Protein: 22g| Fat: 24g| Carbs: 4g

Veal Scallopini with Mushroom Sauce
Time: 30 minutes| Difficulty: Medium| Serving 2

4 veal cutlets (4 oz. each)
1 cup sliced mushrooms
1/2 cup low-sodium chicken broth
1/4 cup white wine (optional)
1 tablespoon capers
1 tablespoon lemon juice
1 tablespoon chopped parsley
1 tablespoon olive oil
Salt and pepper to taste

1. Heat olive oil in a large skillet over medium heat.
2. Season veal cutlets with salt and pepper, sear for 1-2 minutes on each side.
3. Remove veal and set aside.
4. Add mushrooms to the skillet, sauté until golden.
5. Deglaze with chicken broth and white wine, simmer for 5 minutes.
6. Stir in capers and lemon juice.
7. Return veal to the skillet, simmer for another 2-3 minutes.
8. Garnish with parsley before serving.

Per serving
Calories: 220| Protein: 24g| Fat: 9g| Carbs: 5g

Pork Tenderloin with Apples and Cinnamon
Time: 45 minutes| Difficulty: Medium| Serving 2

1 pork tenderloin (about 1 lb.)
2 apples, sliced
1 tsp. cinnamon
1 tbsp. honey
1 tbsp. olive oil
Salt and pepper, to taste

1. Preheat oven to 375°F (190°C).
2. Season pork with salt and pepper.
3. Heat olive oil in a skillet and brown the pork on all sides.
4. Transfer pork to a baking dish, top with apple slices, sprinkle with cinnamon, and drizzle with honey.
5. Roast for 30 minutes or until pork is cooked through.

Per serving
Calories: 295| Protein: 24g| Fat: 14g| Carbs: 18g

Turkey Breast with Apple Stuffing
Time: 1 hour 20 minutes| Difficulty: Medium| Serving 2

1 turkey breast (about 2 lbs.)
2 cups diced apples
1/2 cup diced celery
1 onion, diced
1/4 cup dried cranberries
1 teaspoon dried sage
1 teaspoon dried thyme
Salt and pepper to taste
1 cup low-sodium chicken broth

1. Preheat the oven to 350°F.
2. In a bowl, mix apples, celery, onion, cranberries, sage, and thyme.
3. Season the turkey breast with salt and pepper, and lay flat.
4. Place the stuffing mixture on the turkey, roll up, and tie with kitchen string.
5. Place in a roasting pan and pour chicken broth around the turkey.
6. Roast for about 1 hour or until the internal temperature reaches 165°F.
7. Let rest before slicing.

Per serving
Calories: 290| Protein: 35g| Fat: 6g| Carbs: 22

Sweet Potato Casserole with Pecan Crumble

Time: 1 hour| Difficulty: Intermediate| Serving 2

2 large sweet potatoes, peeled and cubed
1/4 cup coconut milk
2 tablespoons maple syrup
1 teaspoon ground cinnamon
1/2 cup chopped pecans
2 tablespoons coconut oil, melted
2 tablespoons coconut sugar
Salt to taste

1. Preheat the oven to 375°F (190°C).
2. Boil sweet potato cubes until fork-tender, then drain and mash.
3. Stir in coconut milk, maple syrup, ground cinnamon, and salt until well combined.
4. Transfer the sweet potato mixture to a baking dish and spread evenly.
5. In a separate bowl, combine chopped pecans, melted coconut oil, and coconut sugar to make the crumble topping.
6. Sprinkle the pecan crumble over the sweet potato mixture.
7. Bake for 25-30 minutes, or until the topping is golden brown and crispy.

Per serving
Calories: 220| Protein: 3g| Fat: 12g| Carbs: 28g

Herb-Roasted Turkey Breast

Time: 2 hours| Difficulty: Intermediate| Serving 2

2 pounds turkey breast
2 tablespoons olive oil
2 cloves garlic, minced
1 tablespoon chopped fresh rosemary
1 tablespoon chopped fresh thyme
1 tablespoon chopped fresh sage
Salt and pepper to taste

1. Preheat the oven to 375°F (190°C).
2. In a small bowl, mix olive oil, minced garlic, chopped fresh rosemary, thyme, sage, salt, and pepper to make the herb rub.
3. Rub the herb mixture all over the turkey breast.
4. Place the turkey breast in a roasting pan and roast for 1.5-2 hours, or until the internal temperature reaches 165°F (74°C).
5. Let the turkey breast rest for 10 minutes before slicing and serving.

Per serving
Calories: 180| Protein: 30g| Fat: 5g| Carbs: 0g

Roasted Beet and Goat Cheese Salad

Time: 50 minutes| Difficulty: Easy| Serving 2
4 medium beets, peeled and diced
2 tablespoons olive oil
2 tablespoons balsamic vinegar
4 cups mixed salad greens
1/4 cup crumbled goat cheese
2 tablespoons chopped walnuts and Salt and pepper to taste

1. Preheat the oven to 400°F (200°C).
2. Toss diced beets with olive oil, balsamic vinegar, salt, and pepper on a baking sheet.
3. Roast for 30-35 minutes, or until beets are tender and caramelized.
4. Arrange mixed salad greens on serving plates.
5. Top with roasted beets, crumbled goat cheese, and chopped walnuts.

Per serving
Calories: 180| Protein: 5g| Fat: 10g| Carbs: 20g

Turkey Meatloaf with Sage and Onion

Time: 1 hour 30 minutes| Difficulty: Easy| Serving 2
1 lb. ground turkey breast
1/2 cup breadcrumbs
1/4 cup milk (use almond milk for lower fat)
1 onion, finely chopped
2 cloves garlic, minced
1 egg, beaten
2 tbsp. fresh sage, chopped and Salt and pepper, to taste

1. Preheat oven to 375°F (190°C).
2. In a bowl, mix all ingredients thoroughly.
3. Shape into a loaf and place in a baking dish.
4. Bake for about 1 hour or until cooked through.

Per serving
Calories: 265| Protein: 28g| Fat: 7g| Carbs: 18g

Herbed Chicken with Roasted Vegetables

Time: 1 hour| Difficulty: Easy| Serving 2
2 boneless, skinless chicken breasts
1 tbsp. olive oil
1 tsp. dried rosemary
1 tsp. dried thyme
Salt and pepper, to taste
1 cup baby carrots
1 cup Brussels sprouts, halved
1 small sweet potato, cubed

1. Preheat oven to 400°F (200°C).
2. Season chicken with olive oil, rosemary, thyme, salt, and pepper.
3. Arrange chicken and vegetables on a baking tray.
4. Roast for 45 minutes, until chicken is cooked through and vegetables are tender.

Per serving
Calories: 310| Protein: 28g| Fat: 14g| Carbs: 22g

Green Bean Almondine

Time: 25 minutes| Difficulty: Easy| Serving 2

1 pound green beans, trimmed
2 tablespoons olive oil
1/4 cup sliced almonds
2 cloves garlic, minced
1 tablespoon lemon juice
Salt and pepper to taste

1. Bring a pot of salted water to a boil and blanch green beans for 3-4 minutes.
2. Drain and rinse green beans under cold water to stop the cooking process.
3. In a skillet, heat olive oil over medium heat and toast sliced almonds until golden brown.
4. Add minced garlic to the skillet and sauté until fragrant.
5. Add blanched green beans to the skillet and toss until heated through.
6. Drizzle lemon juice over the green beans and season with salt and pepper.

Per serving
Calories: 120| Protein: 3g| Fat: 8g| Carbs: 10g

Cauliflower Mash with Roasted Garlic and Herbs

Time: 45 minutes| Difficulty: Easy| Serving 2

1 large head cauliflower, cut into florets
4 cloves garlic, peeled
2 tablespoons olive oil
1/4 cup unsweetened almond milk
2 tablespoons chopped fresh chives
Salt and pepper to taste

1. Preheat the oven to 400°F (200°C).
2. Toss cauliflower florets and garlic cloves with olive oil, salt, and pepper on a baking sheet.
3. Roast for 25-30 minutes, or until cauliflower is tender and golden brown.
4. Transfer the roasted cauliflower and garlic to a food processor.
5. Add almond milk and blend until smooth.
6. Stir in chopped fresh chives and season with additional salt and pepper if needed.

Per serving
Calories: 120| Protein: 4g| Fat: 7g| Carbs: 14g

3.2 Meals for entertaining guests

Lemon Herb Grilled Chicken

Time: 30 minutes| Difficulty: Easy| Serving 2
2 boneless, skinless chicken breasts
Juice of 1 lemon
2 tablespoons olive oil
2 cloves garlic, minced
1 teaspoon dried thyme
1 teaspoon dried rosemary
Salt and pepper to taste

1. In a bowl, whisk together lemon juice, olive oil, minced garlic, dried thyme, dried rosemary, salt, and pepper.
2. Marinate the chicken breasts in the mixture for at least 15 minutes.
3. Preheat grill to medium-high heat.
4. Grill the chicken breasts for 6-8 minutes per side, or until cooked through.
5. Serve hot with your choice of sides.

Per serving
Calories: 300 kcal | Protein: 30g | Carbs: 2g | Fat: 18g

Garlic Shrimp Linguine

Time: 20 minutes| Difficulty: Easy| Serving 2
200g linguine pasta
200g shrimp, peeled and deveined
2 cloves garlic, minced
2 tablespoons olive oil
1 tablespoon chopped parsley
Salt and pepper to taste

1. Cook linguine according to package instructions until al dente. Drain and set aside.
2. In a skillet, heat olive oil over medium heat. Add minced garlic and cook until fragrant.
3. Add shrimp to the skillet and cook until pink and cooked through.
4. Toss cooked linguine with the garlic shrimp, chopped parsley, salt, and pepper.
5. Serve hot as a main dish.

Per serving
Calories: 400 kcal | Protein: 20g | Carbs: 40g | Fat: 18g

Mushroom Risotto

Time: 40 minutes| Difficulty: Moderate| Serving 2

1 cup Arborio rice
4 cups vegetable broth
200g mushrooms, sliced
1 onion, finely chopped
2 cloves garlic, minced
1/4 cup white wine (optional)
2 tablespoons olive oil
2 tablespoons grated Parmesan cheese
Salt and pepper to taste

1. In a saucepan, heat vegetable broth over low heat.
2. In a separate large skillet, heat olive oil over medium heat. Add chopped onion and minced garlic, and sauté until softened.
3. Add sliced mushrooms to the skillet and cook until they release their moisture and become golden brown.
4. Add Arborio rice to the skillet and toast for 1-2 minutes.
5. If using, pour in white wine and stir until absorbed.
6. Begin adding warm vegetable broth to the skillet, one ladleful at a time, stirring constantly and allowing each addition to be absorbed before adding more.
7. Continue this process until the rice is creamy and cooked al dente, about 18-20 minutes.
8. Stir in grated Parmesan cheese and season with salt and pepper.

Per serving
Calories: 400 kcal | Protein: 8g | Carbs: 50g | Fat: 18g

Grilled Salmon with Lemon Dill Sauce

Time: 25 minutes| Difficulty: Easy| Serving 2
2 salmon fillets
1 lemon, juiced
2 tablespoons chopped fresh dill
2 tablespoons Greek yogurt
Salt and pepper to taste

1. Preheat grill to medium-high heat.
2. Season salmon fillets with salt, pepper, and lemon juice.
3. Grill salmon fillets for 4-5 minutes per side, or until cooked through.
4. In a small bowl, mix together chopped fresh dill and Greek yogurt to make the sauce.
5. Serve grilled salmon with lemon dill sauce on the side.

Per serving
Calories: 300 kcal | Protein: 25g | Carbs: 2g | Fat: 20g

Caprese Stuffed Chicken

Time: 35 minutes| Difficulty: Moderate| Serving 2

2 boneless, skinless chicken breasts
1 large tomato, sliced
4 slices fresh mozzarella cheese
1/4 cup fresh basil leaves
2 tablespoons balsamic glaze
Salt and pepper to taste

1. Preheat oven to 375°F (190°C).
2. Cut a pocket into each chicken breast, being careful not to cut all the way through.
3. Stuff each chicken breast with sliced tomato, fresh mozzarella cheese, and basil leaves.
4. Season the outside of the chicken breasts with salt and pepper.
5. Place stuffed chicken breasts in a baking dish and bake in the preheated oven for 25-30 minutes, or until chicken is cooked through.
6. Drizzle balsamic glaze over the stuffed chicken breasts before serving.
7. Serve hot as a flavorful main dish.

Per serving
Calories: 300 kcal| Protein: 30g | Carbs: 4g | Fat: 18g

Lemon Garlic Shrimp Pasta

Time: 20 minutes| Difficulty: Easy| Serving 2

200g pasta of choice
200g shrimp, peeled and deveined
2 cloves garlic, minced
2 tablespoons olive oil
Juice of 1 lemon
2 tablespoons chopped parsley
Salt and pepper to taste

1. Cook pasta according to package instructions until al dente. Drain and set aside.
2. In a skillet, heat olive oil over medium heat. Add minced garlic and cook until fragrant.
3. Add shrimp to the skillet and cook until pink and cooked through.
4. Toss cooked pasta with the garlic shrimp, lemon juice, chopped parsley, salt, and pepper.
5. Serve hot as a satisfying main dish.

Per serving
Calories: 450 kcal | Protein: 20g | Carbs: 50g | Fat: 18

Sesame Ginger Glazed Salmon

Time: 25 minutes| Difficulty: Easy| Serving 2

2 salmon fillets
2 tablespoons soy sauce
1 tablespoon honey
1 tablespoon rice vinegar
1 tablespoon sesame oil
1 tablespoon grated ginger
1 clove garlic, minced
Sesame seeds for garnish

1. In a small bowl, whisk together soy sauce, honey, rice vinegar, sesame oil, grated ginger, and minced garlic to make the glaze.
2. Marinate the salmon fillets in half of the glaze for 15 minutes.
3. Preheat grill to medium-high heat.
4. Grill the salmon fillets for 4-5 minutes per side, or until cooked through.
5. Brush the remaining glaze over the cooked salmon fillets.
6. Sprinkle sesame seeds on top for garnish.
7. Serve hot as an elegant main dish.

Per serving
Calories: 350 kcal | Protein: 25g | Carbs: 10g | Fat: 20g

Lemon Herb Grilled Shrimp Skewers

Time: 20 minutes| Difficulty: Easy| Serving 2

200g shrimp, peeled and deveined
1 lemon, sliced
2 tablespoons chopped fresh parsley
2 tablespoons olive oil
2 cloves garlic, minced
Salt and pepper to taste

1. Preheat grill to medium-high heat.
2. Thread shrimp onto skewers, alternating with slices of lemon.
3. In a bowl, mix together chopped fresh parsley, olive oil, minced garlic, salt, and pepper.
4. Brush the herb mixture over the shrimp skewers.
5. Grill the shrimp skewers for 2-3 minutes per side, or until shrimp are pink and cooked through.
6. Serve hot as a delightful appetizer or main dish.

Per serving
Calories: 200 kcal | Protein: 20g | Carbs: 4g | Fat: 12g

Stuffed Portobello Mushrooms

Time: 35 minutes| Difficulty: Moderate| Serving 2

4 large Portobello mushrooms
1 cup cooked quinoa
1/2 cup chopped spinach
1/4 cup diced red bell pepper
1/4 cup crumbled feta cheese
2 tablespoons chopped fresh basil
2 tablespoons olive oil
1 clove garlic, minced
Salt and pepper to taste

1. Preheat oven to 375°F (190°C).
2. Remove the stems from the Portobello mushrooms and gently scrape out the gills with a spoon.
3. In a bowl, mix together cooked quinoa, chopped spinach, diced red bell pepper, crumbled feta cheese, chopped fresh basil, olive oil, minced garlic, salt, and pepper.
4. Stuff the Portobello mushrooms with the quinoa mixture.
5. Place the stuffed mushrooms on a baking sheet and bake in the preheated oven for 20-25 minutes, or until the mushrooms are tender.
6. Serve hot as a flavorful main dish or side.

Per serving
Calories: 300 kcal | Protein: 8g | Carbs: 30g | Fat: 15g

Caprese Quinoa Salad

Time: 25 minutes| Difficulty: Easy| Serving 2

1 cup cooked quinoa
1 cup cherry tomatoes, halved
1/2 cup fresh mozzarella balls, halved
1/4 cup chopped fresh basil
2 tablespoons balsamic glaze
1 tablespoon olive oil
Salt and pepper to taste

1. In a bowl, combine cooked quinoa, cherry tomatoes, fresh mozzarella balls, and chopped fresh basil.
2. Drizzle olive oil and balsamic glaze over the salad.
3. Season with salt and pepper to taste.
4. Toss everything together until well combined.
5. Serve chilled as a refreshing side dish or light main.

Per serving
Calories: 300 | Protein: 10g | Carbs: 30g | Fat: 15g

Garlic Herb Roasted Potatoes

Time: 40 minutes| Difficulty: Easy| Serving 2

4 medium potatoes, cut into wedges
2 tablespoons olive oil
2 cloves garlic, minced
1 tablespoon chopped fresh rosemary
1 tablespoon chopped fresh thyme
Salt and pepper to taste

1. Preheat oven to 400°F (200°C).
2. In a bowl, toss potato wedges with olive oil, minced garlic, chopped fresh rosemary, chopped fresh thyme, salt, and pepper until evenly coated.
3. Spread the potato wedges in a single layer on a baking sheet.
4. Roast in the preheated oven for 30-35 minutes, or until potatoes are golden brown and crispy on the outside and tender on the inside.
5. Serve hot as a comforting side dish.

Per serving
Calories: 200 kcal | Protein: 3g | Carbs: 30g | Fat: 8g

Stuffed Chicken Parmesan

Time: 45 minutes| Difficulty: Moderate| Serving 2

2 boneless, skinless chicken breasts
1/2 cup marinara sauce
1/2 cup shredded mozzarella cheese
1/4 cup grated Parmesan cheese
1/4 cup breadcrumbs
1 tablespoon chopped fresh basil
1 tablespoon olive oil
Salt and pepper to taste

1. Preheat oven to 375°F (190°C).
2. Cut a pocket into each chicken breast, being careful not to cut all the way through.
3. Stuff each chicken breast with marinara sauce, shredded mozzarella cheese, and chopped fresh basil.
4. In a bowl, mix together grated Parmesan cheese, breadcrumbs, olive oil, salt, and pepper.
5. Press the breadcrumb mixture onto the top of each stuffed chicken breast.
6. Place the stuffed chicken breasts in a baking dish and bake in the preheated oven for 25-30 minutes, or until chicken is cooked through and cheese is melted and bubbly.
7. Serve hot as a comforting and indulgent main dish.

Per serving
Calories: 400 kcal | Protein: 35g | Carbs: 10g | Fat: 20g

Grilled Vegetable Platter

Time: 30 minutes| Difficulty: Easy| Serving 2

1 zucchini, sliced
1 yellow squash, sliced
1 bell pepper, sliced
1 red onion, sliced into rings
1 cup cherry tomatoes
2 tablespoons olive oil
1 tablespoon balsamic vinegar
1 teaspoon dried Italian herbs
Salt and pepper to taste

1. Preheat grill to medium-high heat.
2. In a bowl, toss sliced zucchini, yellow squash, bell pepper, red onion, and cherry tomatoes with olive oil, balsamic vinegar, dried Italian herbs, salt, and pepper until evenly coated.
3. Thread the vegetables onto skewers or grill baskets.
4. Grill the vegetables for 5-7 minutes per side, or until tender and lightly charred.
5. Serve hot as a vibrant and flavorful side dish.

Per serving
Calories: 150 kcal | Protein: 3g | Carbs: 15g | Fat: 10g

Maple Roasted Brussels Sprouts

Time: 30 minutes| Difficulty: Easy| Serving 2

2 cups Brussels sprouts, trimmed and halved
2 tablespoons olive oil
2 tablespoons maple syrup
1 tablespoon balsamic vinegar
Salt and pepper to taste

1. Preheat the oven to 400°F (200°C).
2. In a large bowl, toss the halved Brussels sprouts with olive oil, maple syrup, balsamic vinegar, salt, and pepper until evenly coated.
3. Spread the Brussels sprouts in a single layer on a baking sheet lined with parchment paper.
4. Roast in the preheated oven for 20-25 minutes, or until the Brussels sprouts are caramelized and tender. Remove from the oven and serve hot as a festive side dish.

Per serving
Calories: 150| Carbs: 20g| Fats: 7g| Protein: 3g

Grilled Vegetable Quinoa Salad

Time: 30 minutes| Difficulty: Easy| Serving 2

1 cup cooked quinoa
1 zucchini, sliced lengthwise
1 yellow squash, sliced lengthwise
1 red bell pepper, halved and seeded
1 red onion, sliced into thick rounds
1 cup cherry tomatoes
2 tablespoons olive oil
1 tablespoon balsamic vinegar
1 teaspoon dried Italian herbs

1. Preheat grill to medium-high heat.
2. Brush zucchini, yellow squash, red bell pepper, and red onion with olive oil and season with salt and pepper.
3. Grill the vegetables until tender and lightly charred, about 4-5 minutes per side for zucchini and squash and 6-8 minutes per side for bell pepper and onion.
4. Remove the grilled vegetables from the grill and let cool slightly.
5. Chop the grilled vegetables into bite-sized pieces and place them in a large bowl.
6. Add cooked quinoa and cherry tomatoes to the bowl with the grilled vegetables.
7. In a small bowl, whisk together olive oil, balsamic vinegar, dried Italian herbs, salt, and pepper to make the dressing.
8. Pour the dressing over the quinoa and vegetables and toss until well combined.

Per serving
Calories: 300 kcal | Protein: 8g | Carbs: 30g |Fat: 15g

Balsamic Roasted Brussels Sprouts

Time: 30 minutes| Difficulty: Easy| Serving 2
2 cups Brussels sprouts, trimmed and halved
2 tablespoons balsamic vinegar
1 tablespoon olive oil
2 cloves garlic, minced

1. Preheat the oven to 400°F (200°C).
2. In a large bowl, toss the Brussels sprouts with balsamic vinegar, olive oil, minced garlic, salt, and pepper until evenly coated.
3. Spread the Brussels sprouts in a single layer on a baking sheet lined with parchment paper.
4. Roast in the preheated oven for 25-30 minutes, or until the Brussels sprouts are tender and caramelized.

Per serving
Calories: 100| Carbs: 15g| Fats: 5g| Protein: 5g

Cranberry Walnut Quinoa Salad

Time: 30 minutes| Difficulty: Easy| Serving 2

1 cup cooked quinoa
1/2 cup dried cranberries
1/4 cup chopped walnuts
2 tablespoons chopped fresh parsley
2 tablespoons olive oil
1 tablespoon balsamic vinegar
Salt and pepper to taste

1. In a large bowl, combine the cooked quinoa, dried cranberries, chopped walnuts, and chopped parsley.
2. In a small bowl, whisk together the olive oil and balsamic vinegar.
3. Pour the dressing over the quinoa mixture and toss until evenly coated.
4. Season with salt and pepper to taste.
5. Serve chilled or at room temperature as a festive salad.

Per serving
Calories: 300| Carbs: 35g| Fats: 15g| Protein: 6g

Cranberry Orange Quinoa Salad

Time: 30 minutes| Difficulty: Easy| Serving 2

1 cup cooked quinoa
1/2 cup dried cranberries
Zest and juice of 1 orange
1/4 cup chopped pecans
2 tablespoons chopped fresh parsley
1 tablespoon olive oil
Salt and pepper to taste

1. In a large bowl, combine the cooked quinoa, dried cranberries, orange zest, chopped pecans, chopped fresh parsley, olive oil, salt, and pepper.
2. Toss until all ingredients are well combined.
3. Serve chilled or at room temperature as a festive salad.

Per serving
Calories: 250| Carbs: 35g| Fats: 10g| Protein: 5g

Mashed Sweet Potatoes with Cinnamon Butter

Time: 45 minutes| Difficulty: Easy| Serving 2

2 large sweet potatoes, peeled and chopped
2 tablespoons unsalted butter, softened
1 teaspoon ground cinnamon
Salt to taste

1. Place the chopped sweet potatoes in a pot of water and bring to a boil.
2. Cook until the sweet potatoes are tender, about 15-20 minutes.
3. Drain the sweet potatoes and transfer them to a mixing bowl.
4. Add softened butter, ground cinnamon, and salt to the bowl.
5. Mash the sweet potatoes until smooth and creamy.
6. Serve hot as a festive side dish.

Per serving
Calories: 200| Carbs: 35g| Fats: 5g| Protein: 2g

Honey Glazed Carrots

Time: 30 minutes| Difficulty: Easy| Serving 2

2 cups baby carrots
2 tablespoons honey
1 tablespoon unsalted butter
1 teaspoon ground cinnamon
Salt to taste

1. In a saucepan, bring water to a boil and cook the baby carrots until tender, about 5-7 minutes.
2. Drain the carrots and return them to the saucepan.
3. Add honey, unsalted butter, ground cinnamon, and salt to the saucepan.
4. Cook over medium heat, stirring occasionally, until the carrots are glazed and heated through.
5. Serve hot as a festive side dish.

Per serving
Calories: 150| Carbs: 30g| Fats: 5g| Protein: 1g

Chapter 4: A 4-weeks Meal Plan for a Gallbladder-Free Lifestyle

1.2. Weekly Meal Planning Strategies & Templates

Planning meals well is essential to eating a balanced, healthful diet. To make a weekly meal plan that satisfies your dietary requirements, follow these steps:

Select Well-Balanced Meals:

Try to eat a good mix of fruits, vegetables, whole grains, and lean proteins at every meal. Use a variety of hues, tastes, and textures to keep your meals interesting and fulfilling.

Utilize Meal Planning Templates:

Use meal planning templates to expedite the process and ensure you cover your nutritional bases. Organize your week's meals into four categories: breakfast, lunch, supper, and snacks. Make sure each meal is nutrient-dense and in line with your dietary objectives.

Prepare Ahead of Time:

Make use of downtime to prepare meals and ingredients. Prepare the week's meals by chopping veggies, cooking grains and proteins, and assembling meals. This lessens the temptation to seek for harmful convenience foods and saves time during hectic workdays.

Chapter 5: Explanation of Weekly Themes:

Week 1: Transition & Getting Acquainted

Day 1:

Breakfast: Greek Yogurt Parfait with Granola and Fruit
Lunch: Turkey and Avocado Wrap with Whole Wheat Tortilla, served with Roasted Brussels Sprouts
Dinner: Lemon Herb Baked Salmon with Quinoa Pilaf and Lemon Garlic Roasted Broccoli

Day 2:

Breakfast: Apple Cinnamon Overnight Oats
Lunch: Tuna Salad Lettuce Wraps, served with Cucumber Avocado Salad
Dinner: Baked Lemon Herb Chicken with Garlic Mashed Cauliflower and Steamed Green Beans with Almonds

Day 3:

Breakfast: Broccoli and Cheese Breakfast Casserole
Lunch: Grilled Chicken Salad with Mixed Greens
Dinner: Beef Stir-Fry with Vegetables served with Quinoa Pilaf

Day 4:

Breakfast: Egg and Vegetable Frittata
Lunch: Mediterranean Chickpea Salad
Dinner: Grilled Swordfish with Mango Salsa served with Lemon Herb Quinoa Salad and Grilled Portobello Mushroom Caps

Day 5:

Breakfast: Berry Chia Seed Pudding
Lunch: Black Bean and Corn Salad with Avocado
Dinner: Turkey Chili served with Garlic Herb Roasted Potatoes

Day 6:

Breakfast: Avocado Toast with Poached Eggs
Lunch: Beet and Goat Cheese Salad
Dinner: Chicken Fajitas with Garlic Mashed Cauliflower

Day 7:

Breakfast: Lemon Blueberry Quinoa Breakfast Bowl
Lunch: Quinoa and Black Bean Salad
Dinner: Pork Tenderloin with Apple Compote served with Lemon Garlic Green Beans

Week 2: Introducing Variety

Day 1:

Breakfast: Apple Cinnamon Overnight Oats
Lunch: Turkey and Avocado Wrap with Whole Wheat Tortilla, served with Roasted Brussels Sprouts
Dinner: Lemon Herb Baked Salmon with Quinoa Pilaf and Lemon Garlic Roasted Broccoli

Day 2:

Breakfast: Mango Coconut Chia Pudding
Lunch: Mediterranean Chickpea Salad
Dinner: Beef Stir-Fry with Vegetables served with Quinoa Pilaf

Day 3:

Breakfast: Peanut Butter Banana Toast
Lunch: Greek Salad with Grilled Chicken
Dinner: Grilled Swordfish with Mango Salsa served with Lemon Herb Quinoa Salad and Grilled Portobello Mushroom Caps

Day 4:

Breakfast: Sweet Potato Hash with Turkey Sausage
Lunch: Black Bean and Corn Salad with Avocado
Dinner: Chicken Fajitas with Garlic Mashed Cauliflower

Day 5:

Breakfast: Protein-Packed Breakfast Bowl
Lunch: Caprese Salad with Basil and Balsamic Glaze
Dinner: Turkey Chili served with Garlic Herb Roasted Potatoes

Day 6:

Breakfast: Lemon Blueberry Quinoa Breakfast Bowl
Lunch: Beet and Goat Cheese Salad
Dinner: Pork Tenderloin with Apple Compote served with Lemon Garlic Green Beans

Day 7:

Breakfast: Spinach and Mushroom Omelet
Lunch: Quinoa and Black Bean Salad
Dinner: Grilled Steak with Chimichurri Sauce served with Herb Roasted Potatoes

Week 3: Building Balanced Habits

Day 1:

Breakfast: Greek Yogurt Parfait with Granola and Fruit
Lunch: Turkey and Cranberry Wrap with a Side of Quinoa Pilaf
Dinner: Lemon Herb Baked Salmon with Steamed Asparagus and Lemon Herb Quinoa Salad

Day 2:

Breakfast: Egg Salad Lettuce Wraps
Lunch: Grilled Chicken Salad with Mixed Greens
Dinner: Beef Stir-Fry with Vegetables served with Garlic Mashed Cauliflower

Day 3:

Breakfast: Avocado Toast with Poached Eggs
Lunch: Mediterranean Chickpea Salad
Dinner: Grilled Swordfish with Mango Salsa served with Roasted Brussels Sprouts and Herb Roasted Potatoes

Day 4:

Breakfast: Berry Chia Seed Pudding
Lunch: Tuna Salad Lettuce Wraps with a Side of Quinoa and Black Bean Salad
Dinner: Chicken Fajitas with Quinoa Pilaf and Garlic Roasted Cauliflower

Day 5:

Breakfast: Lemon Blueberry Quinoa Breakfast Bowl

Lunch: Greek Salad with Grilled Chicken
Dinner: Turkey Chili served with Balsamic Glazed Roasted Carrots and Steamed Green Beans with Almonds

Day 6:

Breakfast: Sweet Potato Hash with Turkey Sausage
Lunch: Beet and Goat Cheese Salad
Dinner: Pork Tenderloin with Honey Mustard Glaze served with Lemon Garlic Green Beans and Herb Roasted Potatoes

Day 7:

Breakfast: Spinach and Mushroom Omelet
Lunch: Quinoa and Black Bean Salad
Dinner: Grilled Steak with Chimichurri Sauce served with Grilled Portobello Mushroom Caps and Lemon Herb Quinoa Salad

Week 4: Mastering the Gallbladder-Free Lifestyle

Day 1:

Breakfast: Greek Yogurt Parfait with Granola and Fruit
Lunch: Turkey and Avocado Wrap with Whole Wheat Tortilla, served with Roasted Brussels Sprouts
Dinner: Lemon Herb Baked Salmon with Quinoa Pilaf and Lemon Garlic Roasted Broccoli

Day 2:

Breakfast: Apple Cinnamon Overnight Oats
Lunch: Mediterranean Chickpea Salad
Dinner: Beef Stir-Fry with Vegetables served with Quinoa Pilaf

Day 3:

Breakfast: Avocado Toast with Poached Eggs
Lunch: Grilled Chicken Salad with Mixed Greens
Dinner: Grilled Swordfish with Mango Salsa served with Lemon Herb Quinoa Salad and Grilled Portobello Mushroom Caps

Day 4:

Breakfast: Berry Chia Seed Pudding
Lunch: Black Bean and Corn Salad with Avocado
Dinner: Turkey Chili served with Garlic Herb Roasted Potatoes

Day 5:

Breakfast: Lemon Blueberry Quinoa Breakfast Bowl
Lunch: Greek Salad with Grilled Chicken
Dinner: Pork Tenderloin with Apple Compote served with Lemon Garlic Green Beans and Herb Roasted Potatoes

Day 6:

Breakfast: Sweet Potato Hash with Turkey Sausage
Lunch: Beet and Goat Cheese Salad
Dinner: Chicken Fajitas with Quinoa Pilaf and Garlic Roasted Cauliflower

Day 7:

Breakfast: Spinach and Mushroom Omelet
Lunch: Quinoa and Black Bean Salad
Dinner: Grilled Steak with Chimichurri Sauce served with Steamed Asparagus and Lemon Herb Quinoa Salad

Chapter 6: Washing and Handling

The importance of proper cleaning
Before getting into the complexities of plant-based cuisine, it's critical to grasp the significance of carefully cleaning fruits and vegetables. This removes dirt, bacteria, and pesticide residues, making your dishes both delicious and safe.

Step-by-Step Guide to Washing Produce:

1. Hand Hygiene: Wash hands thoroughly with warm water and soap before and after preparing fruits and vegetables. This critical step reduces the spread of microorganisms to your food.

2. Make a Vinegar and Salt Solution: In a large dish, combine 1 1/3 cups vinegar and 1 tablespoon salt. Stir the mixture until the vinegar and salt are completely dissolved. Rest certain that the vinegar, a natural disinfectant, and the salt, a microbe-drawing aid, will work together to thoroughly clean your vegetables.

3. Initial Rinse: Wash fruits and vegetables under running water. Gently rub the surface to remove dirt and insecticides. Avoid using soap or chemical cleansers, as these might leave toxic residues if consumed.

4. Soaking times vary depending on the sort of product. Thin-skinned fruits and vegetables, such as berries and leafy greens, require only a 5-minute soak in the vinegar and salt solution. Firm-skinned food, such as apples and squash, should be left in the solution for 10 minutes. This step is crucial to complete disinfection.

5. Scrubbing: Using a clean vegetable brush, gently scrub the skins of complex and textured fruits and vegetables such as melons, carrots, sweet potatoes, and cucumbers. This eliminates trapped dirt and bacteria that a simple rinse may not have removed.

6. Rinsing Post-Soak: After soaking and washing, rinse the vegetables with plain water to eliminate any remaining vinegar or salt. Rinse well to remove any remaining remains.

7. Drying: To dry the fruits and veggies, use a clean kitchen cloth or paper towel. This step is not simply for convenience; it also reduces the possibility of bacterial growth.

8. Inspect and Cut: Check your vegetables for damaged or bruised regions. Cut these away since they can harbor bacteria and degrade the quality and safety of your meal.
Use separate chopping boards for fruits, vegetables, and uncooked meat. After each use, thoroughly clean the board with hot, soapy water.

9. Meat: To avoid cross-contamination, wash your hands, meat, and utensils with soap and hot water, and then pat dry before seasoning or cooking. Follow the right cooking temperatures and times to ensure the meat is safely prepared and cooked to the recommended internal temperature.

Conclusion

Implementing a few key dietary modifications is vital for a smoother recovery after gallbladder ectomy. In addition to substituting certain foods, take the following advice:

1. Do not start eating solid foods right away after surgery. Reintroducing them gradually will help you prevent digestive issues.

2. Eat modest meals throughout the day. Divide your meals because eating too much at once can leave you feeling bloated and gassy. Try to consume five to six small meals every day, spaced a few hours apart. In between meals, have nutrient-dense, low-fat, high-protein snacks. Limit yourself to 3 grams of fat every meal.

3. Substitute popular recipe ingredients. For example, instead of oil, use applesauce in baking, or make an egg substitute by combining flax seeds and water.

4. Consider turning vegetarian. Without a gallbladder, it is often more difficult to digest meats and dairy products, particularly full-fat versions.

5. Stay active; frequent exercise and maintaining a healthy weight help digestion, especially after gallbladder removal. Consider this a reliable source for digestive health enhancement.

Made in United States
Troutdale, OR
07/02/2024

20993307R00064